Reason and Religion

in an

Age of Science

Terry Kelly SJ

Reason and Religion

in an

Age of Science

A Workbook for Senior Students

Terry Kelly SJ

ATF Press
Adelaide

Text copyright © 2007 remains with the author for this volume.

All rights reserved. Except for any fair dealing permitted under the Copyright Act, no part of this book may be reproduced by any means without prior permission. Inquiries should be made to the publisher.

First published 2007

ISBN 978 1 920691 77 6

ATF Press
An imprint of the Australasian Theological Forum Ltd
P O Box 504
Hindmarsh
SA 5007
ABN 90 116 359 963
www.atfpress.com

Contents

Table of Contents	v
Foreword	xi

Chapter 1   The Importance of Science and Religion

1. The problem	1
1.1 Perceptions of the cosmos	1
1.2 The impact of changed perceptions of the cosmos on religion	1
2. The place of religion in the world today	2
2.1 The decline of Christianity in the Western world	2
2.2 A survey of Catholics	3
2.3 A young person's reflection	3
2.4 The ongoing worldwide importance of religion	5
3. Scientific revolutions	6
3.1 The first scientific revolution: when science undermined religion	6
3.2 The second scientific revolution: science finds itself with problems	7
3.3 The revolutionary findings of science	7
4. Other influences on the relationship between science and religion	8
5. The present situation	9
5.1 Science has raised questions perhaps unanswerable by science	9
5.2 The limits of science have been revealed	10
5.3 Is religion believable?	10
5.4 Science and religion: a partnership	10

Chapter 2   The Methods of Science: Its Achievements and Limitations

1. The scientific method: a recent arrival	
2. The extent of scientific influence	13
2.1 Everyday	13
2.2 The invisible and the beyond	14
2.3 The past and the future	15
3. The scientific method	15
3.1 Steps in arriving at a scientific model	15
4. Does the scientific method deliver truth?	17
4.1 Measurements	17
4.2 Laws	17
4.3 Theory	18
4.4 Examples of developments within theories	19
5. The development of instruments: a key to progress	21
6. The role of mathematics in the progress of science	22
7. The explosion of science and technology	24
8. Science as one of the roads to truth	25
8.1 Other roads to reality	25
8.2 What science can do and what science cannot do	26
8.3 Science does not justify itself	27
8.4 Science leads ultimately to counter-intuitive models	27
9. Extension: The philosophy of science	28
9.1 Does the scientific method lead to truth?	28
9.1.1 Science never reaches the truth about nature	29
9.1.2 Science is descriptive	30
9.1.3 Models bring us closer to reality	30
9.2 Emergence or reductionism?	30
9.2.1 Reductionism and the alleged triumph of science	31
9.2.2 Emergence	31

Chapter 3   The Method of Religion: Reflection and Inspiration

1. Definition	35
2. Religion is a human response	36
2.1 Religion is a response to a variety of human experiences	36
2.2 Varieties of response	37
2.2.1 Religious	37
2.2.2 Non-religious	37
3. Evolution of religion	37
3.1 Animism: spirit world of present day hunter-gatherers	38
3.1.1 Chinese folk medicine	39
3.1.2 Australian Indigenous culture	39
3.2 The emergence of more distant gods	40
3.3 The beginning of Greek philosophy: a move from gods towards nature	41
3.4 The emergence of monotheism	41
3.4.1 The West: Judaism, Christianity, Islam	41
3.4.2 East: Taoism, Buddhism and Hinduism	42
3.5 Revelation	44
4. Evidence for religion	44
4.1 Universality of religion	45
4.2 Writing	45
4.3 Mystical experience	45
4.4 Making sense of reality	47
4.5 Other sources of evidence	47
5. Difficulties for religion in the West	48
5.1 Reasons for difficulties	48
5.2 Difficulties lead to dismissive attitudes	49
6. Christ and salvation	50
6.1 The world seeks saviours	50
6.2 Jesus: a challenge for his time	51
6.3 Jesus: a challenge for our times	52
6.4 A new creation	53
6.5 Jesus, the face of God	54
7. The Trinity	54
7.1 God is not the only mystery	54
7.2 Reality as relationship	55
7.3 The threeness of the one God.	55
7.4 God as truly personal	56

Chapter 4   Revolution in the Heavens: The Birth of Modern Cosmology

1. Ancient models	59
1.1 The biblical model	59
1.2 Aristotle's universe	61
1.3 Ptolemy's epicycles	62
2. Copernicus and the sun as centre	63
2.1 Arguments against having the sun as centre	64
2.2 The *Commentariolus*	64
2.3 *De revolutionibus orbium coelestium*	65
2.4 Tycho Brahe's alternative model	65
2.5 Kepler's correction to the Copernican system	65
2.6 Newton provides the convincing argument for the Copernican system	67
3. Galileo's discoveries	67
3.1 What the telescope revealed	67
3.1.1 The moon	67
3.1.2 Jupiter's moons	68
3.1.3 Sunspots	69
3.1.4 The Milky Way	69
3.1.5 Phases of Venus	70
3.2 Summary of Galileo's discoveries	70
3.3 The consequences of Galileo's observations	70
4. Galileo: hero or heretic?	71

4.1 Galileo's position: a paradigm change with theological implications	71
4.2 Galileo supports the Copernican model	71
4.3 Galileo encounters opposition	72
4.4 A preliminary judgment from Rome	72
4.5 'The Dialogue' and its consequences	73

Chapter 5   The Development of Cosmology: The Discovery of a Vast and Dynamic Universe

1. Riddle of the nebulae	80
1.1 Two theories about the nebulae	81
1.2 Hubble found evidence to resolve the question of the nebulae	81
2. The expanding universe	82
2.1 The red-shift	82
2.2 The argument from the force of gravity	83
2.3 Einstein's solution to the implosion	84
2.4 Hoyle's 'steady state' resists the expanding universe	86
3. Microwave background radiation: the compelling evidence	88
3.1 The discovery of the cosmic microwave background radiation (CMB)	88
3.2 The origin of the background radiation	88
3.3 Features of the CMB	88
4. Extension: Chaos	91
4 1 Billiard table thought experiment to illustrate chaos	91
4.2 Chaos in small system	91
4.3 Chaos in systems of innumerable particles	91
4.4 Uncertainty deriving from chaos	91

Chapter 6   The Big Bang: Another Revolution in the Skies

1. The big bang	95
1.1. The theory of an expanding universe leads back to a beginning	95
1.2 The explosion which began the universe	96
2. After the bang	96
2.1 The first three minutes	96
2.2 From three minutes to about 380,000 years after the big bang	98
2.3 380,000 years after the big bang: a creative step, the formation of atoms	98
2.4. Structure begins to form	99
3. Reflections	100
3.1 Scientific: The big bang theory presents problems	100
3.2 Philosophical	101
4. Extension 1: Inflation: a solution to the big bang problems	103
4.1 The meaning of inflation	103
4.2 Big bang problems addressed by inflation	104
4.3 The limitations of the inflation theory	104
5. Extension 2: The role played by dark matter in cosmic evolution	105
5.1 Dark matter in spiral galaxies	105
5.2 The role of dark matter in shaping the cosmos	106

Chapter 7   The Book of Genesis: Modern Scholarship

1. The meaning of myth	109
1.1 Cosmic myths	110
1.2 The prevalence of non-biblical myths and their polytheistic background	110
1.3 The unique character of biblical myths	111
1.4 Differences between biblical and pagan myths: a summary	111
2. Examples of pagan myths	111
2.1 Creation	111
2.2 The battles of the gods	112
2.3 Manipulating and capricious gods	112
2.4 The use of ritual and power to attain favour	113
2.5 The origin of death	113
2.6 The origin of evil	113
3. Biblical myths	114

  3.1 The relationship between biblical and non-biblical myths   114
  3.2 The Bible's first creation story: Genesis 1.1–2.4   114
  3.3 The Bible's second creation story: Genesis 2.5–3.24   115
  3.4 The two Genesis creation stories compared   115
  3.5 A third creation story: Psalms and the Book of Job   116
  3.6 Why are there three different creation stories?   117
  3.7 A summary of what the biblical creation stories tell us   118
  3.8 The philosophical view of creation   118
 4. The bible as the word of God   119
  4.1 How was Genesis 1–11 written?   119
  4.2 How are these chapters the word of God?   120
  4.3 What the Bible teaches   120

Chapter 8 The Stars: Instruments of Creation

 1. Two gigantic leaps forward   123
  1.1 The skies appear static   123
  1.2 The cycle of life and death in the skies   123
  1.3 Creationism is not the answer   124
 2. The stars   124
  2.1 How did the stars form?   125
  2.2 A balancing act between implosion and explosion   126
 3. Formation of the elements   127
  3.1 A large star: a stellar cooker   128
  3.2 The syntheses of the remaining elements   130
  3.3 The death of a large star: supernova   131
  3.4 The formation of solar systems   132
  3.5 Life-giving carbon   133
 4. The death of the sun   134
 5. The end of a superstar: a black hole   137
 6. Extension: The neutrino coincidence   138

Chapter 9 The Anthropic Universe: Science at its Limits

 1. The universe   143
  1.1 General possibilities for a universe   144
  1.2 Evolution of the universe   144
  1.3 The anthropic question   145
 2. The arrow of time   145
  2.1 The pessimistic arrow of time   146
  2.2 Optimistic arrow of time   147
 3. The fine-tuning of the laws of nature   149
  3.1 Some examples of the fine-tuning needed for life to emerge   149
  3.2 Is the fine-tuning a chance occurrence?   151
 4. The anthropic principle   152
  4.1 The strong anthropic principle   152
  4.2 The weak anthropic principle   152
 5. The multiverse solution to the fine-tuning   153
  5.1 Different styles of multiverse speculation   154
  5.2 Some reflections on the multiverse   154
 6. The design solution   155
 7. Other approaches to fine-tuning   158
  7.1 A fluke   158
  7.2 A given   158
  7.3 A necessity   159
 8. Extension 1: Reasons for and against the multiverse theory   159
  8.1 Reasons against the multiverse theory   159
  8.2 Reasons for the multiverse theory   160
 9. Extension 2: String theory   161
  9.1 Michio Kaku   161
  9.2 Arguments in favour of string theory   162
  9.3 Arguments against string theory   163
 10. Extension 3: 'Intelligent design'   163

Chapter 10 The Resurrection: The Redemption of Creation

1. The foundational belief	167
1.1 The quest for the historical Jesus	167
1.2 Christological controversies	168
1.3 Resurrection interpretations	168
2. He is risen!	168
3. The Resurrection of Jesus	169
3.1 The belief	170
3.2 The evidence for the belief	170
3.3 Inconsistencies in the evidence	172
3.4 The inconsistencies can be seen to increase credibility	173
3.5 The transformation of the apostles	173
3.6 The birth of Christianity	174
4. Alternative explanations for the transformation of the apostles	175
4.1 The apostles deliberately made up stories in order to feel better	176
4.2 The swoon theory: Jesus was not dead	176
4.3 The story as an imitation of earlier dying and rising gods	178
4.4 The story as symbol in the minds of the apostles	178
4.5 The apostles were hallucinating	178
5. The meaning	179
5.1 Jesus is the living Lord	179
5.2 Resurrection is the answer to life	180
5.3 Resurrection is not earthly utopia	180
5.4 The risen one: the spirit he released transforms us	180
5.5 The promise of personal resurrection	181
5.6 The final revelation of God and God's purpose	181

Conclusion: The Fruitful Conversation between Science and Religion

1. Is science our salvation?	183
2. The many fruits of science	184
3. Serious problems remain for a large proportion of the human population	185
4. Reason in a world of science	185
5. A danger emanating from the success of scientific reasoning	185
6. How to view the relationship between science and religion	187
6.1 The conflict model	187
6.2 Contact, conversation and confirmation	187
6.3 A parallel approach	188
7. Concluding comment	188

Glossary   191

Foreword

This text has three intertwined lines of enquiry. Firstly, it attempts to acquaint students with the methodology of science and some of its achievements. In particular it seeks to facilitate an appreciation of some of the extraordinary findings of modern cosmology. Secondly, it reflects on the origins and universality of religion and specifically focuses on the new message of Christianity. Thirdly, it brings both science and religion into a dialogue. In doing this it attempts to show that religious and philosophical reflections on the findings of science point to concerns whose answers cannot be gained by the scientific method. There are critical issues in life, and indeed within the universe as we know it, where science itself has to acknowledge its inability to proceed. As Stephen Hawking said, 'Why is there anything at all? When we have answered this question we will know the mind of God.'

While this text looks to questions raised by cosmology and physics, similar lines of enquiry could equally engage the other sciences of evolution and ecology and the growing sciences of Human consciousness and genetics.

The text has been developed for a course delivered to Year 12 students as a part of their Religious Education studies at a Jesuit college in Adelaide. I have been teaching variations of this course, along with senior physics and philosophy, for over thirty years. It brings together my deep commitments and enthusiasms: for Christianity, for the sciences of physics and cosmology, and for philosophy. It hopes to address some of the questions in students' hearts and minds as they grapple with their particular life situations on our planet.

The universe has evolved. It has passed through many, more simple stages before arriving at today's complexity. Each new stage appears to have contained something new, something that was not in the preceding stage. Could stars have been predicted from the featureless world of hydrogen and helium? Could dinosaurs have been predicted from fish? Could animal evolution have predicted the amazingly fast development of the human brain? Looking backwards, could intelligent awareness have been predicted at all? At each stage there has been an emergence of new forms and new laws, not reducible to the properties of the constituents of the preceding stage, though dependent on their functioning. The apostle Paul wrote that 'all creation is groaning in one gigantic act of giving birth'.[1] Marvellous matter reveals new secrets at each stage of its progress.

Many students have only little knowledge of the nature and development of the universe, but realise it differs markedly from the simple creation stories of the Bible. They hear and read reports about an alleged conflict between religious beliefs and scientific discoveries, without knowing how much work has been done over the last century in understanding and interpreting the Bible as a unique text. There is a temptation to allow their ultimate assertions to be consonant with scientific scenarios and to dismiss religious knowledge as a thing of the past. However many scientists and theologians see no contradiction between their concerns and are happy to see the relationship between science and religion as a fruitful dialogue. We need multiple perspectives when dealing with the mysteries of life.

It is important for all of us, and especially young adults, to appreciate the new thoughts and interpretations which are widely known in theological circles. It is important to remember that many aspects of our lives demand constant reviewing and reflection. We have a lifetime of learning.

Because of science's tremendous achievements, some assume that knowledge attained through the scientific method is the only true source of knowledge. This text is an attempt

---

1. Paul, *Letter to the Romans*, 8:22.

to show that religion plays a significant role in our thinking. It hopes to enlighten students in their knowledge of the cosmos and to link this knowledge with an intelligent appreciation of what the Bible, at its deepest level, is actually saying.

1

The Importance of Science and Religion

Chapter overview

- The problem for religion in an age of science
- A student's perception of religion
- Religion, as a worldwide phenomenon, is still important today
- The first scientific revolution and the problems presented to religion
- The second scientific revolution and the problems presented to science
- Religion and science are both forced into conversation

1 The problem

1.1 Perceptions of the cosmos
Christian belief began 2000 years ago, arising out of Jewish faith and claiming to be its fulfilment. All Israel's prophecies and hopes were realised in the person of Christ. For one and a half millennia, Christianity's beliefs were expounded in terms reflecting the cultural milieu, in terms preceding the scientific revolution. The sky was a transparent sphere with stars fixed to the inside of this sphere which revolved around the earth: God was above and beyond the sphere of stars; the earth was the centre of creation; the moon was made of Aristotle's *quintessence*; angels moved the planets which were also made of the same heavenly *quintessence*. God created everything in seven days and we are all descended from a single couple who sinned and ruined life for all of us. This medieval view is far removed from what we know today (see chapter 4).

Primitive though it seems, all this was a big advance from the pagan beliefs that the moon, stars, sun and forces of nature were gods: that the gods were very human and sometimes preyed on humans or ignored them; that creation began with wars between gods.

1.2 The impact of changed perceptions of the cosmos on religion
As science accelerated in the eighteenth and nineteenth centuries, consequent upon the first scientific revolution (see chapter 4), religion's previous fields of knowledge were invaded more and more by science. But after the second scientific revolution (of the twentieth century), science itself has encountered walls which it may not be able to scale; questions have been raised which invite a new look at religion. Religion, having abandoned the medieval framework, is invited to take into its field the findings of science. However it needs to beware of attaching itself too strongly to them, as there will almost certainly be further scientific advances. Religion itself has been strengthened by new approaches to the scriptures which

include serious studies of the cultural contexts of the texts and an attempt to understand the types of literature with which those texts were engaging at the time of writing.

Philosophical thinking on creation begins with the data presented by science. When philosophy draws conclusions from the natural world today, there is an enormous difference between the data it interprets today compared with the data presented fifty, a hundred, 200, 400, 2000, 2500 years ago. Theology, too, must be able to be combined felicitously with scientific conclusions. Our scriptures emanated within a scientifically primitive world. That primitive worldview was replaced by the philosophy of Aristotle, and later by Ptolemy's universe. Some of doctrines, as we have them today, were formulated, developed and explained in a culture permeated with Aristotelian thought. But our perception of the universe is unlike Aristotle's perception and that of the times when the scriptures were written. The dismantling of the cosmology of Aristotle and Ptolemy, and the increasing credibility of the theory of evolution have demanded a reformulation of doctrines, not at their essence, but of what culturally enshrouds them. They need to be able to be understood within our cultural context but that does not mean they are to be made into scientific propositions. Much of this work of interpretation and understanding has been taking place for decades now but its fruits are not always widely appreciated. Science may indeed have more surprises awaiting us, like the recent revelation that the universe is not only expanding but its expansion rate is accelerating.

2. The place of religion in the world today

2.1 The decline of Christianity in the Western world
The decline in religious belief and practice in Europe and Australia is real. Many people consider themselves culturally Christian but take it no further than that. Religious practices are a low priority for the majority. Christianity by some is seen to be linked to prior mythic practices, such as seeing the resurrection at Easter as a reflection of pagan full moon festivals. Many see that a belief in the resurrection challenges the modern worldview. We no longer link cosmic events with God's immediate action.

There are many reasons for such a decline in belief:

- The understanding of nature has progressed so much that areas that were previously reflected on and answered by religion, have now been taken over by science. Science has delivered so much about the past, about the cosmos, about the history of humankind, about disease, about computation, about thought and emotions and about the future that other forms of knowledge are seemingly dwarfed. For some, the only source of truth is the scientific method.

- The origins of religious beliefs are seen to be shrouded in myths and to have come from an age of superstition.

- The church is seen as an old fashioned institution, out of touch with present-day realities. The Galileo controversy is a warning for many: the church resisted the beginnings of the scientific revolution and is seen to have not changed since.

- Some see the basis of Judeo-Christian religion in the Book of Genesis with its stories of creation, flood and sin. These events seem, for some, so cosmic and foundational that it is difficult for them to see them as stories with a message. Even for Judaism, God's intervention in Israel preceded the writing of Genesis. People had experienced God in the divine saving acts performed for them, and in the words of the prophets.

Biblical studies have shown that these stories have a message and, as with the parables from the New Testament, are not presumed to have actually happened (see chapter 7). For some literal minded people, to assume that something in the Bible did not actually happen is to assume that the Bible is untrue.

- In the media religion is often identified with a fundamentalism which steadfastly and aggressively promotes literal interpretations of the scriptures. However mainstream Christian theology has long moved beyond this approach. Genesis does not teach science. It teaches that whatever happened in the beginning, God was the master. The theory of the big bang and God as master are not in conflict.

2.2 A survey of Catholics

A sample of 18,000 Australian Catholics surveyed in 1996[1] found that 5,500 of these had stopped going to mass. Some of the reasons cited were: occupations involving week-end work, household chores, attending children's sporting events and the week-end being the only time for family. Also, and importantly, disagreements with some church teachings, irrelevant homilies from the pulpit and scandals involving the church were also given as reasons. A more limited survey in 2006 produced a similar spread of reasons.

2.3 A young person's reflection

An article recently published in the Adelaide *Sunday Mail*, written by a secondary school student, presents a host of impressions that people may have picked up concerning mainly contemporary Christianity. The letter reads:

> To me, religion involves well-meaning people who muddle positive ideas with actions that are bumbling, odd and often offensive.
>
> Lately Christianity, Judaism and Islam seem to be so blundering they could be taken for the Three Stooges.
>
> I remember last Sunday watching as families poured out from an Adelaide church. While concerned I might have been missing out on some act of spiritual transcendence inside those four walls, I was comforted while sitting out Easter's holy celebrations when I recalled the recent intelligent design debate, the ultra-conservative politics of the American bible belt, and the Church's role in the AIDS and anti-abortion debates.
>
> I am basing my arguments around the obvious—the world's largest and most powerful religions are all horribly ancient, with morals and stories foreign to many of us today.
>
> At the same time, I'm frequently disappointed by those in positions of authority in these religious codes who have the power to reinterpret their existing doctrines to make them more relevant.
>
> In every case we've seen these leaders swing away from modernisation and embrace outmoded and uninformed fundamentalist attitudes. Is this some sort of absurd competition, a struggle for each religion to resist the modern world more completely?
>
> Christianity and Islam particularly seem behind the times. It's as if to believe the Bible or Koran are not texts for literal interpretation would be to undermine their religion's entire belief system.
>
> With the US intent on a brutal ideological battle with its expeditions into the

---

1. http://www.acbc.catholic.org.au/bishops/confpres/20061201472.htm

Middle East, it's difficult for me to see, in terms of raw suffering, how the world could be any worse off without religion.

But could I live in a world without spirituality? Could anyone? The air of spiritual deadness that pervades our commercialised consumer culture is frightening and I'd rue the day we replaced churches with mega-malls.

It would be nice if religion wasn't so darn silly.[2]

Questions: As a student, do you relate to the views of a fellow student expressed in the above letter?

....

....

....

....

....

....

Do you see fundamentalism as a significant part of Christianity?

....

....

....

....

....

Do you think the church has an obligation to keep up with current thinking? Is there a place in the churches where scholarship is seriously pursued?

....

....

....

....

....

....

---

2. *Sunday Mail,* Adelaide, 23 April 2006.

Which church-based organisations which help others in trouble do you know about?

....

....

....

....

....

....

Is the Iraq war a religious war?

....

....

....

....

....

....

2.4 The ongoing worldwide importance of religion

Despite sentiments such as these, on a worldwide scale religion is very important. Its adherents number billions: Hindus, Muslims, Christians and Buddhists would make up over sixty per cent of the world's population. Religion is a sign of hope as well as a sign of division.

Despite Christianity's decline in Europe and in Australia, it is influential in the United States, rapidly increasing its numbers in Africa and in Asia,[3] strong in areas in Indonesia and India, supported by the vast majority in South America and the Philippines, and has survived in China and Russia despite significant pressures on its adherents. (In fact the number of people professing some religious belief in China is estimated at 300 million, some of whom are Christian.[4]) No one today can be unaware of the strength of Islam as it forms a belief system for millions in the Middle East and South East Asia with significant personal and political influence in those places. Islam is also a growing phenomenon in Europe. Hinduism affects the culture and belief of hundreds of millions in India and Buddhism is a feature of the East, and growing in Australia.

---

3. http://www.cathnews.com/news/702/77.php, accessed 14 February 2007.
4. http://www.asianews.it/index.php?l=en&art=8423&size=A, accessed 9 February 2007.

If we wish to come to grips with our religion today, to understand and justify it, it seems that we need have a knowledge of how to interpret ancient texts.[5] The books of the Bible are ancient texts, spanning over a millennium, written in ancient languages and against the backgrounds of ancient cultures. What did they mean for the folk for whom they were written? What of substance can they tell us today? In this context we will have a look at the early chapters of the Book of Genesis.

Religion must engage itself with the modern world, and hopefully some of the issues raised in the column from the *Sunday Mail* will be addressed in the following chapters.

3. Scientific revolutions

Science has undergone two momentous revolutions, two extensive changes of worldview. As a broad base to the considerations of this text, it would be helpful to look at these two revolutions.

3.1 The first scientific revolution: when science undermined religion
It was not until the seventeenth century that science became based on the scientific method. Up until this time, to study science had meant to study the biology and physics of Aristotle (384–322 BCE), the cosmology of Ptolemy (c90–168 CE), and the anatomy of Galen (c130–200 CE).[6] It was largely a deductive pursuit; that is, it was not based on the results of experiment, but more on the method of philosophy. The church condemned the atomic theory of Democritus (c460 BCE). Purposeless atoms in an infinite void ran contrary to a cosmos imbued with divine purpose and was thought to be a threat to the real presence in the Eucharist. As pressure for a radical change gathered, the church clung to Aristotle as the official science, because much theology had been expounded in the context of a geocentric (earth as centre) universe.

Before this revolution, it was thought that the earth did not move; it was the centre of creation and everything else rotated around it. God created all species directly, including Adam and Eve. Life was explained by a vital principle which organised the parts of plants and animals to make them work together and to give them life. Knowledge was gained by studying perennial truths which resided in the works of philosophers and the teachings of the church.

After the first revolution, the sun was firstly seen as the centre of the universe with the earth revolving around the sun, and eventually the sun was one of many stars in the universe, a universe which was thought to be identical with the Milky Way Galaxy. From this scientific method also came theories of evolution: all present day species had evolved over long periods of time from other species. Humans had evolved from earlier species and *homo sapiens* had been around for hundreds of thousands of years. The understandings gained through physics and chemistry began to be applied to the understanding of life. The scientific revolution banished God from the universe. God was no longer required at creation because the universe was seen as eternal; God did not create the species, nor the first parents. The power of the scientific method exalted scientific knowledge above other forms, relegating philosophy and theology to matters of diminished importance. The whole notion of a spiritual dimension to humankind began to be questioned.

---
5. Chapter 6.
6. Galen was a Greek physician and founder of experimental physiology. About one hundred of his medical writings survive.

3.2 The second scientific revolution: science finds itself with problems

The first revolution can be thought of as being completed by about 1900. The world of science imagined everything had now been solved. In 1894 Michelson stated:

> The most important fundamental laws and facts of physical science have all been discovered, and these are now so firmly established that the possibility of their ever being supplemented in consequence of new discoveries is exceedingly remote . . . our future discoveries must be looked for in the sixth place of decimals.[7]

Newton's mechanics accounted for the everyday world; Maxwell's theory of electromagnetic radiation described light and heat very well; there was now an atomic theory for the micro-world, and, for the big picture, a universe of the solar system, embedded in a huge Milky Way galaxy. Everything seemingly was explained.

But many things were soon to come that would overturn this cosy picture. Thomson's 1897 discovery of the electron, indicating that the atom was a construct, opened the way to the undreamt of physics of the sub-atomic: nuclear and particle physics. A few unexplainable observations about radiation, after investigation, pointed the way to the quantum theory, which displaced Newton's billiard ball mechanics and the predictability in the micro-world. The failure of the Michelson-Morley experiment to detect the ether, an all-pervading invisible medium which transmitted life through space, was a surprise: if light were a wave, which it clearly seemed to be, it needed a medium; it could not go through empty space. This medium was the ether. But alarmingly, there was no ether as at about the same time as the electron's discovery, its existence was disproved. This jettisoning of the suggested all-pervading medium, which allowed for the transmission of light through space, led to the special theory of relativity, with its restrictions on speed, dilation of time and conversion of matter into energy. New astronomical observations with better equipment indicated a vast, dynamic, self-creating universe. Theoretical science was totally changed in the space of three decades.

3.3 The revolutionary findings of science

- Cosmologists have discovered an immensely vast and expanding universe. This universe had a beginning, a cosmic evolutionary development and will come to an inevitable end.

- Einstein's special relativity revealed there was an absolute maximum velocity, that of light, beyond which nothing could go faster. Relativity implied that the rate of time varied with speed, so that time went slower as you moved faster (for example at nine tenths of the speed of light, for the traveller, one second becomes 2.4 seconds); and also relativity implied that mass could be converted to energy ($E = mc^2$), and this was amply demonstrated at Hiroshima, and is demonstrated on a daily basis in France where seventy per cent of its power is generated by changing mass into energy.

- Einstein's general relativity proposed that gravity affects the rate of time, that gravity can affect light, and that gravitational forces are the result of curvature in space-time. The testable predictions of general relativity have been progressively verified.

---

7. Hanbury Brown, *The Wisdom of Science* (Cambridge: Cambridge University Press, 1988), 66.

- Quantum mechanics rules the micro-world. While Newton's laws reign supreme in everyday life, they do not rule the micro-world. The micro-world is the realm of atoms, nuclei and molecules. The mathematics of quantum theory has yielded perfect results for seventy years, but the reality behind the mathematics is difficult to imagine, and seems to defy common sense. In this foundational reality, out of which a common sense world is constructed, the same set of circumstances can produce different results; the reality is not actually determined until an experiment is performed, and separated particles generated under certain conditions communicate instantaneously, faster than light signalling, even if they are metres or even kilometres apart. Einstein called this latter property 'spooky action at a distance'.

- DNA, life's blueprint, has been analysed and the whole human code laid bare.

4. Other influences on the relationship between science and religion

- Archeological, anthropological and historical understandings were expanding. The discovery of non-biblical creation and flood myths in many cultures led to a conclusion that perhaps Genesis was a collection of myths, and had no more value than the myths of other cultures. (This will be discussed in Chapter 7.)

- Philosophers started to question the concept of God. Atheistic philosophers like Ludwig Feuerbach (1804–1872) proposed that God was the invention of the human mind, the idealisation of many good human qualities. He saw God as the answer to human wishes: we want to live on, so we invent God to fulfil this wish. Karl Marx (1818–1883) declared religion to be 'the opium of the people' meaning that religion is used by the ruling classes to oppress the working class who can be content with poor wages and bad conditions if they are promised future bliss. Friedrich Nietzsche (1844–1900) declared defiantly that 'God is dead'.

- The church throughout this time became defensive. It generally condemned new revolutionary theories, such as Copernican theory and evolution. And the situation of Galileo became a symbol of the church's incompatibility with science. Galileo had been placed under house arrest and threatened for his support of the Copernican theory of the universe. (Ironically at the same time, the heliocentric model (sun-centred) was being taught by the Jesuit Matteo Ricci[8] to Chinese intellectuals.) Areas of knowledge once the province of religion have been shown to be more adequately explained by scientific theorising; for example, the orbiting of planets around the sun, once thought to be the work of divinities, or angels, is now known to be a combination of inertia and other natural forces; mental illness, once viewed as the work of the devil, is now seen to have its base in biochemistry and environmental factors.

   The alleged incompatibility between science and religion has long gone. The church now works with science as demonstrated by its institutions (such as the Vatican Observatory, the Templeton Foundation and the Centre for Science and Religion), its official statements (such as those from Pope John Paul II and George Coyne, SJ) and its publications (such as in books by John Haught, John Polkinghorne, Ian Barbour and Alister McGrath). As stated in *New Scientist*:

---

8. Vincent Cronin, *The Wise Man from the West* (London: Rupert Hart-Davies, 1955).

> The idea that science necessarily entails an assault on religion has long been rejected by theologians and scientists such as Stephen Jay Gould and Francis Collins. The very success of science raises a profound and complex question that can be seen to point to the existence of a deity: why is the world explicable at all?[9]

- There has been a huge increase in material benefits to humanity. The progress of science in producing useful for technology has been almost unlimited. Scientific research has discovered laws about nature—electricity, magnetism, gravity, atomic theory, semi-conductors—which have allowed all sorts of new processes, products, medicines, amusements and computing facilities. The quality of life for the lucky third of humanity continues to increase exponentially. Science has uncovered ancient humans, hominids, ice ages, the geological history of the earth, the birth of the sun. Science reaches to thirteen billion light years away, is able to project five-sixths of the way back to the beginning of time, declares the age of the universe itself, and finally predicts the end of the sun and of the solar system and ultimately the end of the universe itself.

5. The present situation

5.1 Science has raised questions perhaps unanswerable by science

- There seems to have been an initial nothingness. How can something come from nothing?

- The universe is contingent. This means two things: it does not have to be, and it does not have to be as it is. Why does it exist if it does not have to be?

- Why is the universe like it is if it doesn't have to be like it is?

- The universe has been furnished with special matter and special laws which have enabled an evolution from an initial superdense speck of energy to matter, atoms, galaxies, stars, supernovae, new stars, planets, chemicals, complex chemicals, life, higher forms of life, consciousness, and mind. The universe is dynamic and creative. From each stage of its evolution emerges a new stage, not reducible to the stage out of which it emerged.

- The quantum nature of matter is a mystery. The ultimate theory of matter works superbly mathematically, but the reality corresponding to this is bizarre.

- Is there a purpose for a universe which began and will end?

- The existence of ghostly realities. Cosmological discoveries have necessitated the invention of dark matter, and dark energy of the vacuum, neither of which have actually been encountered directly experimentally. More speculative final theories envisage strings vibrating in eleven dimensions. These strings would be trillions of time smaller than atoms; this is really small, considering millions of atoms fit on the point of a pin.

---

9. Bryan Appleyard, 'The Delusion is All Yours', *New Scientist* 193/ 2593 (2007): 47.

- The existence of contradiction. Quantum mechanics (micro-world) and general relativity (cosmic world) work in their own realms, but their conclusions are incompatible if extended beyond these.

5.2 The limits of science have been revealed
Although science applies to things and processes in a remarkably powerful way, it is not all-powerful (see chapter 2).

- Science's theories are always provisional. The scientific landscape is crowded with abandoned theories.

- Science cannot answer questions about meaning.

- Science cannot create morality.

- Science does not justify itself—its method is justified from philosophy.

- Scientific laws are descriptions of nature, but do not explain themselves.

- Scientific models are constructs of the human mind, leaps of creative imagination following on evidence and may not mirror reality.

- Science has not saved the world; despite the remarkable achievements of science, poverty, injustice, oppression, hunger, greed, violence are no less alive than they were before the first scientific revolution.

5.3 Is religion believable?
John Polkinghorne likens the religious search to something like the scientific search—clearly not identical, but religion is not fabricating something out of nothing.[10] There is a large body of evidence associated with each system of belief. This is not scientific evidence, but it is still evidence. There are events, writings, religious experiences, mystical phenomena, beliefs passed down, practices, moral systems and lives of outstanding adherents to each faith. Did the resurrection happen? Did God intervene in Israel? Have people really met God in prayer? In particular, does Christianity meet the new scientific world with confidence? To conclude whether religion is believable or not, it is necessary to investigate the evidence. In Christian teaching, this will not deliver faith, but it can be a preparation for receiving this gift from God.

Alister McGrath, professor of historical theology at Oxford University, in a recent book charts the rise and fall of disbelief in the modern world. He concludes: 'the future looks nothing like the godless and religionless world so confidently predicted forty years ago'.[11]

5.4 Science and religion: a partnership
John Haught, professor of theology at Georgetown University, proposed four models for the relationship between science and religion in his book *Science and Religion: From Conflict to Conversation*:[12]

---
10. John Polkinghorne, *One World* (Princeton: Princeton University Press, 1987), 26–38.
11. Alister McGrath, *The Twilight of Atheism* (London: Random House, 2004), 278.
12. John Haught, *Science and Religion* (New York: Paulist Press, 1995), 27–46.

- Conflict: Either one or the other is correct. For a religious fundamentalist, science is wrong when it conflicts with religion. For a materialist scientist, religion is wrong when it conflicts with science.

- Contact: They both have their areas of competence. They both have a lot to contribute, but their spheres of action are separate. They address different questions in ways appropriate for each discipline.

- Conversation: Religion should listen to science and take its findings into account in the elaboration of its beliefs. God's creation should take into account the present findings about the history of the universe. Science should recognize its findings can be the basis for philosophical speculation.

- Confirmation: The religious person finds his/her idea of the intelligence and power of God confirmed by the findings of scientific research.

For many people the picture of the universe that they have discovered is breath-taking. A transition in perception has taken place from the eternal and infinite static universe of the 1920s to a seemingly miraculous cosmos with a beginning from nothing, a self-development from utter simplicity through various stages eventually arriving at beings capable of unravelling the marvels hidden in matter itself.

For those content with science alone, the picture is a fascinating one, spurring many onto further research and generating an eagerness to hear of the latest hypothesis.

For the open-minded religious person this scientific picture fits in well with the creator God, and the already known intelligent God. Each new scientific step adds to the knowledge of God's intelligence, creativity and subtlety. We are the recipients of an enormous gift from the all-powerful one—a cosmos given beautiful laws and a freedom to find itself.

Further reading

Connie Barlow, editor, Evolution Extended: Biological Debates on the Meaning of Life (London: MIT Press, 1994).

John D Barrow, *Impossibility: The Limits of Science and the Science of Limits* (Oxford: Oxford University Press, 1998).

Simon Conway Morris, *Life's Solution: Inevitable Humans in a Lonely Universe,* (Cambridge: Cambridge University Press, 2003).

Michael J Denton, Nature's Destiny: How the Laws of Biology Reveal Purpose in the Universe (London: The Free Press, 1998).

Kitty Ferguson, *The Fire in the Equations: Science, Religion and the Search for God* (London: Bantam Press, 1994).

Alister McGrath, *The Twilight of Atheism* (London: Random House, 2004).

Robert Osserman, *The Poetry of the Universe: A Mathematical Exploration of the Cosmos* (London: Phoenix, 1995).

Michael Poole, *A Guide to Science and Belief: How Science Works, Explaining the Universe, Faith Evidence and Chance* (Oxford: Lion Publishing, 1994).

Murray Rae, Hilary Regan and John Stenhouse, editors, *Science and Theology: Questions at the Interface* (Edinburgh: T&T Clark, 1994).

Christopher Southgate and others, *God, Humanity and the Cosmos: A Textbook in Science and Religion* (Edinburgh: T&T Clark, 1999).

Margaret Wertheim, *Pythagoras' Trousers: God, Physics, and the Gender Wars* (London: Fourth Estate, 1997).

2

The Methods of Science:

Its Achievements and Limitations

Chapter overview

> - The fabric of our lives springs from scientific discoveries:
>   - Work, play, health
>   - The beyond, the invisible
>   - The past, the future
> - The scientific method
> - Reasons why it is a recent arrival in the history of *homo sapiens*:
>   - Development of instruments
>   - Development of more sophisticated mathematics
> - Does the scientific method deliver ultimate explanations?
> - The limits of the scientific method
> - Extension: An overview of the philosophy of science

1. The scientific method: a recent arrival

We in Western culture live in a time that is enlightened, enlivened and saturated through and through by science. Almost everything we do has been influenced by something whose very possibility goes back to a scientific discovery. Technology arising from science is part and parcel of our work, our play, our sickness and our health. Technology has the power to move us through space, to investigate the past and the future.

We look back on the history of thought and ask how the human race could have been so ignorant, so taken up by beliefs in gods and myths, as to ignore the laws of nature which seem so obvious to us. We can see that in the past we could construct cities, armies, ships and aqueducts; we could pursue trade, develop agriculture, blossom into empires such as those of Egypt, Rome, Greece. Yet while there were many great achievements in that time, the ultimate explanation for events for much of that time has rested on myth, with little understanding of the bases of science. It has only been very recently that we have developed the mathematics, the methodology and the instruments of technology at the heart of science. Wasn't it all too obvious that the sun and the stars were going round the earth?

When we reflect on the overwhelming impact of science on our lives it leads to asking this question: is science so powerful that its way of knowing overshadows all other ways of knowing and even condemns them to irrelevancy?

2. The extent of scientific influence

2.1 Everyday

All our daily activities—cooking, getting about, learning, working, entertainment and relaxing—all our work and play have been underpinned by science: the electric light, the fridge, the car, the plane, the amplifier, the television, the computer, the barcode, the iPod, the digital camera. The following chart indicates the basic scientific principles that underlie some of our everyday activities.

Product	Scientific principle
alarm clock	electrodynamics
radio	quantum theory, electromagnetic waves
hot shower	thermodynamics
cassette player	electromagnetic induction
car	kinetic theory of gases
television	Thomson's e/m experiment, electromagnetic waves
computer	semi-conductors, quantum theory
luminous watch	radioactivity
cereals	organic chemistry, genetics
medicine	biochemistry
mobile phone	electromagnetic waves, semi-conductors, quantum theory
CD	laser, wave theory
electric stove	Ohm's law, energy conservation

2.2 The invisible and the beyond

We know of the existence of bacteria, viruses, and can often deal with them when they threaten our well-being. For example, in 2003, the world was threatened by a plague, SARS. But internationally coordinated research led to the isolation of the virus responsible, and the quick elimination of it as an immediate plague threat.

We find out what lies under the earth (coal, oil and gas) and bring it to the surface for our use. Perhaps soon we will be able to exploit subterranean hot rocks as a non-polluting energy source. We detect and analyse the ubiquitous cosmic microwave background (CMB) (see chapter 5), and through close analysis of the CMB learn much about the evolution of the universe.

Robots have crawled around the surface of Mars for over a thousand days, and have sent back pictures and other data. Spacecraft have visited Venus and taken photos, satellites have been put into orbit around Neptune and its moon Triton. We have intercepted Halley's comet, spied on asteroids, and even videoed the last minutes of a comet as it crashed into the mighty Jupiter as the great planet exercised its role of solar system junkyard.

Telescopes have enabled us to photograph the spiral arms of the Milky Way, companion galaxies, walls of galaxies, voids, clusters and filaments up to over ten billion light years away. We have clear pictures of supernova remnants (see chapter 8).

We penetrate matter to its smallest particles—to the atom, the nucleus, the proton and the quark—and in the process we find myriad particles of exotic matter. We can seen the effects but do not know understand the mysterious dark matter which binds the stars into galaxies, and are seeking to explain the more mysterious dark energy[1] which seems to be accelerating the universe's expansion rate. There is still much that we do not know.

---
1. Stuart Clark, 'Heart of darkness', *New Scientist* 193/2591 (2007): 28–33.

2.3 The past and the future

Cosmology takes us back almost to time's beginning (see chapters 5 and 6). Biology and palaeontology have shown us microfossils of bacteria 3.5 billion years old, other early life forms, dinosaurs, the great extinctions, the Cambrian explosion, hominids.

Geology reveals the history of the earth, ice ages, greenhouse times, tectonic plates, the structure of the inside of the earth.

Science predicts the death of the earth, the death throes of the sun, and the eventual end of the universe. We find it more difficult to make even short-term predictions about human history. Modern prophecies are usually gloomy, and notoriously wrong. For example Dr Paul Erlich, in his *The Population Bomb*,[2] in the 1960s forecasted widespread starvation and wars over resources for the 1980s, which never came to be. We cannot absolutely predict the outcome of such things as global warming.

Question: Is global warming the result of human activities? Are its gloomy predictions well-founded?

3. The scientific method

The scientific method was pioneered by Galileo Galilei (1564–1642) in the seventeenth century. He introduced experimentation, and successfully applied mathematics to his observations. The scientific method involves a series of steps which are applied to an aspect of reality. Part of learning through science's methodology is to be aware of its limitations.

3.1 Steps in arriving at a scientific model

- Observation: Science begins with an observation which arouses curiosity as to 'why is it so?' and this leads to the question 'what is actually happening here?'. For example: there is the observation that apples fall off trees leading to the question of 'why do the apples fall after they become detached from trees?'. Newton's (1642–1727) response was that the earth exerts a force on the apple propelling it to the ground.

---

2. Paul Erlich, *The Population Bomb* (New York: Ballentine 1968).

- Experiment: An experiment is then set up, a controlled observation in which the correlations between quantities involved in the phenomenon are investigated, to see if there is a relationship, and to find out what the relationship is. Galileo found that all objects, small and large, fell at the same rate. The rate of falling does not depend on mass: light things fall as fast as heavy things. Any differences are fully explained by air resistance. A forty kilogram mass falls at the same rate as an eighty kilogram mass. Clearly such an experiment involves measuring instruments such as clocks.

- Law: If a relationship is found, the relationship is called a law. For example, the relationship between force and acceleration. If you pull on a cart, it accelerates. If you double the force you double the acceleration ($F = ma$). Another example would be the relationship between gravity and distance from the earth. The further away a rocket gets from the earth, the less is the force of the earth's gravity on the rocket (if you double the distance from the earth's centre, you quarter the force). The earth's gravity at the moon is 1/3600 of the force of gravity on the earth's surface. That is because the moon is sixty times further from the centre of the earth ($1/60^2$).

- Model or theory: The scientist then asks again more pointedly *why is it so?* Why is reality behaving in this lawful matter? So having determined a law, the scientist constructs a model, a theory intended to mimic the inner workings of a system to which he/she has no direct access. This is a mental activity. The scientist goes beyond the data and proposes a theory (see examples section 4.4). This leads to the question, are scientific models anything more than useful mental constructs? (See section 9.)

- Prediction: The theory is then tested. This is done by making a prediction from the model which can then be tested. The prediction is an aspect of behaviour of the system which has never been observed, but if the model is correct, this behaviour would be observed. General relativity predicts that light and time are changed by gravity. Both have been found to be true, lending credence to the theory of general relativity.

- Experiment: The scientist then thinks out an experiment to test the model. If the prediction is verified by experiment, the model, theory gains in stature. If the prediction turns out to be false, the theory has to be amended by a new feature to account for this finding. A prediction from Einstein's special relativity theory was that matter could be converted to an enormous amount of energy, $E = mc^2$. This prediction was verified for all to see in the devastating bombing of Hiroshima in 1945. An addition termed inflation theory to the big bang model has enabled the model to deal with some explanatory difficulties (see chapter 6, extension 1). Einstein's general relativity theory produced many predictions which have been progressively tested as more sophisticated apparatus is invented. So far they have all been verified.

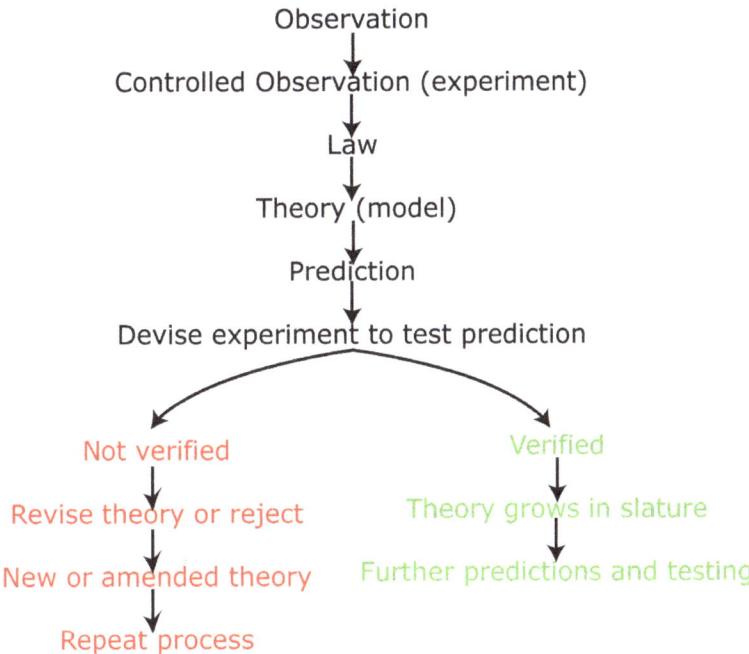

Scientific method

Observation → Controlled Observation (experiment) → Law → Theory (model) → Prediction → Devise experiment to test prediction

- Not verified → Revise theory or reject → New or amended theory → Repeat process
- Verified → Theory grows in slature → Further predictions and testing

4. Does the scientific method deliver truth?

Each of the steps in the method can be assessed in its truth-delivering capacity.

4.1 Measurements

Doing an experiment we make measurements, and these can be done with great precision. But however precise these measurements may be, they are never unlimitedly precise—the last decimal place always contains uncertainty. You might say the height of the fence is exactly 5.0 metres. But could it be 5.01 metre? No, it is 5.00 metre. Well could it be 5.001? Yes it could. But it could even be 5.004. You can always get to a decimal point where there is uncertainty. But measurements are certain up to a limit. This restriction leads to what is known as *chaos theory* (see chapter 5, extension).

4.2 Laws

Laws are constant ways of behaving in physical systems. A good degree of certainty is found here. In fact, the knowledge of laws has enabled computer and calculator technology, human travel to the moon and spacecraft to circle Neptune. But we must always be ready for some observation that calls the law into question. Any eighteenth-century British person would have agreed that *all swans are white*. Such a statement had to wait for the observation of black swans in Australia to show the falsity of this law.

- Laws are descriptions of underlying regularities, and do not express fundamental necessities. The law of apples falling to earth does not tell us that apples *must* fall to earth. The law just says that they will fall with an acceleration of 9.8 ms^{-2}:

  > The laws cannot be said to be the source of the behaviour nor of the constraints on behaviour—they model or describe it. Although the laws of nature do reveal and describe fundamental patterns of behaviour and regularities in the real world, we cannot consider them

the source of those regularities, much less attribute to them the physical necessity these regularities seem to manifest.[3]

- Laws prescind or abstract from other aspects of reality—personal relationships, for example, should not influence a scientific law. And they are tested in idealised and special circumstances, in 'experimental conditions', governed by laboratory standards.

- We do not know why we have these laws and no others.

4.3 Theory

Having determined a law, the scientist constructs a model intended to mimic the inner workings of a system. Models capture part of reality, but what the reality is in itself, we don't know fully. Maybe we don't know at all.

Models are mental constructs which then can be used to unify data, and charter the way into previously un-thought-of possibilities. Mathematical and scientific theorist Roger Penrose proposed a classification of theories into superb, useful and tentative:

> Superb theories: Apply to a wide range of phenomena, and over a long period of time. Newton's laws of motion, Euclid's geometry.
>
> Useful theories: Results are in harmony with the theory, but the theory needs further testing, fine-tuning, even to the point of future rejection. For example, big bang origin of the universe, present theory of nucleus.
>
> Tentative theories: Interesting speculations, which help direct research: various big bang models, wormholes, multiverse, branes, string theory.[4]

Theories and models change over time. In the light of new observations they are modified, and then remodified and so on until the original theory can no longer be accepted. A new theory is needed. This happened for the theory of the nature of light. Newton had proposed the corpuscular theory—light consists of tiny particles. In 1803, Thomas Young produced convincing evidence that light did not consist of particles; rather, it was a wave phenomenon, a travelling vibration like sound. When you hear a sound, you are not struck by particles, but a vibration of the air sets your eardrums vibrating. Similarly light as a wave impacts on the retina. But this was not the final answer. In 1905, Einstein showed light was seemingly something of a particle phenomenon as well. It seemed to be sometimes a wave, sometimes a stream of special particles called photons. This solution addressed the question of how a vibration could pass through empty space.

Theorists consider how the world works and build models of reality, and experimentalists test the models by comparing them with reality.

The scientific method gives us models which may not be the last word. Joseph Polchinski (University of California) remarked that 'our job is to find out the way nature is, not to tell it how to behave. Every five to ten years we learn something that surprises us, which shows we don't have the full picture.'[5]

---

3. William Stoeger, 'Contemporary Physics and the Ontological Status of the Laws of nature', in CJ Isham, *Quantum Cosmology and the Laws of Nature*, edited by Robert John Russell and Nancey Murphy (Vatican City State: Vatican Observatory Publications, 1999), 222, 208.
4. Roger Penrose, *The Emperor's New Mind* (Oxford: Oxford University Press, 1990), 152.
5. Steve Nadis, 'Making Multiverses', *Astronomy* 33/10 (2005): 38.

4.4 Examples of developments within theories

The discovery of gravity

Observation	Things fall to earth. Earth holds moon in orbit. Things fall to earth. Earth holds moon in orbit.
Hypothesis	The same gravity is doing both: holding the moon in orbit, and making things fall.
Law	It was found gravity fell off rapidly as you left the earth: go double the distance and gravity is quartered, three times the distance and gravity is only 1/9 of value at earth. Force exerted by the earth's gravity varies as $1/d^2$.
Theory	Newton's theory: any two masses anywhere will exert forces of attraction on each other. Two passing cars exert forces on each other, but they are negligible. When large masses are involved, the force is significant. Earth's mass causes other masses to fall. Earth's mass exerts force on moon's mass, and holds moon in orbit. $\mathbf{F = GM_1M_2/d^2}$
Prediction	This force can be detected and measured in the laboratory with sensitive equipment.
Test	Investigate if there are forces between two known masses. Verified by Cavendish.
Decision	Accept Newton's theory.
Further prediction	Gravity will not affect light because light does not have mass.
Test	Indications that light is affected by gravity.
Decision	Reject Newton's theory
New theory	Einstein's theory of general relativity
General relativity predictions	Gravitational lensing, precession of orbit of Mercury, black holes.
Tests	All predictions are verified.
Decision	Accept general relativity theory. Newton's theory is true for 'ordinary' situations.

The discovery of the universe

(See also chapter 4)

Apparatus	Evidence	Model
Eye	everything circles earth	earth as centre; spheres
Keen observation	planets' retrograde motion	epicycles for planets
Mathematical analysis	planets could circle sun	sun as centre? *Rejected*
Galileo's telescope	Jupiter's moons phases of Venus millions of stars at varying distances	earth not always the centre Venus circles the sun stars not on same sphere
Kepler's further maths	planets revolve in ellipses	sun at focus; planets go around sun
Telescopic evidence	myriad of stars nebulae identified	Milky Way = universe within Milky Way or beyond?
Further observations	Cepheid variables	Nebulae huge distances away; therefore different galaxies
Spectral analysis	red shift	expanding universe beginning when/how? expansion rate must slow down
Accidental discovery	microwave radiation	big bang 'confirmed'
COBE satellite	microwave intensity variations	galaxy seeds: initial quantum ripples
1998 intensity analysis	supernovae evidence dark energy	expansion accelerating
WMAP satellite	subtle variations in μ wave	questions for model

Question: Are we getting closer to the truth, or will the truth forever elude us?

....

....

....

....

....

Question: Science is a two-edged sword: it works, but does it tell us what is in reality?

....

....

....

....

....

....

....

5. The development of instruments: a key to progress

Galileo Galilei was a key figure in the development of science. He formally began the scientific method, by making his first step measurement, and then progressing from measurement to law. By timing various motions he laid the foundation for Newton's Laws of Motion. Because of the lack of time-measuring instruments Galileo was forced to improvise by measuring time with his pulse rate.

Nicholaus Copernicus (1473–1543) proposed a neat sun-centred universe to replace the universe with the earth as centre. Despite its greater simplicity, its radical reorientation of the religiously supported earth-centred universe was not accepted until decades later, when the telescope, a suitable instrument for observing the universe, was developed. Galileo improved an instrument that had been invented in Holland and observed a number of features of the heavens that were to provide a radically new direction for astronomy (see chapter 4).

Robert Hooke (1635–1703) discovered cells using the newly invented microscope. The pendulum clock enabled accurate timing; the thermometer, barometer and air-pump enabled an expansion of the knowledge of the behaviour of gases.

> Histories of science are often written in terms of outstanding people like Newton and Einstein so that they give the impression that the progress of science depends largely on the development of new theories. It would be nearer the truth to say it depends largely on the development of new instruments, so on new materials, and new ways of making things.[6]

Since then, every advance in astronomy and cosmology has come about through advances in technology. Since the 1920s we have had radio telescopes, ultra-violet (UV) and infra-red (IR) receivers and the Hubble Space telescope. These revealed to us many hitherto unknown features of the universe culminating in the surprise revelation of its accelerating expansion. As Steve Nadis states:

> Cosmology's shift has come about through advances in technology. Armed with new precision tools, astronomers seek to chart the

---

6. Hanbury Brown, *The Wisdom of Science* (Cambridge: Cambridge University Press, 1988), 7.

history of the universe and determine its size, shape, structure and composition.[7]

In addition an artificial satellite, the Wilkinson Microwave Anisotropy Probe (WMAP), can discern a difference of one millionth of a degree in temperature in the cosmic microwave background radiation (CMB). Its highly precise analysis of the CMB, among other findings enabled it to pin down the age of universe to 13.7 billion years ±1%.

The Wilson cloud chamber, the liquid hydrogen bubble chamber and the cyclotron have catalysed the study of atoms and particles and we now have the standard model, a comprehensive theory of atoms and their constituents. Today long circular tunnels accelerate particles to unbelievable speeds, and sophisticated analytical tools reveal what happens when the particles collide and break apart, revealing to us the nature of reality as more than corpuscles, more than different types of unbreakable units.

The Anglo-Australian 2dF Galaxy Redshift Survey collected 220,000 galaxy distances. The Sloan Digital Sky Survey (SDSS) created a three dimensional map of a million galaxies. This information should help in solving the puzzle of how galaxies are formed.

Question: The development of sophisticated instruments for the exploration of space is hugely expensive. 18,000 children die every day from poverty and malnutrition. Would it be better to spend the billions on them?

....

....

....

....

....

....

....

6. The role of mathematics in the progress of science

Wilhelm Röntgen (1845–1923), the accidental discoverer of X-rays, thought there were three things necessary for scientific progress: the first was mathematics, the second was mathematics and the third was mathematics. No doubt he did not wish to exclude observation and interpretation.

Centuries ago, not only were there no calculators, but also mathematics had not been developed. Pythagoras, who died about 497BCE discovered the theorem that bears his name, but also discovered irrational numbers (π, √2) and found relationships between the periods of heavenly bodies, though these were found to be not significant. He even held that numbers are the basic reality.

Plato believed there to be a world, where the ideas themselves existed apart from any mind. In this way mathematical truths existed. Today Roger Penrose imagines humans do

---

7. Steve Nadis, 'Measuring the Universe', *Astronomy, Origin and Fate of the Universe* (November 2004): 6.

not invent theorems, but they enter a world of abstractions, in contact with which they discover the theorems. Penrose would perhaps believe that Pythagoras did not invent his theorem, but actually entered the ideas world of mathematical truths and discovered his theorem already existing. He certainly believes this to be the case *at least for the more profound mathematical concepts*[8].

In the third century BCE, Euclid lived and worked in Alexandria, in northern Africa, which was then the world's main cultural centre. He ran the 'museum' which was an early 'multiplex'—a shrine, a place of instruction and a huge library. Here he founded a school of mathematics. This immense cultural centre burnt down in 391 CE. Euclid's *Elements* is a synthesis of geometry and is the second most published book in history (the most published book being the Bible).

The Arabs at the start of the ninth century CE introduced our present numerals, adopting the system based on tens. Also they developed algebra and trigonometry. Their mathematics found its way into Europe during 1600s.

Building on this, in the seventeenth century Descartes founded analytical (coordinate) geometry, Newton and Leibnitz (1646–1760) invented (or discovered?) calculus, and Newton compiled a gigantic synthesis of physics (owing much to Galileo) when in 1687 he published *Mathematical Principles of Natural Philosophy*.

Earlier, before such advances in mathematics, Johannes Kepler (1571–1630) showed the planetary orbits were ellipses rather than circles. Lacking calculus, he needed eight years and 900 pages of problem solving to do this. Newton in his book, justified Kepler's ellipses, by showing that elliptical trajectories necessitated the existence of centrally directed force towards central mass and the inverse square law of force.

The progress of mathematics and its role in the development of empirical science is aptly summarised by Hanbury Brown:

> The techniques of mathematics were also advanced in the seventeenth century making it increasingly possible to turn qualitative speculation into quantitative science and to tackle problems that could not be solved in words.[9]

Question: Do we discover or invent mathematics?

---

8. Penrose, *The Emperor's New Mind*, 97
9. Brown, *The Wisdom of Science*, 12.

....

....

....

7. The explosion of science and technology

Progress from this solid base was considerable in the eighteenth century, but exploded in the nineteenth century. Armed with mathematics, and with efficient instruments, science yielded applications which changed the daily lives of populations, and gave birth to industries. Technology is applied science, the application of scientific laws to inventions. Electrical theory led to electric lighting, heating, washing machines; quantum theory has led to computers, digital cameras; electromagnetism has led to storage of data on tapes.

A summary of the relationship between scientific achievement and technological application is shown in the following table.

Science and technology

Scientist	Science	Discovery	Application
Volta, Faraday, Ampere, Ohm	electricity	current flow	electric light(1820), industrial electrolysis, telegraph(1836)
Maxwell Hertz	electromagnetic waves	nature of light	wireless telegraph radio (later)
Joule	heat	heat is energy (1850)	liquefy gases, freezing industry
Pasteur	medicine	bacteria	disease cure and prevention, vaccines
Darwin	zoology, biology	evolution(1859)	
Mendel	genetics (1866)	inheritance	understanding of some diseases, genetics
Dalton	chemistry organic (1828)	atomic theory(1808)	refining of metals synthetic industry

Question: Is there anything left for any other form of knowledge?

....

....

....

....

....

....

....

....

8. Science as one of the roads to truth

Although we make copious use of the fruits of science in our work, our recreation and in our recovery from sickness, scientific truth is not our only guiding light. Our own intuition, commonsense, the words of others, art, philosophy, religion also play a part in shaping our beliefs and values.

8.1 Other roads to reality

The success of science leads to a widely-held contemporary assumption that science is the ultimate road to truth. It is easy to think that science will lead us to the complete knowledge of everything—the 'theory of everything'—that will solve all our problems. Experimental evidence becomes the ultimate test for everything.

Although science is a powerful tool which leads to advances in knowledge, know-how, and life style, it does not necessarily lead to advances in being human. Scientist Peter Atkins surely exaggerates wildly when he says:

> Reductionist science is omnicompetent. Science has never encountered a barrier it has not surmounted. We can reasonably suppose it has power to surmount and will in due course be equipped to surmount any barrier'.[10]

Our values, need of purpose, sense of the transcendent, and the justification for the scientific method itself are not found in science and cannot be found there. There are many other ways of encountering reality, many windows into reality.

There are many other sources of knowledge: literature, art, history, personal experience, intuition, religion, philosophy and the word of others.

Each side of the octagon in the following diagram represents a window on to reality, a field of knowledge or a way of looking at the world. It is only possible to grasp reality with the combined application of all of these views.

---

10. Peter Atkins, 'The Limitless Power of Science' in *Nature's Imagination* (Oxford, Oxford University Press, 1995), 195.

Windows to reality

Diagram: An octagon labeled 'REALITY' containing Matter, Ideas, People, Politics, Spirit, God, with arrows pointing inward from: Philosophy (top), Science (upper left), Literature (upper right), Art (left), Personal — self-knowledge, trust, partnerships, interests and concerns (right), Religion (lower left), Art (lower right), Conscience (bottom).

Modern science may appear as the most powerful form of knowledge ever. In some ways it seems to make all other forms of knowledge irrelevant. However, this is far from the whole picture: many crucial aspects of our lives are dealt with by other forms of knowledge. Whom do I trust? What are my interests? Whom will I marry? What is my life's purpose? Faith, self-knowledge, values, purpose of the universe, God and conscience: these are not conclusions obtained by the scientific method.

8.2 What science can do and what science cannot do

Science leads to a knowledge of matter and certain processes. In doing so, science unveils the laws of nature—if only partially. Science leads to technology, which underpins how we live, work and play. But science is a limited form of knowledge.

Science cannot lead to statements of value. Science can undermine our value systems: as the theories, models, gained from the scientific method are always transitory, open to correction, even to abandonment, so too we might transfer this aspect of scientific knowledge to our value systems, conscience and morality (see conclusion). Science has little to do with relationships, with love and hate, with good and evil.

Science is powerless to speak of purpose. Cosmic evolution (see chapter 5) is a remarkable process of complexification from chaotically moving particles to stars and planets. Science lays bare this process, but can go no further. Its method cannot locate purpose. Animal evolution has revealed progress from inert matter to life, from one-celled life to colonies, to primitive animals to reptiles to mammals, to hominids to *homo sapiens*. Science once again is powerless to speak of purpose. There is no experiment to be conducted whose result is purpose. Philosophy and/or religion may then reason to a purpose behind everything.

In *The Goldilocks Enigma* Paul Davies remarks:

> (The universe) appeared to (Fred) Hoyle as if a super intellect had been monkeying with the laws of physics. On the face of it, the universe does look as if it has been designed by an intelligent creator expressly for the purpose of spawning sentient beings.[11]

---

11. Paul Davies, *The Goldilocks Enigma* (London: Penguin, 2006), 3.

A few sentences later Davies states: 'No scientific explanation for the universe can be deemed complete unless it accounts for this appearance of judicious design'. Seemingly Davies is looking for a statement of purpose as a scientific conclusion which cannot be delivered by the scientific method. In other writings Davies had concluded philosophically:

> The contrived nature of physical existence is just too fantastic to take on board as simply 'given'. It points forcefully to a deeper underlying meaning to existence. Some call it purpose, some design. but that it is about something I have absolutely no doubt.[12]

Question: How does one come to the knowledge of values?

....

....

....

....

....

....

....

8.3 Science does not justify itself
The validity of the scientific method cannot be demonstrated by the scientific method. There is no experiment that can be performed whose conclusion would be to validate the scientific method. So there must be truths outside the method.

Kurt Gödel's incompleteness theorem showed that no system of mathematics justifies itself. There is no complete system of maths that stands by itself. Mathematical systems must be justified by truths outside the system. Such proofs outside the system may or may not exist.

Similarly, science itself rests on foundations outside itself: the intelligibility of nature, its constancy, the cogency of inductive logic, the efficacy of mathematics, the principle of contradiction, and the principle of sufficient reason.

8.4 Science leads ultimately to counter-intuitive models
A counter-intuitive model is one which goes contrary to commonsense. It may appear bizarre, absurd, non-comprehendible, impossible and unbelievable. Examine these conclusions emanating from the scientific method:

- The big bang is when time and space began, and the whole universe was contained in a volume smaller than an atom. There was no before. Time began 13.7 billion years ago. So we cannot ask the question of what was there before the big bang.

- Space (rather *space-time*) is curved.

---
12. Paul Davies, 'The Sacred Maning of Science', *The Australian*, 4 May 1995

- 'Spooky action at a distance': certain particles can communicate with each other over large distances, faster than light signalling, even instantaneously. If two particles come from the same process they are forever joined. One may journey metres, kilometres from the other. Make a change in one, and the other will change immediately. There has been no message exchanged.

- The Heisenberg uncertainty principle. There are fundamental uncertainties in certain combinations of position, energy and time at the quantum level. For example if we know everything about the speed of a particle we have no idea where it is.

- String theory: ultimate particles are different vibrations of strings trillions of times smaller than nuclei, vibrating in ten dimensions. Each particle is the same string, but vibrating differently.

- Space contains seventy-three per cent of all reality in the form of dark energy—the energy responsible for the acceleration of the universe's expansion. Dark matter, never yet encountered directly, makes up twenty-two per cent. The hundred billion galaxies only make up about five per cent of the matter/energy of the universe.

- The expansion of the universe is the expansion of space itself, which is dragging the galaxies with it. Some parts of space are expanding faster than light.

- In the centre of a black hole there is a singularity, a point of no volume but with the mass of a star of infinite density.

- The atom itself is largely space. The nucleus is like a peanut in the centre of a circular football arena.

- If you travel fast enough time goes slower relative to a stationary observer.

Question: Can such counter-intuitive models be the stuff of reality?

....

....

....

....

....

9. Extension: The philosophy of science

9.1 Does the scientific method lead to truth?

Early philosophy books, written in Latin, defined truth as *adequatio inter intellectum et rem*, meaning that truth is a congruence between the thought and what the thought represents. Aristotle defined truth in this way 'a statement is true when it says of what is that it is, and of what is not that it is not. It is false when it says of what is that it is not, and of what is not that it is'.[13] The trouble here is how do we know this? Emmanuel Kant (1724–1804) taught that the mind confers on outside data the perception of space and time, which do not actually exist out there.

Let us go beyond such problems and assume there is a world out there as we perceive it. The problem with scientific models is that they go beyond our ordinary experiences and profess to get to the untouchable reality beneath what we experience. Do atoms exist? Are photons real? Did a big bang actually take place? Is the sun a nuclear furnace?

What makes an assertion true is not whether we think it is true. It is true if it accords with reality. Are there intelligent beings elsewhere? We don't know, but there is a correct answer. Science presumes reality is one way rather than another.

Science works. But the question here is this: is science leading us into the nature of reality and its processes?

In the scientific method we go from perceptions to laws to models of reality. When can we say the model is reality? There is a wide range of opinions on this issue.

9.1.1 Science never reaches the truth about nature

- According to David Hume (1711–1776) inventing models is a rational exercise following perceptions. It is going beyond perceptions. It is thus pure and simply a mind exercise resulting in ideas. Any result of such rationalising is going beyond experience and hence is merely a product of the mind. Thus Hume also did not believe in the mind, cause and effect or God.

- According to Karl Popper a model is never the final truth. It is useful until an observation runs counter to it. It can never be verified as true. You can say so far the model is not false. You can never say we have conclusive evidence. The model can only be falsified. It is always awaiting an observation which would show it is not the final answer. It is always awaiting *falsification*. If a theory is not open to falsification, it is not a scientific theory—it cannot be investigated experimentally. The statement 'there is a God' cannot be experimentally falsified. You cannot conduct an experiment to show there is a God or that there is not a God. God's existence or non-existence cannot be accessed by science.

- According to Thomas Kuhn a theory forms part of an overarching scientific *paradigm*, the set of concepts shared by the scientific community. For example, the standard theory of matter is the current paradigm. It includes theories about atoms, molecules, nuclei, sub-atomic particles, quarks, anti-matter, nuclear forces. New observations, laws, and models are fitted into the paradigm. If they do not fit the paradigm exactly, features are added to the paradigm, or subtracted from it so that the overall paradigm still mirrors reality. When the paradigm becomes overburdened with *ad hoc* changes, it is abandoned in favour of a new paradigm.

    At present a group of cosmologists think the big bang model of the universe has become overburdened with *ad hoc* additions such as inflation, dark matter, and dark energy, invented to deal with theoretical difficulties, and anomalous observations. They are proposing a paradigm shift. But they don't know to what (see chapter 6).

    Historically, Galileo's observations plus Newton's theoretical work forced the final abandonment of the geocentric universe, in favour of the heliocentric model (see

---

13. Richard E Creel, *Thinking Philosophically* (Oxford: Blackwell, 2001). Quoting Aristotle's 'Metaphysics', IV.

chapter 4). Einstein's work on light caused the change of the ultimate theory of light from a wave to a particle phenomenon.

Many models thought to be the final answer have had to give way to newer, more accurate models. For example: the Milky Way was seen as the totality of the universe, but in the 1920s it was found that this was not so; it was assumed that the expansion rate of the universe must decrease, but in 1998 this was found to be wrong.

Models challenge our common sense intuition: particles with wave properties; quantum 'spooky action at a distance'; dark energy of the vacuum; and the big bang theory. Can models be what is real if they seem to be incomprehensible?

9.1.2 Science is descriptive
We gather information about how nature is acting, but we do not acquire a true picture of what is within nature to make it behave the way it does, or know why nature is thus constructed. As Stoeger says:

> Although the laws of nature do reveal and describe fundamental patterns of behaviour and regularities in the real world, we cannot consider them the source of those regularities, much less attribute to them the physical necessity these regularities seem to manifest.[14]

9.1.3 Models bring us closer to reality
Each new model brings us closer to reality, because it takes into account all the features the previous model explained, but also deals with additional features unexplainable by the old model.

Writer, nuclear scientist and Anglican priest John Polkinghorne subscribes strongly to this view:

> Our understanding of the physical world will never be total but it can become progressively more accurate . . . The result is a tightening grasp of a never completely comprehended reality.[15]

Closeness to reality can be signalled by elegance and simplicity. The *elegance* of a theory involves attractiveness and simplicity. Is there an attractiveness associated with a certain solution? Is there *beauty* in the equation? String theorist Michio Kaku once said that he was almost reduced to tears when he first read the Dirac equation, such was its beauty. (The Dirac equation is the electron's relativistic wave equation.) Einstein thought the simpler the equation to describe a phenomenon, the more likely it was to represent reality.

If a simple new idea resolves an otherwise difficult problem, this is evidence of getting closer. Ptolemy with his epicycles is certainly elegant, but not simple. The idea of the sun as centre is simpler than that of the earth as centre, and on this count is more likely to be true.

9.2 Emergence or reductionism?
'Reductionism' in science maintains that all phenomena are explainable in terms of the properties of the basic constituents. 'Emergence' maintains the behaviour of living things are not fully explainable in terms of the laws regulating the most basic constituents.

---
14. Stoeger, *Quantum Cosmology and the Laws of Nature*, 208.
15. John Polkinghorne, *One World* (Princeton: Princeton University Press, 1987), 17.

9.2.1 Reductionism and the alleged triumph of science
The success of science leads to the contemporary belief that science will lead us to all knowledge of everything and solve all our problems. Experimental evidence is our unique guide to truth.

An underlying idea here is reductionism. Reductionism maintains everything can be explained in terms of bottom level laws of physics. One can go up the scale of entities, from the simplest to the more complex, in stages. Reductionism would assert each stage could be explained fully in terms of the lower stages. Ultimately everything could be explained by the laws involved with stage one: quarks, gluons, electrons and neutrinos. Much can be learned about the cell by studying its chemistry. But does that explain its aliveness, or additional properties of working together for the good of the whole?

Can the behaviour of a complex system be entirely understood by knowing fully the laws involving the constituents of the complex system?

Reductionism would explain the origin of life in this way: if we were to factor in everything about the prebiotic 'soup' and its environment then we could predict life from the laws of physics.

Francis Crick defines reductionism for the biological context when he says in *The Astonishing Hypothesis*:

> You, your joys and your sorrows, your memories and your ambitions, your sense of personal identity and free will, are in fact no more than the behaviour of a vast assembly of nerve cells and their associated molecules. As Lewis Carroll's Alice might have phrased: 'You're nothing but a pack of neurons'. This hypothesis is so alien to the ideas of most people today that it can truly be called astonishing.[16]

This would include thought, consciousness and free will.

9.2.2 Emergence

The ladder of increasing complexity/ascending awareness

Mind, intelligent consciousness, thought, free will
↑
Sensation: seeing, feeling, hearing, memory, taste, smell
↑
Groups of cells coordinated together
↑
Cells
↑
Macromolecules
↑
Molecules
↑
Atoms
↑
Protons, neutrons, electrons
↑
Quarks, gluons, electrons, neutrinos

> Each group's potentialities depend on the previous groups' laws. But for each group, new properties and laws emerge, which are not reducible to the laws of the lower groups.

---

16. Francis Crick, *The Astonishing Hypothesis* (New York: Charles Scribner's Sons, 1995), 3.

The contrary theory to reductionism is *emergence*. At each stage in the above nine-step scheme, new laws emerge to explain each new stage. These laws are not reducible to the laws governing the previous stage. Though they depend on the continued working of the previous stage's laws, they are new laws. The new laws are only there when the new stage of complexity comes into being. The livingness of a cell is not reducible to the properties of quarks, gluons, electrons and neutrinos. Human thought is very different to reactions between atoms, but nevertheless relies on chemistry and physics.

Paul Davies argues for emergence. He distinguishes weak emergence from strong emergence:

- Weak emergence: occurs in complex systems like weather patterns. No irreducible new laws emerge but the overall behaviour of the system cannot be predicted. The behaviour of many complex systems cannot be predicted mathematically. Their evolution is probably caused by the behaviour of components, but predictive calculations are too hard. We need to watch and see how they evolve, for example, a hurricane.

- Strong emergence: a living cell develops properties which cannot be reduced to the properties of the individual atoms. As Paul Davies says, writing for the *New Scientist*, 'Some complex systems may be understood only by taking into account additional laws or organising principles that emerge at various levels of complexity.'[17] An example of this is life, the behaviour of any living organism.

    Davies distinguishes this type of emergence from the behaviour of chaotic systems, such as weather patterns. Weather could be understood if we knew all the motions of all the air particles, which we cannot. The livingness of a cell is more than all the chemistry. Something new has emerged.

---

17. Paul Davies, *New Scientist*, 5 March 2005.

Further reading

Hanbury Brown, *The Wisdom of Science* (Cambridge: Cambridge University Press, 1988).

AK Dewdney, *Beyond Reason: Eight Great Problems that Reveal the Limits of Science* (Hoboken New Jersey: John Wiley and Sons, 2004).

Chris Imprey and Catherine Petry, editors, *International Symposium on Astrophysics Research and on the Dialogue between Science and Religion* (Italy: Vatican Observatory, Castel Gandolpho, 2002).

Leon M Lederman and David N Schramm, *From Quarks to the Cosmos: Tools of Discovery* (New York: Scientific American Library, 1995).

John Maddox, *What Remains to be Discovered* (London: Macmillan, 1998).

Abraham Pais, *Inward Bound: Of Matter and Forces in the Physical World* (Oxford: Oxford University Press, 1988).

John Polkinghorne, *Science and Creation: The Search for Understanding* (London: SPCK, 1988).

John Polkinghorne, *Science and Christian Belief: Theological Reflections of a Bottom-up Thinker* (Cambridge: Cambridge University Press, 1994).

John Polkinghorne, *Beyond Science the Wider Human Context* (Cambridge: Cambridge University Press, 1998).

John Polkinghorne, *Science and Providence: God's Interaction with the World* (Philadelphia: Templeton Press, 2005).

Michael Redhead, *From Physics to Metaphysics* (Cambridge: Cambridge University Press, 1996).

W Mark Richardson, Robert John Russell, Philip Clayton and Kirk Wegter-McNelly, editors, *Science and the Spiritual Quest: New Essays by Leading Scientists* (London: Routledge, 2002).

Jeane Staune, editor, *Science and the Search for Meaning*: Perspectives from International Scientists (Philadelphia: Templeton Press, 2006).

Dava Sobel, *Longitude: the True Story of a Lone Genius Who Solved the Greatest Scientific Problem of His Time* (London: Fourth Estate, 1996).

Lee Smolin, *The Trouble with Physics: The Rise of String Theory, the Fall of Science and What Comes Next* (London: Penguin, 2007).

3

The Method of Religion:

Reflection and Inspiration

Chapter overview

- Religion is more than working for a cause
- Religion has evolved:
    - Animism: spirits everywhere
    - Gods: human-like beings beyond
    - The *other:* an incomprehensible absolute
    - Revelation: God speaks to humanity
- Evidence for religion is not scientific evidence, but nevertheless is evidence
- Difficulties experienced by Christianity in the West today
- Christ: the answer for the world's need for a saviour
- The Trinity

1. Definition

Religion in general is a response to mystery; it is a response to mystery which affirms that there is more to reality than meets the eye.[1] A religious person is one whose life includes a response to an unseen reality. A religion is an organisation in which there is a structured response to some sort of ultimate reality whether this be prayer(s), worship, call to conversion or reform, explanations of reality, deeper reality, ethical code, enunciation of purpose—one, some or all of these, or others that may be left out. A spiritual person may not necessarily be a member of an organised religion.

Organisations such as Greenpeace, or causes such as feminism, in which people work in their own way for the perceived good of society, are not religions.

Question: How many religions can you name?

....

....

....

....

---
1. Michael Barnes, *In the Presence of Mystery* (Mystic, Connecticut, Twenty-Third Publications, 1991), 2.

Question: Do you think there is a difference between spirituality and religion? If so, what do you mean by spirituality?[2]

2. Religion is a human response

2.1 Religion is a response to a variety of human experiences

- Tragedy: Death, poverty, violence and sickness motivate a search beyond the pains, pleasures and superficialities of life, leading to a deeper appreciation of self, and to a transcendent (beyond the material) reality.

- The unexplained: Before the emergence of science, phenomena of nature such as thunder, earthquake, floods and the power of the ocean were attributed to unseen powers. Today the existence of the universe, the order in the universe, its fruitful history and the purpose of the universe can all lead to thoughts of transcendent being.

- Sense of the sacred: Religion is more than dealing with death and pain. It can be an 'encounter with the objective dimension of mystery . . . the person responding to a "presence"'.[3]

- Revelation: God has spoken to the human race. In the Old Testament, God revealed godself through prophets, and through participating in Israel's history. In Islam, God's final and decisive prophet was Mohammad. In Christianity it is God in Jesus Christ.

---

2. David Tacey, *The Spirituality Revolution* (Sydney: HarperCollins, 2003), 30–46.
3. John Haught, *What is Religion?* (New York: Paulist Press, 1990), 20.

Question: The level of everyday comfort in developed countries raises up everyday life from the gloom of daily squalor and tragedy. With squalor absent and tragedy moved into the background, what need is there for religion?

....

....

....

....

....

....

....

....

....

2.2 Varieties of response

2.2.1 Religious

- Monotheism: there is one God only.
- Dualism: there is one supreme principle of good, and one supreme principle of evil.
- Polytheism: there are many gods.
- Animism: the world is alive with spirits, good and evil.
- Emanationism: there is one God. Creation is the spilling over of divine substance.
- Pantheism: the world is part of God.
- Monism: Only God is real. Everything else is illusory appearance.
- Deism: God created the world, but is now totally remote and uninvolved.
- Process: God pre-exists, but God's 'consequent nature' evolves with the world.
- Agnosticism: The reasons for God's existence or non-existence are not conclusive. The agnostic person is sincerely searching.

2.2.2 Non-religious

Atheism: From this point of view there are good reasons for saying there is no God. For some people this will become the basis of a life that is focused on their own betterment and selfish concerns. For others it will be cause for a nihilistic depression or powerless fatalism. However many atheists find meaning within ethical and moral principles through which they work for the common good.

3. The evolution of religion

The human response to mystery has changed throughout history. It has progressed from multitudes of spirits, to many equal gods, to a high god who lorded it over other gods, to an unintelligible absolute,[4] and to an understanding that the Absolute has revealed godself to the human race.

---

4. Barnes, *In the Presence of Mystery*, 9.

3.1 Animism: spirit world of present day hunter-gatherers

Animism is the belief that all natural objects possess a soul and that all natural happenings, such as the ripening of fruit or a storm, can be attributed to spirit. All aspects of life are spiritual. The world is alive with personal and non-personal unseen forces. They are equally as real as what you can see. It is conjectured that this type of religion was the religion of humankind in its hunter-gatherer phase. Animism is practised and studied today amongst the Kalahari Desert people, the Congo Pygmies, some dwellers of Amazonian rain forest, tribal areas of New Guinea, in Australia. For these people, there are numerous spirits which are conscious invisible personal forces with thoughts, feelings and wills. They are in living things in places of power (such as mountain tops) and in places of fear (such as dark caves). They take on the character of whatever they inhabit: the spirit of the babbling brook is talkative. Just as there are no great chiefs in these hunter-gatherer cultures, so in the world of their gods, there are no great overriding powerful gods but rather dispersed energies. The demarcation line between religion and secular does not exist; all life is in the realm of the sacred.

People have attendant personal spirits. Some spirits are pests; they make you trip and break a leg, or cause the apples to rot, or the milk to go sour; they cause disease and death. The spirits of the dead are at the edge of the campsite, or in the land of the dead. They can come back to the camp for various reasons, as may the spirits of the original ancestors. Each human being is a spirit being.

A child is taught how to hunt and, equally importantly, how to deal with spirits: not to tread on taboo ground; to know which rocks and trees have spirits; to care for your good spirit, or for the spirit of the place by pouring drink onto the ground; how to drive away pest spirits with crackers, gongs, clattering sticks, the figure of a cross or star, or with garlic.

Human diseases and crises are closely related to the existence of spirits. For instance, in offending nature or spirits and causing disorder in the supernatural realm, one can experience physical illness and symptoms.

When sorcery combines with religion and philosophy the doctrine of folk medicine becomes more systematised although its belief in the cause of disease remains. Folk medicine regards the person's life, death, and fortune as divine experiences.

Question: Is animism anything more or less than living in God's presence?

3.1.1 Chinese folk medicine

Echoes of animism are found in Chinese folk medicine, which is still practiced today in China and throughout the world.[5]. It may include a wide variety of practices such as acupuncture, herbal medication, aromatherapy, bee venom therapy, energy therapy, foot reflexology, massage Zen contemplation, fasting, organic foods, yoga and meditation. Many different kinds of illnesses are recognised, some of which are attributed to spirits. As many of its practices are calming and balancing they may have powerful calming effects on the immune system.

Practices may also pertain to the paranormal: soothsaying, divinations, drawn sticks, appeasements, consecrated water, and use specialists in the paranormal such as spiritual mediums or Taoist practitioners.

Chinese folk medicine is still an important part of people's lives and has long been a part of Chinese culture. Its influence is strong and even found among the educated. Chemistry professor Frank Buldenhozer, in writing of the Taiwan situation from Taipei's Fu Jen University, reports that whenever he sets a task on science and religion, students often see this in terms of folk medicine.

3.1.2 Australian Indigenous culture

A traditional Aboriginal creation story shows some similarities with animism:

> The Earth is uncreated and eternal. From eternity, the earth was a bare plain, like the Nullarbor Plain, nothing more. Under this plain, eternally sleeping, dwelt a great multitude of supernatural beings. These supernatural beings emerged from eternal sleep. (Under the Nullarbor Plain are caves and water.)
>
> The supernatural beings created all the physical features—sand-hills, rivers, ranges, rocks. Each Aboriginal group depicted their supernatural being, their ancestor as an animal. Native cat ancestor while fashioning the landscape moved about in human form, but could turn at will into a native cat. And from him all cats in the district came as well as humans in the region. This is similar for snakes, kangaroos, emus in other regions. Humans in the region are regarded as re-incarnations of the ancestor, or his supernatural children. Each supernatural being was linked invisibly with a plant or animal. At end of labours supernatural beings returned to earth or changed into rocks, trees etc. They sleep the eternal sleep they'd slept before from eternity.
>
> Sacred sites are the places from which the beings emerged. They became waterholes, soaks, claypans, caves. Though asleep, the ancestors retain the power to send down rain, fill the earth with plants, or with animals of their own totem. They do this whenever they are summoned by rites.
>
> Everything on earth is continued gift. The people did not have to work, only collect the gifts. The people firstly implore their ancestor to give the gifts in a sacred dance a 'corroboree'. Corroborees are ceremonies in which these humans, re-incarnations of the ancestors, intoned the sacred verses that the supernatural beings themselves had first sung during their own labours of creation. Aborigines believe they enter into, continue the creative activity of their ancestors. Ceremonies—corroborees—re-enact what had

---

5. Chi-Meng Cheng, 'Scientific and Cultural Aspects of Folk Medicine, in *Religion and Science in the Context of Chinese Culture*, edited by Tak-kwong Chan, Yi-Jia Tsai and Frank Budenholzer (Adelaide: ATF, 2006), 81–106.

gone before so that the events became present again. The ceremonial was the tribe's work, and they then hunted or collected what they had previously created, through their ceremony.

A group in Western Australia, as reported in the *Australian*, after twenty years perseverance have succeeded in gaining title to large tracts of land recognised. Some of the interest in gaining land title is to have these sacred sites preserved.[6]

3.2 The emergence of more distant gods
With the development of agriculture and the consequent establishment of areas of permanent settlement, chiefs and kings became features of cultures. Mirroring the culture, gods appeared among the spirits as chiefs. As a tribe now had a chief, its god was imagined as a chief. As various classes of people became evident within the culture, so there developed a hierarchy of power among the gods.

The gods have personality, thoughts, feelings, wills and relationships between each other; they experience peace and strife. They can be helpful and kind, or petty and destructive. The more powerful gods are not like your neighbour, but more like a chief whom you respect or fear. They are more remote than the spirits of animism—living in the sky, the sea, or under the earth. The local spirits, who inhabit everyday space are now under the control of the chief god. For example, the sea god rules the underwater cave spirits. The chief god is often the highest god, the one able to dominate most other gods. Each major cilvilisation has its own high god.

In Indo-European culture, the sky was conceived as the dominant realm, because the power of the sun and the storm overwhelmed all else. Therefore, the sky god is the high god. In ancient Greece the high god is Zeus. Under the high god, the other gods divide up territory: Poseidon took the sea, and Hades the underground. In ancient Egypt Ra is the sun god.

> In Egypt, Ra the sun god was the high god. The sun as the giver of light was also perceived as the giver of life and so, had the most important god associated with it. Each morning Ra, as the sun, rose in the east and set off across the world to sink below the horizon in the west.
>
> The sun is in the solar barque. The solar barque is supported by Shu and the sun is received by the sun goddess Nut.
>
> Ra had an origin. In the time of chaos, the celestial goose, the great cackler (whose cackling broke the silence of the universe) came to the mound of Hermopolis and laid an egg from which was born Ra, sun god and creator of the world.
>
> The Nile Delta was home to many snakes, and wild cats were treasured and welcomed into homes because they were snake killers. Bast was the cat goddess. Bast accompanied the solar barque through the regions of night and nightly gave battle to the serpent Apep, the enemy of Ra. Each night Ra went over the horizon showing the way to the world of the dead.[7]

Gods have their own passions and pride; they can be emotionally immature. They are not always gracious and can go on the rampage causing disasters such as floods and epidemics.

---

6. Paul Albrecht, *Aboriginal Creation Story*, edited version of a talk to the Lutheran Youth of Australia Assembly, Canberra, 1 August 1988.
7. Richard Patrick and Peter Croft, *Classic Ancient Mythology* (London: Hennerwood Publications Ltd, 1987), selections from 32–52.

The classic tale of *The Odyssey* narrates the stories of the impact of the whims of the gods on humanity.

3.3 The beginning of Greek philosophy: a move from gods towards nature
Around 600 BCE, with the move towards larger settlements, some people were freed from labour, and there was leisure to look beyond the everyday, systematic modes of thought arose in many major cultures.

In Ionia at this time, there arose a democracy, with its potentialities for freedom. Miletos and Ephesus were two great ports on the Aegean Sea, and there were trading connections with Egypt, India and China. Commerce gave rise to intellectual curiosity. All these factors contributed to a fertile ground for philosophical and scientific thinking. A new attitude of mind emerged. Philosophy and science arose at the same time; they were intermingled. Curiosity and the critical mind can only flourish in a climate of free discussion. Ionia thus was the centre for great thinkers: Thales (c624–c546 BCE), Pythagoras (c560–c480 BCE), Heraclitus (c535–47BCE), Empedocles (c490–430 BCE) and Zeno (490–430 BCE).

Investigations were going beyond mere utilitarianism for day-to-day living. Problems were studied for their own sakes. Intellectual work was perceived as noble and pleasurable and mathematics developed. Natural explanations were sought for natural phenomena. So Thales, the first known Greek thinker not to appeal to the gods, proposed that lightning was caused by wind cutting through clouds. An angry Zeus was no longer seen as a sufficient cause of lightning and thunder. Earthquakes were now seen as a consequence of subterranean rivers shaking the ground rather then an enraged Poseidon. But at this point the origin of the universe was not a question because it was thought to have always existed. In this climate, thoughts of a being not representable by images arose.

3.4 The emergence of monotheism

In the centuries before the birth of Christ totally separate and uncommunicating cultures came to the same conclusion: they saw that supporting all reality is an incomprehensible absolute. This absolute was not human or animal but an unseen transcendent entity. At the base of many of these views were these principles:

- There is an ultimate unity to all things.
- The source of this unity lies beyond or beneath complexities and changes, beyond the limits of the world.
- The source is a reality of total perfection.
- Such perfection must be an incomprehensible absolute.[8]

3.4.1 The West: Judaism, Christianity, Islam
The first great monotheistic religion, a religion which has just one absolute God, was Judaism. With the establishment of Christianity and then six hundred years later the emergence of Islam, there are three main monotheistic religions. In the West, the absolute possessed the following features:

- God has unlimited power.
- God created the universe: there being no pre-existing material God created the universe out of nothing.
- God's knowledge is unlimited or omniscient: God knows everything that is happening now, everything that happened in the past, and everything that will happen.

---
8. Barnes, *In the Presence of Mystery*, 48.

- God is good: God is compassionate, understanding, and is not manipulative in relationships with created beings.
- God is personal.[9]

God is thus the infinite incomprehensible fullness, beyond any limitation. The Western absolute is personal, rules the universe, and communicates its Self through prophets and through intervention in historical events. God is concerned with the right ordering of the world, and with right relationships between people. God is eternal and exempt from conditions of time and space, but shows godself in time and space. Salvation is from sin and evil. If you do not comply with God's will you do not achieve salvation.

3.4.2 East: Taoism, Buddhism and Hinduism

The Eastern absolute is eternal and unchanging, non-personal and having the stillness that is the source of all activity. Salvation is salvation from the human condition: from the cycle of suffering, death, and decay.

- Taoism arose sometime in the first millennium BCE.[10] Reality is a manifestation of *yin* and *yang*. *Yin* is female, *yang* is male. The colliding and interaction of *yin* and *yang* led to the formation of heaven, earth and air, which produced all else. The dregs formed a static earth in the centre. Beneath *yin/yang*, there is a non-personal ultimate, self-existent; one supreme force, unable to be spoken, formless: this is the *tao*. It was the *tao* that put its power (*teh*) into a movement of *yin* and *yang*. *Tao* is in all and all is in it. The earth is the centre of an infinite universe. All life pass through cycles of birth, decay and rebirth.

- Buddhism is a varied system of practices and beliefs begun by *Suddhodana Gautama* (c560–c480 BCE) in his search for deliverance from pain.[11] The 'four noble truths' of Buddhism are:

    o Human existence is pain.
    o Pain is caused by desire.
    o Pain can be overcome by victory over desire.
    o This is to be done by means of the 'eight-fold path': 'right views, right intentions, right speech, right action, right livelihood, right effort, right mindfulness and right concentration'.[12]

In Buddhism, the individual self is not distinct from the one life permeating all beings. Whether this one life is seen as God, depends on the particular Buddhist tradition. Buddhists will sometimes say their creed is not a theology but a way of life.

> If by religion we mean the quest for transcendent reality, or the sense of god, or the sacred, or even the 'One' of Hinduism, then Buddhism does not look much like a religion, at least initially. However, Buddhism may still be called a religion. Like other religions, it holds out a way to ultimate salvation, to a final liberation or fulfilment. It may not speak explicitly of God or the sacred. But in its very advocacy of 'silence' about ultimate

---

9. Barnes, *In the Presence of Mystery*, 55–7.
10. Cheng, *Religion and Science in the Context of Chinese Culture*.
11. Haught, *What is Religion?*, 46–59.
12. Haught, *What is religion?*, 51.

reality it nonetheless promotes in its participants a movement of self-transcendence.[13]

- Hinduism embraces many local and common gods, but ultimately there is one transcendent reality, Brahman. It is often necessary to relate to Brahman through intermediaries, such as Vishnu and Shiva. Other gods are manifestations of Brahman. Hindus have thought deeply for five millennia, and there are many writings. For them, the absolute is not personal but totally, utterly different: remote, impersonal, and incomprehensible, without attributes. 'There is one supreme and ultimate reality, infinite and incomprehensible, that lies behind the entire universe, a reality to be called Brahman. It is the ocean of Being, the fullness of Power, the Really Real.'[14]

  We are generally ignorant of the real inner nature of our being. The reality is that we are in a state of identity with Brahman, or Brahman is very close to us within. We suffer because we do not realise our inner nature, and salvation means becoming aware of our oneness with or closeness to Brahman.

Question: Is the evolution to one overriding principle in Judaism, Taoism, Hinduism, and others, a process of significance? (Islam and Christianity are then developments from Judaism).

....

....

....

....

....

Question: To what extent can the differing claims of the world's religions be understood as culturally conditioned responses to the same reality ?

....

....

....

....

....

....

....

---

13. Haught, *What is religion?*, 55–6.
14. Barnes, *In the Presence of Mystery*, 65.

3.5 Revelation

Judaism maintains that God revealed godself to the nation through intervening in Israel's history, through leading figures such as Abraham, Moses, David, and through the prophets.

Judaism holds God to be the God of the Old Testament. Christianity holds the God of the New Testament, claiming the transcendent God of the Old Testament became man in Jesus Christ, the second person of the Trinity. Muslims accept the Old Testament and the New Testament,[15] but declare that Mohammad (570–632 CE) was God's final and definitive manifestation, Jesus being but another prophet.

Question: How can one respond to the claim of the prophetic religions to have originated from a revelation from God ?

....

....

....

....

....

4. Evidence for religion[16]

It is not self-evident that religion can be dismissed, as some pundits today might think. There is an identifiable sphere of human interaction with reality which can be attributed to the religious experience of the human race.

Religion is not a matter of believing the unbelievable, nor is faith believing because there is no reason. Faith is not an unexamined leap into the void. Nor is faith a certain conclusion like $1 + 3 = 4$, or the acceleration due to gravity is $9.8 ms^{-2}$. There are reasons for theistic belief in general, and for believing specific systems of faith.

Richard Dawkins asserts there is no evidence:

> After all, what is faith? It is a state of mind that leads people to believe in something—it doesn't matter what—in the total absence of supporting evidence. If there were good supporting evidence then faith would be superfluous, for the evidence would compel us to believe it anyway.[17]

Question: What evidence is there for your faith?

....

....

....

....

---

15. Except where they contradict the *Qur'an* and then Islam claims the texts have been corrupted in these parts.
16. John Polkinghorne, *One World* (Princeton: Princeton University Press, 1987), 26–38.
17. Richard Dawkins, *The Selfish Gene* (Oxford: OUP, 1989), 330.

4.1 Universality of religion

As shown in the section on the stages of religious thought, religion has been a significant part in every age of humankind's development, and it is a significant feature of the human race today in every part of the world. Even in secular Western Europe and Australia over half the population still adheres to a faith and almost all of those in the Americas count themselves believers. Today Christianity continues to spread in Africa. Islam is a very strong presence throughout the Middle East, Indonesia and other parts of Asia. Seventy years of enforced atheism in Russia did not manage to obliterate people's faith, nor has state opposition annihilated religion in China. Most Taiwanese are religious, and Catholicism has become strong in South Korea.

4.2 Writing

There are many records of experiences, collections of reasoning, statements of values, accounts of history and stories. The Judeo-Christian scriptures are collections of various styles of writings and immense amounts of study have been put into interpreting these ancient documents over the last seventy years. There are writings of academics, saints and holy people.

In Judaism the Bible is accompanied by an oral tradition which, once written down, is called the *Midrash*. The *Zorah* is the collection of mystical texts and the *Kabbalah* the collection of ritual practices.

The Islamic sacred text is the *Qur'an* and its oral and ritual tradition is in the *Hadiths*. Some key Islamic commentators, such as Al-Farabi (c870–950), Avicenna (980–1037) and Averroes (1126–1198), were not just important to Islamic culture but also important to Christianity.

Hinduism provides a wealth of writings. Its sacred texts include the *Vedas* which were written fifteen hundred years before the birth of Christ and the *Upanishads* which go back to 600BCE.[18]

4.3 Mystical experience

In encounter with the mysterious *other*, usual barriers between the individual and the absolute are broken. The experience is unable to be put into words. There is a similar methodology for acquiring mystical experiences common to Judaism, Hinduism, Buddhism, Christianity and Islam. In Christianity some examples of mystical experiences are Ignatius Loyola's *Spiritual Exercises* and *Autobiography* (which are records of what he attributed to be experiences between himself and God) and Teresa of Avila's *Interior Castle* (where she describes how at its deepest levels consciousness reflects a profound in-touchness with the divine).

We all have awareness, and some would say that each of our individual awarenesses is rooted in a larger common principle of consciousness which we can barely begin to appreciate.

These mystical experiences are not only to be found in the past. At times they may occur without deliberate practices to induce them.

> Will Meecham was a surgeon in San Francisco. His life was going very well until he had a major mental breakdown. And he went to hospital for a month. You might think this was a horrible time, and you'd be right, he said. But in the midst of it all I found a pearl of the divine. God literally touched me. One night I was in abject despair, praying to a God I didn't really believe in. I was so desperate for help I prayed: God, 'you just have to exist, you have to

---

18. Haught, *What is Religion?*, 34.

help me, or I can't go on'. 'I repeated this over and over all night long. When morning arrived, a whole series of fantastic coincidences and visions occurred around me. This went on for days, but at the most profound moment, my eyes opened up to a shimmering window of light, and a penetrating calm swept over me leaving me awed at complete peace. I knew that God was there, God cared, and I was going to make it through these hard times'.

Meecham asked: 'Can God come to a person through a disordered brain?' He answered: 'Mystics and spiritual leaders throughout history have described experiences that sound a lot like my visions. The advances in knowledge about the brain make it easy to ascribe all mental states to patterns of neuronal activity. Depressed? There may be a disorder in serotonin modulation. Is your child too dreamy? Maybe we can fix that with Ritalin. God manifests before you? There must be a problem in your temporal lobe? Is there a place for the spirit separate from ceaseless electrical and chemical activity in the brain? There is an enormous gap between firing of neurons and awareness, between chemicals jumping between synapses and feelings of happiness, depression, anxiety, determination, spiritual peace.'

Despite these reflections based on his medical knowledge, he reflected 'following my visions my faith in God was absolute; I went from a state of studied agnosticism to complete surrender to the divine. My gratitude for these gifts was all-consuming. With the passage of time, doubts sometimes trouble me. But on the deepest level I know that within me there is the seed of something grand and powerful. What have I done since? The direct fruit of my passage through this profound period was my conversion to Catholicism. My resulting relationship with Christ has given the trials of five years ago inexpressible importance. My life fell apart, but when it came back together I was in the company of God.'[19]

Question: Meecham was well aware of the importance of brain chemistry in connection with this experience. Yet he was convinced that it was an overwhelming experience of a spiritual reality. Discuss.

---

19. *National Catholic Reporter*, 25 November 2005.

Mystical experience, an 'encounter with the numinous presence of an Other',[20] has a universal dimension:

> The overcoming of the usual barriers between the individual and the Absolute is the great mystic achievement. We become one with the Absolute and we become aware of our oneness hardly altered by difference of clime or creed. In Hinduism, in Neoplatonism, in Sufism, in Christian mysticism, we find the same recurring note, so there is about mystical utterances an eternal unanimity which ought to make a critic stop and think.[21]

In a less dramatic way ordinary faith experiences of trust, reading and prayer give rise to feelings of certainty about belief. Submitting oneself to the scriptures brings contact with the sacred.

4.4 Making sense of reality

When order is introduced into a realm of experience by use of a certain concept (for example: gravity, quantum theory, electromagnetic waves and atoms), there is a *prima facie* case for believing in the entities to which the concepts refer. In the same way, creation and cosmic evolution—an evolution resulting in intelligent beings—and the purpose of the universe are explained by the concept of a Being who transcends this creation.

Question: Is science is unable to answer questions of purpose? Has religion a role here?

....

....

....

....

....

....

....

4.5 Other sources of evidence

- Religion gives answers to some questions posed by science and unanswerable by the scientific method. Religion offers an answer for questions such as: Why is matter endowed with such creative qualities? Whence the fine-tuning of the universe to produce life? Why is the universe intelligible? Does the mathematical intricacy of reality demand an intelligence? Where did the laws come from? Why was the big bang fruitful? Why is there anything at all? (Chapters 6, 8, 9.)

---

20. Polkinghorne, *One World*, 29.
21. Polkinghorne, *One World*, 29. Quoting from William James, *The Varieties of Religious Experience* (New York: Longmans, Green and Co, 1923).

- The convergence of the major religions. Is the evolution in the same era to one overriding mysterious being in Judaism, Islam, Christianity, Taoism, Hinduism, and others, a process of significance?

- The resurrection (see chapter 10).

5. Difficulties for religion in the West

5.1 Reasons for difficulties

That organised religion in industrialised consumerist societies is under pressure at this time is beyond dispute. Some of the reasons would be the following:

- Much of religion comes from the past, and its wisdom is necessarily mixed with archaic concepts.

- Religion is considered as fixed and, therefore, unchangeable in an era of great change. But people are ignorant of the research work of theologians. The fruitful work of scholars is not always handed on.

- Early in the scientific revolution, the church saw science as a threat, and fought against it. Great scientists were threatened and silenced by the church's power to excommunicate and put to death So religion is still perceived as an enemy of science, despite the great benefits brought by science. Often evidence is not sought, and the discussion begins and ends with Galileo (full discussion in chapter 4).

- The retreat of the church in the earlier stages of the scientific revolution. After the damaging Galileo affair, the church was seen to oppose or belittle scientific progress, and resisted the theory of evolution. Darwin's *On the Origin of Species* was condemned by the Council of Cologne. In 1887 Abbe Leroy proposed that evolution was not contrary to faith, and that it did not imply a denial of God; he was summoned to Rome where the authorities insisted he change his view.[22]

    Books such as *Wayfarers in The Cosmos*[23] by Vatican Observatory director George Coyne, SJ, and a series on *Scientific Perspectives on Divine Action* published by Vatican Observatory Publications along with statements by Pope John Paul II and Pope Benedict XVI indicate that the Catholic Church has parted ways with such historically affected positions.

- Many of life's problems were seen as being amenable to religious solutions. Now we have psychologists, psychiatrists and social workers (as well as sport and entertainment and affluence). These can be perceived to have superseded the effectiveness of religious solutions. Yet spiritual concerns deal with the relationship between an individual and something beyond science, and hence are inaccessible to psychologists. There is still a significant role for the spiritual director: Psychiatrist Gerald May explores the role of the spiritual director at length and points to differences in the roles of psychotherapists and spiritual directors. A quote shows the direction of his thinking:

---

22. Jean-Pierre Lonchamp, *Science and Belief* (Middlegreen UK: Guernsey Press, 1993) 109–10.
23. George Coyne, SJ, *Wayfarers in the Cosmos* (New York: Crossroad, 2002).

> Psychotherapy often seeks to bolster an individual's capacity to gratify needs and desires and to achieve a sense of autonomous matter over self and circumstance. In contrast spiritual direction seeks liberation from attachments and a self-giving surrender to the discerned power and will of God. In the harshest medical model of psychiatry, the physician assumes the role of healer. In spiritual direction, however, the true healer, nurturer, sustainer and liberator is the Lord. [24]

- The chemical DNA, which is the basis of life, has been isolated and manipulated. It is said life, consciousness and spirit are electrical and chemical so there is no need for soul and spirit.[25] Yet the phenomena of consciousness, free will and the sense of self transcend the physics and chemistry on which they depend.

- Science, by some, is seen to be the only valid form of thinking. When this position is firmly held it is called scientism. Throughout the nineteenth century, there developed a euphoria flowing from the constant progress of science, and confidence in its unlimited powers. Anything not science was devalued. Religious truths were called outdated prejudices. Science was declared to be the only road to truth. Today writers such as biologist Richard Dawkins loudly proclaim the pre-eminence of science and in addition speak strongly against religion:

    > In a universe of blind physical forces and genetic replication, some people are going to get hurt, other people are going to get lucky, and you won't find any rhyme or reason in it, nor any justice. The universe we observe has precisely the properties we should expect if there is, at bottom, no design, no purpose, no evil and no good, nothing but blind pitiless indifference. As that unhappy poet AE Housman put it 'For nature, heartless, witless nature, will neither know nor care'. DNA neither knows nor cares. DNA just is. And we dance to its music.[26]

5.2 Difficulties lead to dismissive attitudes
The difficulties facing religion in this age, when science is such a powerful form of knowledge, is accompanied by popular attitudes which tend to dismiss religion without closely examining its credentials. Many people hold versions of the following views:

- Religious faith is believing the unbelievable.
- Religious faith is believing in what has been disproved.
- There is no evidence for religious faith—if there were, it would not be faith.
- Religious faith is nothing but the meaning you want to give something.
- At its best religion is irrelevant.

---

24. Gerald May, MD, *Care of Mind Care of Spirit* (New York: Harper Collins, 1992), 17, 18.
25. Francis Crick, *The Astonishing Hypothesis* (New York: Charles Scribner's Sons, 1995), 3.
26. Richard Dawkins, *River Out of Eden* (London: Orion Publishing Group, 1995), 133.

Question: Do you identify with any of these statements? Would you say religion is 'up to you' and has nothing going for it in terms of evidence or logical argument?

....

....

....

....

....

Question: Do you think most people lead their lives on principles derived from the scientific method, or rather on 'certainties' they have derived from elsewhere?

....

....

....

....

....

....

....

6. Christ and salvation

6.1 The world seeks saviours

Human stories are full of salvation, both historical and fictional. Historical versions are the imagined triumphs of the victors in world wars and the successes of political leadership (Mao was seen as China's saviour). Fictional versions include *Batman, Spiderman, Superman*, and the heroes of *Star Wars* and *The Matrix*. After the events of 9/11, the West seeks salvation from *terror*. Even if there is no real threat, the media will invent one, and leave us fascinated and perhaps worried.

There is promise of a saviour at the end of the paradise and fall story. And in every chapter of early Genesis, this is the answer. Humans will mess it up, but God enters to save. For Christians, to right the wrongs in the world is beyond human power. The results of sin—injury, resentment, hostility and alienation—radiate like ripples from a pebble thrown in a pond. Christ's refusal to meet hostility with hostility, sin with sin, is the antidote to the endless cycles of revenge and violence. Salvation can be individual and personal. When someone responds to Christ, God is acting decisively within the experience of the person, not to bind the person, but to free the person; to free the person from prejudice, from jaundiced views of others, from greed and to remove blindness to self.

6.2 Jesus: a challenge for his times.

Wherever he went, Jesus changed people. Jesus was a challenge: he challenged those embedded in mediocrity; he challenged those crippled by legalism; he challenged his friends to rise above petty jealousies; he challenged their faith by his death.

Jesus challenged the 'establishment' by eating and drinking with tax collectors and other sinners; tax collectors were notorious as extortionists. Jesus challenged the tax collector Matthew. He did not consider him, as our newspapers say, 'disgraced', but rather said 'follow me'. Matthew responded to the challenge and Matthew changed.

He challenged the rich young man. He had too many of the good things, so did not respond to the challenge. He did not change. He challenged the Samaritan woman. She approached him when he was sitting on the well and he asked her for a drink. He then raised the subject of the spirit within, which he called living water, and mentioned her life-style. She accepted him and told the whole town about him, and changed.

When confronted by the sick and the down and out, he challenged them to believe in themselves: 'Has anyone condemned you?' 'Go and sin no more'. Those he cured he challenged to think well of themselves.

One day he was speaking in the synagogue, and all sorts of people were there. When a man with the deformed hand approached him, he challenged the doctors of the law. He looked them in the eye and said publicly in the hearing of all: 'Is it lawful to heal on the Sabbath?' No one replied. He healed the man, challenging the closed minds and the jealous hearts of the leaders. After that they began to plot his downfall.

Jesus was not a conformist, but rather somewhat of a stirrer. He could not be shrugged off and put in his place. A group of Jewish scholars tried to better him. They approached him with the question of whether or not it was lawful to pay tribute to Caesar. If he said 'yes', the Jews would be angered; they resented the army of occupation. If he said 'no', the Romans would become interested in this influential person and he could be arrested. But he turned it back on them when he asked the questioner to show him a coin. There were two currencies, the local currency and the more valuable Roman coins. The questioner pulled out a coin. It was a Roman coin. On it was the head of Caesar. He had implicated himself with the occupiers of the land by using their currency instead of the local coins. The questioner showed himself as a collaborator and was caught out.

Jesus taught differently to the rabbis. He taught on his own authority. 'You have heard it said . . . but I say to you . . . '[27] Exasperated they ask him on whose authority did he teach. They were not seeking information, but to reduce his influence. He responded by asking them whether or not John the Baptist was a prophet. If they said 'yes', they were endorsing him because John had declared his support for Jesus. If they said 'no', they would lose face before the people, many of whom had gone to the Jordan to be baptised by John, and believed him a true prophet. They said they could not answer, they did not know. He said, 'neither will I tell you the authority by which I teach'.

Question:. Why do you think Christ had such influence over people that he could change them?

....

....

....

---

27. Matthew 5.

6.3 Jesus: a challenge for our times

The values that receive attention in the media include power, wealth, narcissism, immediate gratification, creature comforts, sex appeal, pride, greed, competition and escapism. Universal values on the other hand include love, truthfulness, fairness, freedom, unity, tolerance, responsibility and respect for life.[28]

Question: Is this being too hard on the media? Look at today's morning paper. On which side of the ledger did it fall, media values or universal values?

What does Jesus, the risen one, think of the world today? Today he himself challenges us. Enjoy the wonderful things science has given us and try to make sure that everyone gets a share. But look beyond these to the giver of all gifts, and to the paths that bring enduring happiness, self-knowledge, self-belief and the ability to be generous to others.

---

28. Hugh Mackey, Research on Australian's Traditional Value, 'Back to Basics'.

Question: He has described himself as 'the way, the truth, the life'. How accurate is his self assessment?

....

....

....

....

....

....

Not only does he show the way, but he also enables us to follow the way. Paul exclaimed:

> So I find this rule: that for me where I want to do nothing but good, evil is close at my side. In my inmost self I dearly love God's law, but I see that acting on my body there is a different law which battles against the law of my mind. So I am brought to be a prisoner of that law of sin which lives inside my body. Who will rescue me from this body doomed to death? God—thanks be to him—through Jesus Christ our Lord.[29]

6.4 A new creation

Jesus Christ is seen not only as one who has the recipe and strength for a better human society, but also as the conqueror of death; not only of his own death but of the death of everyman and everywoman. As Paul said, 'But what could be the new heaven and the new earth?' As resurrected humans this would not be a 'disembodied, timeless eternity',[30] but something suitable for resurrected humans. If one examines all the stages of the evolving cosmos, one can see it was not possible to predict each succeeding stage from the one that went before it. Could you predict stars from hydrogen, the ninety-two elements from stars, the accelerating universe from the nature of matter or human beings from proconsul?[31] Physicists predict the demise of the universe, but maybe it has more surprises in store. Maybe God's final plan is prewritten into the laws of physics. If not, the new creation could be something springing from the present through God's creative action, 'the new will be to the old as the flower is to the seed, as the butterfly is to the chrysalis'.[32]

For the human person an act of God is necessary, as it was in the case of Jesus' resurrection. Jesus' new life was not the resuscitation of a corpse, but a transformation to a new form of existing; his friends knew him but sensed him as very different. New life is resurrection of the body, eternal life for the same person and, just as it was for Jesus, a 'new mode of physicality, over and above the present one'.[33]

The confession that Jesus is the Christ is the Christian answer to the question of salvation and redemption. In his life, death and resurrection something happened that has fundamental

---

29. Paul, *Letter to the Romans* 7:22–5.
30. Marcus J Borg and NT Wright, *The Meaning of Jesus: Two Visions* (San Francisco: Harper Collins, 2000), 197.
31. A tree dwelling mammal thought to be a human ancestor.
32. Borg and Wright, *The Meaning of Jesus*, 198.
33. Borg and Wright, *The Meaning of Jesus*, 200.

importance for the entire human race and even for the whole of created order. The story of the incarnation is unique: the love of God shown in the dreadful fate of God made man. The resurrection is the hope of transcendent fulfilment.

6.5 Jesus, the face of God.
Today people rightly ask the question: 'Who was Jesus?' Many books have been written about differing aspects of the life of Jesus and there are many interpretations of his personality and mission. Jesus is moral preacher, humanist, social reformer, revolutionary, demagogue, superstar and free man. *Time* magazine has had a feature concerning 'Jesus and the Internet'. The teaching of the Christian church is that Jesus is truly a man and truly God. The Christian view is the Christmas view as sung in the popular carol: 'Veiled in flesh the godhead see, hail the incarnate Deity! Pleased as man with man to dwell, Jesus our Emmanuel'. We try to pin him down with labels and fit him into categories. Labels may capture individual aspects, but never the whole phenomenon of Jesus.

The Christian God is the God revealed in Jesus of Nazareth. Not one exercising huge powers over such things as floods or earthquakes, but one accepting others as free, setting forth the love of God in word and action, appealing to people to rise above hate and revenge, and one willing to go to a horrible death proclaiming the message of God's love. Although meditations on the ultimate lead us to some understanding of how different is God, we gain access to something more of the nature of God by contemplating Jesus. As the source of all existence, God remains shrouded in otherness, but we have an inkling of something wonderful in the person of Jesus.

Question: What is your concept of heaven?

....

....

....

....

....

7. The Trinity

The Christian belief is that there is an absolute, but with a difference. Through Christianity there is a revelation of God's self: the absolute is the Trinity. In the Trinity, God is not a static essence, but a community. This itself is a mystery. How can one be three? How can one transcend time?

7.1 God is not the only mystery
The incomprehensibility of God should not be reason for dismissal, for it is not only God who is incomprehensible. The ultimate theories of matter are also incomprehensible. With *quantum theory*,[34] the maths is infallible, yet the reality behind the maths is unimaginable. Einstein spent his last thirty years trying to disprove quantum theory, but despite his paradigm-shifting work on light and gravity, he failed. And we still fail fifty years after Einstein's death.

---

34. John Gribben, *Schroedinger's Kittens* (London: Weidenfeld & Nicolson, 1995). 198–9. See also *What the Bleep Do We Know?*, DVD.

Yet the bizarre quantum model allows so much that is new in technology and a part of our everyday lives: transistors, computers, iPods, MP3s, mobile phones.

Incomprehensible also is the nature of the recently proposed dark energy of the vacuum. This all-pervasive entity is the necessary ingredient of an accelerating universe. *New Scientist* recently explored dark energy, 'the biggest mystery in the universe' in a cover story, and asked 'What is behind the mysterious force we call dark energy?'.[35] At the micro level, string theory speaks of one-dimensional strings vibrating in ten dimensions which gives coherence to particle phenomena.

So too is God mysterious: our minds are like small jugs and it is impossible to put all of the water in a dam into a small jug. Surely the Being behind the universe, which is so full of mystery, should have within an even more profound mystery. Through the Trinity we know that relationship is the very fabric of God's being.

7.2 Reality as relationship
In his book *Life of the Cosmos* Lee Smolin has a chapter entitled 'The world as a network of relations'. In this he says that 'string theory, if it is to succeed, must be reformulated as a theory of pure relations'.[36] For Smolin, even fundamental particles are defined by their relationships. Space too is relational: 'we know from our basic principles that this description (of space) must be entirely relational; there must not be any fixed or absolute structure of space'.[37]

For human beings too, relationships are at the heart of our essence. The formation of a healthy personality crucially depends on good relationships between parent figures and children at the stages of infancy, childhood and adolescence. Our enduring happiness depends on good relationships with family, friends, work companions and our neighbours and community.

7.3 The threeness of the one God
In Christ's discourse after the Last Supper, he speaks of an intimate union between himself and the Father. They are distinct yet one.[38] The Spirit is affirmed in the same discourse.[39] Jesus the Son, makes it quite clear his mind is the same as the Father's, and the Spirit is at one with the Father and the Son, as the Spirit will make plain to the disciples.

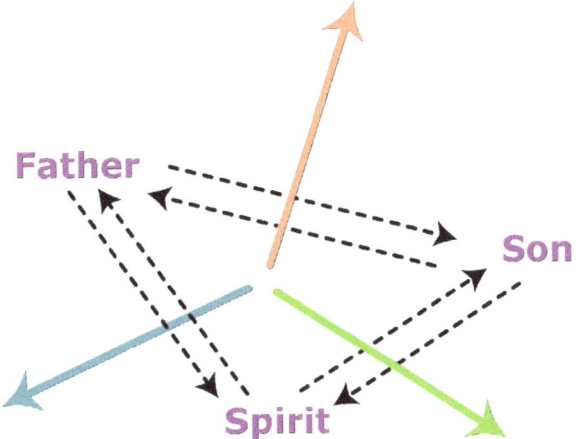

---

35. Stuart Clark, 'Heart of Darkness', *New Scientist* 193/2591, 17 February 2007: 28–33.
36. Smolin, *The Life of The Cosmos*, 284.
37. Smolin, *The Life of The Cosmos*, 278.
38. John 1:10–11, 28; 15:1, 9, 15.
39. John 14:16–17, 26.

God shares by creating

The one God has worked in creation. The same God works as three in redemption. The Father sent the Son who showed us the face of God, and who showed himself as 'the way the truth and the life' for us. The Spirit is sent to enlighten and strengthen believers in the way Jesus has shown to be the Father's will.

The Son, Jesus, made it quite clear he cared about the welfare of others. This was part of the Father's plan, to show that the divine persons cared not only about each other, but also about those created in their image. That care is extended to all by the Spirit who urges people to care beyond themselves: for the poor, for the imprisoned, for the sick and even for their enemies. This care is a reflection of divine love, which is loving without seeking a reward.

7.4 God as truly personal

God is not a distant force, but rather is a vibrant community. We can understand something. The ultimate is a Thou. As Andrew Greely wrote in *The Great Mysteries*, 'the Christian experience of graciousness is an experience of a Thou to whom one can respond'.[40] And, more than that, it is a realisation that the ultimate is a supreme relationship, an enormous activity, sharing life and existence with us, freely giving us this world—to intrigue us, to challenge us and finally to bring us to a life with the same Trinity.

---

40. Andrew Greely, *The Great Mysteries* (New York: Seabury Press, 1976), 11.

Further reading

Karen Armstrong, *A History of God* (London: Mandarin, 1994).

Ian G Barbour, *When Science Meets Religion: Enemies, Strangers, or Partners* (San Francisco: Harper, 2000).

Michael Barnes, *In the Presence of Mystery* (Mystic, Connecticut: Twenty-Third Publications, 1991).

A van den Beukel, *More Things in Heaven and Earth: God and the Scientists* (London: SCM, 1991).

Hilary M Carey, *Believing in Australia: A Cultural History of Religions* (Sydney: Allen and Unwin, 1996).

Tak-kwong Chan, Yi-Jia Tsai and Frank Budenholzer, *Religion and Science in the Context of Chinese Culture* (Adelaide: ATF, 2006).

Paul Davies, *God and the New Physics* (United Kingdom: JM Dent, 1983).

Jose Mario Francisco, SJ, and Roman Miguel de Jesus, editors, *Science and Religion and Culture in the Jesuit Tradition: Perspectives from East Asia* (Adelaide: ATF, 2006).

RA Gilbert, *The Elements of Mysticism* (Longmead: Element Books, 1991).

Bede Griffiths, *A New Vision of Reality: Western Science, Eastern Mysticism and Christian Faith* (London: Fount, 1992).

John Haught, *What is Religion?* (New York: Paulist Press, 1990).

Jean-Pierre Lonchamp, *Science and Belief* (Middlegreen: St Pauls, 1993).

Alister E McGrath, *Science and Religion: An Introduction* (Oxford: Blackwell, 1999).

Alister E McGrath, *The Future of Christianity* (Oxford: Blackwell, 2002).

Alister E McGrath, *The Twilight of Atheism: The Rise and Fall of Disbelief in the Modern World* (London: Rider, 2004).

Alister E McGrath, *Dawkins' God: Genes, Memes, and the Meaning of Life* (Oxford: Blackwell, 2005).

Gerald May, *Care of Mind, Care of Spirit* (New York: Harper Collins, 1992).

Michael Mason, Ruth Webber, Andrew Singleton and Philip Hughes, *The Spirit of Generation Y, 2003–2006*. Reports at: http://dlibrary.acu.edu.au.research/ccls/spir/sppub.htm (accessed 24 May 2007). To be published in September 2007, by John Garratt, Melbourne.

Michael Peterson, William Hasker, Bruce Reichenbach and David Basinger, *Philosophy of Religion: Selected Readings* (Oxford: Oxford University Press, 1996).

John Polkinghorne, *Belief in God in an Age of Science* (New Haven: Yale University Press, 1998).

4
Revolution in the Heavens: The Birth of Modern Cosmology

Chapter overview

- An ancient model of the universe, found in Genesis and other writings
- Aristotle's universe: the solution for two millennia
- Ptolemy's response to planetary retrograde motion: the epicycles
- The sun as centre: a discounted new idea of Nicolas Copernicus
- Galileo Galilei: the telescope's discoveries deliver plausibility to Copernicus
    - The flawed answer of Tycho Brahe
    - Kepler's ellipses, a necessary correction to Copernicus
    - Isaac Newton's clinching proof
- Galileo, hero or heretic?

The nature of the universe has puzzled thinkers from the dawn of history. While we today see philosophy, science and religion as discrete areas of study this was not so in the past. Even today there is a blurring at the edges of these disciplines. To go beyond what the eyes could see required not just a new thinking but new instruments for more sophisticated observation and a method that allowed more objectivity and the possibility of results being duplicated.

1. Ancient models

Before the advent of science in the sixteenth century, various models of the universe based on observation and speculation were put forward. The models describing the universe have changed over the millennia, slowly at first, and more rapidly in the twentieth century.

Religious truths concerning creation have been expressed in terms of mythic or philosophic models of the universe. The demise of a model does not necessarily entail the demise of the religious truth.

1.1 The biblical model
The writer of Genesis, in chapter one of the Bible, built up a simple picture of the cosmos. The world was like a bubble in the primeval waters. The cosmos was like an upturned transparent salad bowl within these waters. The sides and the top of the bowl were called the firmament, or the vault. The sun, moon and stars were fixed into the firmament. As the sky was blue, and the sea was blue, and water came from the sky, there must be an ocean above the firmament. Rain occurred when the *sluice gates* opened. As one found water by digging into the earth, there must also be an ocean below.

This image of the universe is clearly false, and so the assertion behind the myth has also been branded fanciful. The assertion behind this myth is that God is the master, God created from nothing. It is simple to dismiss the literality of the myth, but not so easy to dismiss the assertion behind the myth.

The big bang story of origin is open to the notion of a creator.

Biblical universe

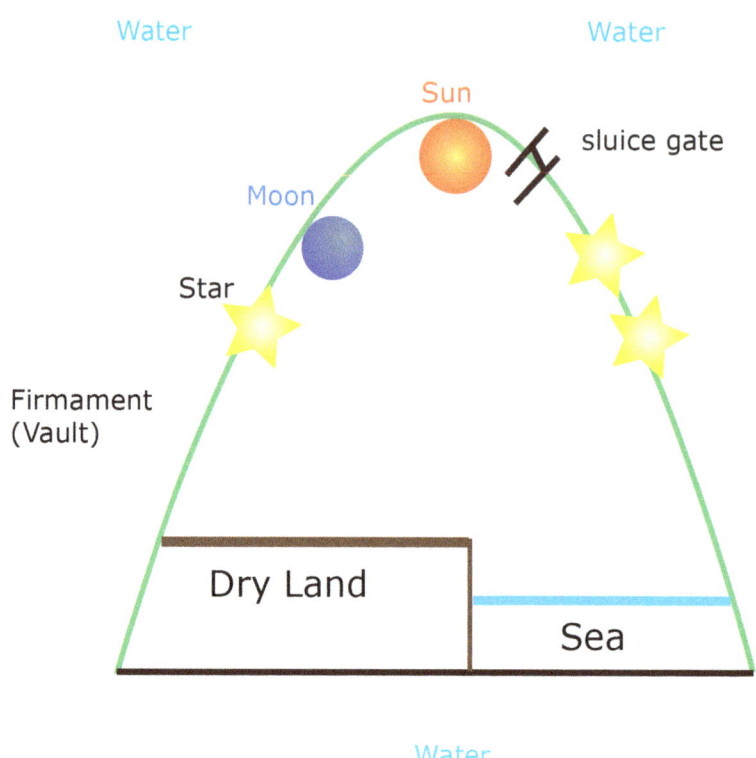

Question: Can you abstract the religious assertion from the primitive cosmology?

....

....

....

....

....

....

....

1.2 Aristotle's universe

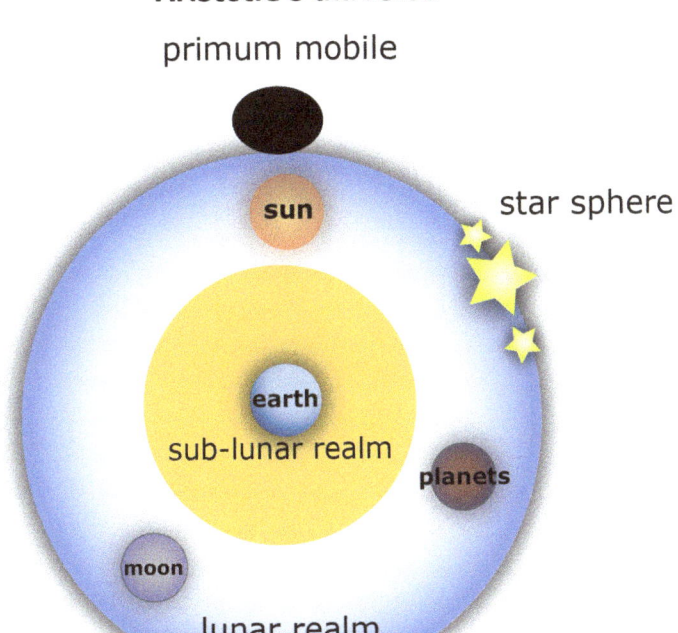

Aristotle (384–322 BCE) distinguished the lunar realm, from the sub-lunar realm. The sub-lunar realm included the earth and the adjacent sky. The lunar realm began further up and was a totally different region. Following Empedocles' (c490–430 BCE) theory, everything on earth and within the imperfect sub-lunar realm was made of different combinations of the four basic elements of earth, air, water and fire. These elements in pure form had natural places in the sub-lunar realm: earth the lowest, then air, water, and finally fire. Water was higher than air because the blue sky sat above the air. Fire was beyond this, because smoke and sparks travelled upwards.

Above the sub-lunar realm, in the lunar realm everything was perfect; none of the four elements intruded into this region. Anything solid (the moon, for example) was made of a heavenly substance called quintessence. All orbits were perfect (that is, circular) and all shapes also were perfect (that is, spherical).

The sun and moon were attached to rotating transparent crystalline spheres, and the planets were also encased in rotating spheres. Finally, there was a sphere containing the fixed stars. Aristotle had no idea of the great number of stars we now know exist. The only stars were those visible to the naked eye. Outside of the final sphere, was the source of all motion, the unmoved mover, the *primum mobile*.

Aristotle's cosmos

Sub-lunar realm	-	Consists of earth, air, fire water
Lunar realm	-	'Heavenly' • orbits circular • shapes spherical • consists of 'quintessence'
Final sphere	-	Contains fixed stars
Outside final sphere	-	'Primum Mobile'

Empedocles: sub-lunar realm

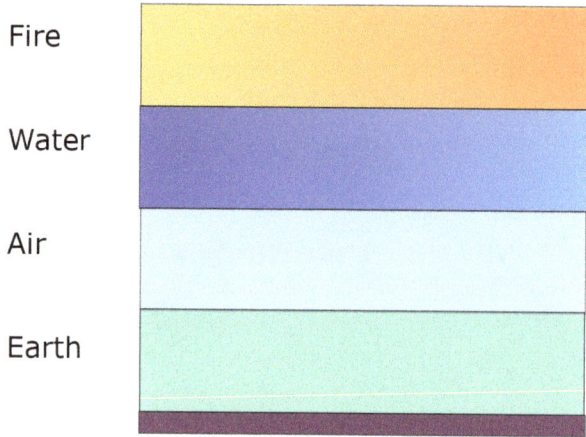

Fire
Water
Air
Earth

Question: The human being then was just as intelligent as the human being now. Why did educated people accept such a fanciful idea of the cosmos for almost two thousand years?

....

....

....

....

....

1.3 Ptolemy's epicycles

It was noted that the planets did not move in simple circles around the earth, but their overall circular orbits also incorporated a series of backward or retrograde movements. (We observe a simple apparent retrograde motion daily. If you are in a car which is travelling at 100 km/hr and it is catching up to one doing 60 km/hr, the car being overtaken, from the point of view in the faster car, appears to be moving backwards. From the faster car, if you did not know you were moving, you would assume that the slower car was moving backwards.)

Today, we can explain the apparent retrograde motion of Mars through a more complex relative motion. We see the planet's circular orbit around the sun as relative to our earth's circular movement.

Ptolemy's epicycles

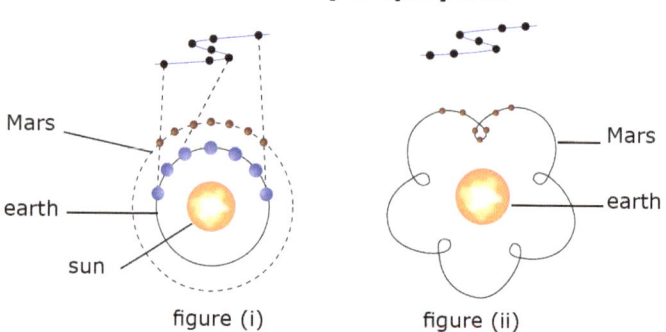

figure (i)   figure (ii)

Figure (i) shows both earth and Mars moving around the sun. A sun-centred observer would see them both moving in circular fashion around the sun. Mars has further to go and in addition has a lower orbital speed. Its year is over 600 days. The figure (i) shows both earth and Mars in seven contemporaneous positions. The earth begins behind Mars and ends up in front because of its greater speed and shorter orbital distance, its smaller circumference. An observer on the earth observes Mars backtracking from positions three to position five. The actual path relative to the Earth-based observer is shown in figure (ii).

Claudius Ptolemy (c90–c168 CE) wrote an astronomical text which remained in usage for 1400 years, being the basis of Western and Islamic calculations. It was a model which accurately predicted planets' positions:

- Simple concentric spheres for the planets were abandoned, because these could not account for variations in brightness of planets and their retrograde movements. To account for these,

- Ptolemy developed a complex system of cycles to account for irregular motions and irregularities of brilliance of the planets. Planetary epicycles became the accepted model.

- Ptolemy's geocentric system formed the astronomical paradigm for centuries.

To solve this problem, Ptolemy among others, adopted a model which still had the planets moving in circular fashion around the earth. But each planet had an additional circular motion called an epicycle. The planet revolved around the centre of the epicycle. The centre of this epicycle went around the Earth in circular mode. The result was the observed retrograde motion. This is a good example of a scientific model which explains the facts, but does not represent reality.

Ptolemy's model was expressed in his book *Almagest* or *The Great Treatise*.

Ptolemy's system

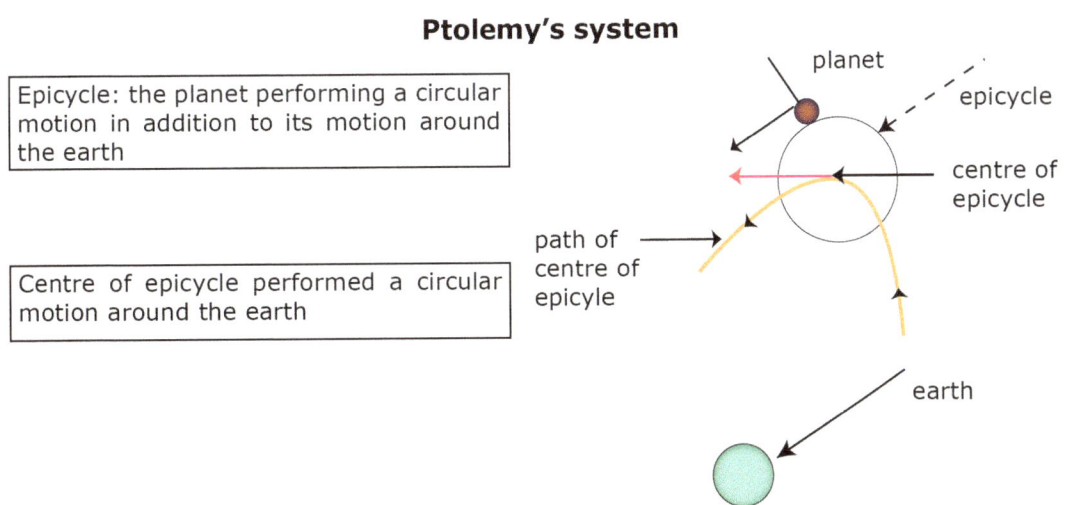

2. Copernicus and the sun as centre

The world was happy with the Ptolemaic system for over a millennium. It described the heavens in a common-sense way, and allowed accurate predictions to be made of the positions of stars and planets. Theology adopted the model, with God outside Aristotle's final sphere, angels moving the stars and planets, and the centre of the universe, earth, being the home of the highest point of creation, the human being. In the quiet recesses of Poland, Nicolaus Copernicus had other ideas.

Nicolaus Copernicus (1473–1543) studied medicine, law and economics, and was canon at the Cathedral in Frauenberg, Poland. He was attracted to a revolutionary idea, first proposed by Aristarchus of Samos in the third century BCE: the sun was the centre of the universe and the earth went around the sun.

2.1 Arguments against having the sun as centre

The arguments against the sun-centred universe (*heliocentric*) were strong.

- Everything was observed to go around the earth, the sun, the moon, the stars and the planets.

- To move the earth and keep it moving would require an extraordinarily large constant force.

- If you threw something up, it would not return to you but would land behind you because you and the ground were moving.

- You would feel a constant wind.

- The Bible in a number of places affirmed the sun moved and the earth was still. 'You fixed the earth on its foundations, for ever and ever it should not be shaken.'[1]

But there had been so much tinkering with the geocentric (earth-centred) system, with more and more epicycles needed to square with better and better observations, Copernicus felt that despite these arguments, the sun as centre would provide a better model. He constructed a mathematical model on this basis, and found it could be used to predict the movements of the planets.

2.2 The Commentariolus

In 1514, he wrote a small work called the *Commentariolus (Little Commentary)*, which was not widely known, but succinctly expressed his ideas. In it were seven axioms:

- Heavenly bodies do not have a common centre.

- The centre of the earth is not the centre of the universe.

- The centre of the universe is near the sun.

- The distance between the earth and the sun is insignificant compared with the distance between the earth and the stars.

- The apparent motion of the stars is due to the earth's rotation on its axis.

- The apparent movements of the sun is the result of the earth's rotation around the sun.

- The apparent retrograde motion of planets is the result of our position as observer on a moving earth.[2]

---
1. Psalm 104:5.
2. Simon Singh, *Big Bang* (Netley: Griffin Press, 2004), 38.

This work was circulated among a few in 1514 and then worked on for next thirty years. It challenged the results of 1500 years of Astronomy.

2.3 De revolutionibus orbium coelestium

In 1533 he published a limited work outlining his ideas. Finally his defining work, *De revolutionibus orbium coelestium*, was published in 1543.

This implied Aristotelian physics was wrong: that the certainties of 1500 years were ill-founded, that the heavens were not immutable and that certain biblical texts were in error. This also seemed to fly in the face of common-sense observations, and to call into question the whole arena in which human salvation was to be worked out.

An unsigned preface was added to Copernicus' work evidently to soften the likely reaction from the church. The preface implied the heliocentric (sun-centred) theory was not a model of reality, but merely a device to aid calculations. The authorship of the preface is not clear.

In contrast to its enormous subsequent influence *De revolutionibus* had little immediate impact. In the twenty years following its publication while it was reprinted twice, Ptolemy's *Almagest* was reprinted one hundred times. While still alive Copernicus kept a low profile and once he died he was all but forgotten. The book had a dense style that made reading it very difficult and was presented merely as a calculating device. Because it did not include the important ellipses the Copernican scenario was not as accurate as Ptolemy's in predicting the paths of the planet. So although some people, at various stages throughout history, were aware of such models they were not useful enough as calculating devices. And overall it was too radical a departure from what had been taken as true for such a long time.[3]

2.4 Tycho Brahe's alternative model

Tycho Brahe (1546–1601) was born just after Copernicus' death. He made a series of astronomical observations which, using the latest instruments, measured positions of stars, and planets to within a precision of one thirtieth of one degree.

He knew of Copernicus' book but could not accept the heliocentric view. Nevertheless, he abandoned features of the medieval model, especially the view concerning the unchangability of the heavens. In his book *De Stella Nova* he described the movement of a bright star which shone as brightly as Venus in the constellation of Cassiopeia in 1572. Yet in 1574 it was no longer visible. 'Apparently something was wrong with the idea that celestial bodies never change.'[4]

The short-lived star was a supernova, a large star in its explosive death throes. In 1577 a comet appeared. Where was it? If near the moon, it was in the lunar realm. Therefore change had occurred in the unchanging heavens, forbidden according to the standard Aristotelian cosmology. Various measurements showed that the comet was beyond the moon, in the lunar realm where allegedly nothing could change. A new model was being called for. Tycho Brahe proposed one which kept the earth static, the sun rotating around the earth, and explained the phases of Venus (see later in this chapter). This was a model which was consistent with observations. How did he do this? He explained that the sun went round the earth, but the other planets went around the sun.

---

3. Singh, *Big Bang*, 44.
4. Hanbury Brown, *The Wisdom of Science* (Cambridge: Cambridge University Press, 1988), 46–7.

Brahe's universe

- The earth is the centre
- It does not move
- The moon circles the earth
- The sun circles the earth
- The other planets circle the sun
- Sun drags planets round earth

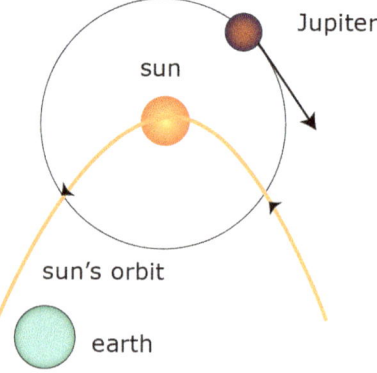

This has the earth as centre, the moon circling around the earth, the other planets circling around the sun, and the sun circling the earth. The sun therefore dragged the planets around with it. This model, as well as Copernicus', accounted for the observed motions of the sun and planets and the phases of Venus.

This is another example of a scientific model which explained observations, but was not correct.

Tycho Brahe destroyed one feature of the Aristotelian system, according to which the planets revolved around the earth because they were fixed to solid crystalline spheres which rotated. The sun also was in such a sphere. From the above diagram it can be seen the sun's crystalline sphere would intersect at times with Jupiter's. Also the comet of 1577 would have smashed the spheres.

2.5 Kepler's correction to the Copernican system

Johannes Kepler (1571–1630) was an assistant to Brahe. After Brahe's death he availed himself of all Brahe's previously hidden meticulous observations. Kepler supported the sun-centred model. He was a trained mathematician, and was aware that the Copernican sun-centred model produced less accurate predictions of the planetary positions than did the Ptolemaic model. Kepler declared he would solve the heliocentric orbital inaccuracies in eight days.

Eight years later, after nine hundred pages of calculations,[5] he produced his results. The orbits were not perfect circles. All the planetary orbits were ellipses, with the sun, not at a central position, but at one of the foci of the ellipses.

The orbit of each planet was an ellipse or an oval. Mathematically, any true ellipse has two points each of which is termed a focus. If you take a point on the ellipse and draw straight lines from this point to each of the foci, and if you then add these distances together, the answer will always be the same no matter which point you take on the ellipse.

Ellipse

Ellipse: sun is at one focus

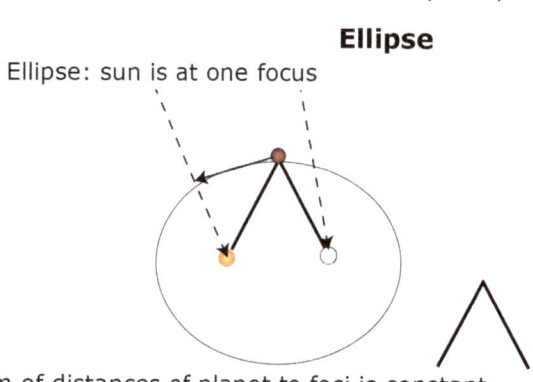

Sum of distances of planet to foci is constant

---
5. Singh, *Big Bang*, 53.

In 1609, Kepler published his results in a work entitled *Astronomia Nova*. The ellipse model gave very good results for predicting the motions of planets. It corrected the inaccuracies of the model based on circular orbits. However, the intelligentsia, both lay and clerical, could not cope with the abolition of circles in the heavens. Kepler also proposed a force similar to gravity which kept the planets in orbit.

Before the advent of Kepler and his ellipses, Galileo Galilei—the founder of modern science and key promoter of the Copernican system—had provided persuasive evidence for the heliocentric system, using the telescope which he had perfected for the purpose. Brahe's unwieldy model was, however, still a scientific possibility. Cardinal Bellarmine of the Inquisition kept insisting that theories be proposed as hypotheses until convincing evidence was presented.

2.6 Newton provides the convincing argument for the Copernican system

In 1684 Isaac Newton described a coherent planetary system with the sun as central body, based on his law of gravitation. And he justified Kepler's Laws mathematically. His law of gravitation clearly accounted for why things fell to earth, why the moon circled the earth, and how the sun kept all the planets in elliptical orbits. His law enabled the speeds of planets and the length of each planet's year to be accurately calculated. Newton's solution involved gravity forces which Galileo had rejected as in the realm of the nonsensical and superstitious.

In general, Newton's mechanics put paid to many ancient assertions. For example, Aristotle had declared that there was no vacuum, because zero resistance would have things moving at infinite speeds. Newton's other work disproved this. Galileo asserted the moon could not affect tides. The effect of the moon on tides was a conclusion of Newton's theories. With Newton came the proof lacking in 1633.

3. Galileo's discoveries

Galileo's observations with his upgraded telescope proved the catalyst for the eventual acceptance of Copernicus' sun-centred (heliocentric) model of the universe.

Galileo transformed the design of an imported rudimentary telescope, giving it a magnification of sixty and used it to make a number of previously unperceived observations. This breakthrough was an indicator of how scientific advancements depend on the capability of the instruments used.

3.1 What the telescope revealed

3.1.1 The moon

Galileo's moon observations

Galileo looked at the moon with a primitive telescope and saw little spots of light, which were the tops of mountains, which indicated the moon was made of matter like that on earth

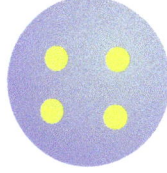

The moon was not made of quintessence. It was not perfect, not heavenly, nor was it perfectly spherical. It was composed of the same sort of matter as the earth. The notions of the lunar realm and the elemental structures (of earth, air, water and fire) were under serious threat.

Question: Imagine you are alive in the sixteenth century, and interested in religion, science and philosophy. Describe your feelings about the whole world and the possibility of your faith beginning to waver.

....

....

....

....

....

....

3.1.2 Jupiter's moons

Galileo's Jupiter observations

In January 1610, Galileo turned the telescope onto Jupiter. He was surprised to see *little stars*. Next day they were on the other side, having moved in the direction opposite to Jupiter. Each day they were in new positions on either side of Jupiter, and finally there were four of them. He got the idea that they were companions of Jupiter, going around the planet.

(First viewing)

(Second viewing)

He had shown that the earth was not the centre of rotation for every object there was. Earth was not the undisputed centre of the universe.

Question: Galileo's observations spelled the beginning of the end of a science which had persevered for almost two millennia. What difficulties faced scientists and theologians?

....

....

....

....

....

....

3.1.3 Sunspots

Galileo focused the instrument on the sun and let its image fall onto paper. He made the observation that there were black spots moving across the sun. Again the notion of a perfect heavenly body was challenged.

Galileo's sun observation

Dark spots that appeared to move across the sun
The conclusion was perfect heavenly body, nor was it changeless

3.1.4 The Milky Way

Galileo's Milky Way observations

When Galileo focused his telescope onto the Milky Way, he saw lots more stars than the known ones and they were seemingly at different distances.

Stars not on a final sphere

This observation pointed to the fact that the stars were not all on a final crystal sphere. Also there seemed to be countless numbers of them.

3.1.5 Phases of Venus

Galileo's Venus observations

A series of observations of Venus went through phases, like those of the moon (full venus, half venus, new venus). This meant that Venus, like the moon, was sometimes between the sun and earth, and sometimes on the other side of the sun

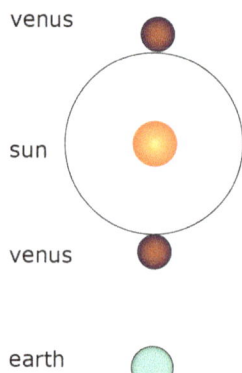

Phases of Venus

This was good evidence for Venus' going round the sun, but not that the earth moved.

3.2 Summary of Galileo's discoveries

- Moon: mountains and planes revealed. Therefore the Moon is not perfect or quintessence.
- Sun: moving blemishes or sunspots. Therefore the Sun is not perfect or changeless.
- Jupiter: four orbiting moons. Therefore not everything circles the earth and the earth cannot be the centre of the universe.
- Venus: phases pattern. Therefore Venus orbits the sun.
- Milky Way arm: many more stars. Therefore there is no crystal sphere.

3.3 The consequences of Galileo's observations

The importance of Galileo's observations was not immediately universally recognised. However, they could not be generally ignored in the same way as was the model in the writings of Copernicus seventy-five years earlier. The observations led to continuing debate, which eventually turned into a damaging conflict. His undiplomatic manner, the serious threat to what was known in science and the implications for a religion anchored in the geocentric scientific paradigm resulted in the celebrated, infamous confrontation between Galileo and the church. Ever since this confrontation detractors of the church have seen the church as hostile towards science.

Question: Given the evidence, why did people still opt for Brahe's model?

....

....

....

....

....

4. Galileo: hero or heretic?[6]

4.1 Galileo's position: a paradigm change with theological implications[7]

For at least twelve centuries popular and some educated perception had placed God in heaven somewhere beyond the spheres: the stars were like decorations on the ceiling. If the heliocentric idea were allowed in, where is heaven? But much Christian theological tradition spoke against placing God anywhere near the spheres. As Clement of Alexandria said: 'The First Cause is not then in space, but above both space, and time, and name, and conception'.[8]

The scriptures literally affirmed an earth-centred cosmology. Galileo's battle was centred around a monumental change of paradigm with significant ramifications for religion. It was a quest for truth which brought in its wake a battle with authority.

4.2 Galileo supports the Copernican model

Galileo was attracted to Copernicus' idea. While teaching in Padua in 1609 he taught the geocentric model, but also the mathematics of the heliocentric model. He heard about peddlers selling an object which made objects appear closer. He did not see one, but worked out how to make one of these telescopes himself, making a hundred of them (two of which are in the History of Science Museum in Florence). He demonstrated it to members of the Venetian senate.

His discoveries using the telescope made him a supporter of the Copernican model, and he sought hereafter to gain credence for it. One of the objections to Copernicus was how does the earth take the moon with it? Galileo's response was: 'Look at Jupiter'. He thus helped make Copernicus more plausible.

He became mathematician to Cosimo de' Medici, the grand duke of Venice, but wanted to be seen also as the duke's philosopher, so that he could really talk about his idea.

His series of observations revealing the phases of Venus and satellites of Jupiter were confirmed by the Jesuit mathematician and astronomer Christopher Clavius (1537–1612) but Galileo wanted to make all the discoveries, so he did not publish this immediately. But he wrote to Cosimo's brother an encoded statement: 'the mother of love imitates the shapes of Cynthia'.[9] By this he meant that Venus ('the mother of love') is like the moon ('Cynthia'), in that it has phases. He also sent an encoded version to Kepler.

---

6. Owen Gingerich, *The Great Copernican Chase* (Cambridge, Massachusetts: Sky Publishing Corporation, 1992) 105–22.
7. As well as the above reference, the author is using summaries of talks given by Gingerich at conferences in Dunedin, New Zealand(1993) and Adelaide (2002).
8. *Stromateis* V: 11.
9. Gingerich, *The Great Copernican Chase*, 102.

4.3 Galileo encounters opposition

Galileo eventually published his results. The church began to become involved, and Cardinal Bellarmine counselled Galileo to be cautious. Galileo thought the church might condemn the heliocentric idea so in 1616 he journeyed to Rome to lobby for his cause.

While in Rome, Galileo called on Bellarmine who told him to stop speaking forcefully on behalf of Copernicus, and to present the geocentric view as mainstream. He advised that Galileo should propose any such idea as an hypothesis. It was against the church's best interests to propose Copernicus as fact, because this model had not yet been proved and its acceptance would imperil the faith of many not skilled in science or theology. The reasons against it seemed overwhelmingly convincing (see 2.1). He was told Copernicanism was false, and against the scriptures, but never that it was heretical. Bellarmine was aware there was a chance of the heliocentric system's being verified, but his judgment was that the chance was minimal. If it were ever demonstrated as true, proposed Bellarmine, much care would have to be taken in how to explain the scriptures.

There were rumours that Galileo had been told to abjure his ideas. Galileo was upset by these, and asked Bellarmine to write a letter explaining his position, which Bellarmine did.[10] This letter was an injunction to not teach Copernicus as truth but as an hypothesis. Assuming it to be hypothesis was good for the mathematician; but as a statement of reality, it was irritating to philosophers and challenged the scriptures.

The letter was not signed, nor was it obvious it was ever formally served on Galileo. Galileo, who did not want to be charged with heresy, obeyed.

4.4 A preliminary judgment from Rome

The feeling among some in Rome was that Galileo was no more than an amateur theologian, and so could not tell professionals how to interpret the scriptures. For example the *Book of Joshua* clearly taught that the sun moved:

> In the presence of Israel Joshua said: 'Sun, stand still over Gibeon, and moon, you too, over the Vale of Aijalon'. And the sun stood still, and the moon halted until the people had taken vengeance on their enemies. The sun stood in the middle of the sky, and delayed its setting for almost a whole day.[11]

The literal inerrancy of the scriptures was considered paramount:

> I can hardly emphasise this point enough. The battleground was the method itself, the route to sure knowledge of the world, the question of whether the Book of Nature could in any way rival the inerrant Book of Scripture as an avenue to truth . . . Galileo's procedures were essentially inductive and therefore potentially fallacious. Such contingent arguments were insufficient to force a reinterpretation of scripture that might erode the concept of the inerrancy of Holy Writ.[12]

Any scientific argument was of its very nature inductive. Induction was known to be an imperfect guarantor of truth. In the case of the phases, the argument went like this:

---

10. Owen Gingerich, *The Book Nobody Read* (Sydney: Random House, 2004), 72–3.
11. *The Book of Joshua*, 10: 12–13.
12. Gingerich, *The Great Copernicus* Chase, 113.

If the planetary system is heliocentric, Venus should show phases.
Venus shows phases.
Therefore the planetary system is heliocentric.[13]

This is not logically valid; there could be other reasons for the phases. Another possible reason was shown by Tycho Brahe who had put forward a model that saved the earth as centre, but also had Venus showing phases.

The result was that Galileo was cautioned, and that Copernicus' book *De revolutionibus orbium coelestium* was censored, and placed on the Index (an official list of forbidden books), but only until the Index gave direction about how the book was to be corrected before it could be distributed. It had to talk of hypothesis. The sun-centred model had to be regarded as giving the basis for a simpler method of making calculations about the positions and periods of planets. The censored version was distributed in Italy, but the uncensored version was found in the rest of Europe.

4.5 'The Dialogue' and its consequences

In 1623 Urban VIII became pope. He had been a member of a small discussion group with Galileo. After he became pope he met with Galileo in the gardens. Urban thought it would be a good idea if Galileo wrote a book which would be a technical explanation of both the geocentric and heliocentric positions, thus allowing him to fully propose the previously forbidden position.

Responding to this suggestion, in 1632, Galileo published *The Dialogue*. This was a discussion of the cosmological ideas of Aristotle, Ptolemy, and Copernicus. It presented no proof, but argument after argument piled up in favour of the heliocentric view. More immediately important, the words of Aristotle were put into the mouth of the monk Simplicio who was a sixth century commentator on Aristotle. And Simplicio was less than this commentator, he was truly simple; Urban's advisers said Simplicio was Urban himself. Urban was outraged, and ordered Galileo to come to Rome and face the consequences.

The Inquisition found Bellarmine's (now dead) letter in the archives which did not pronounce heliocentrism as heretical, so Galileo could not be declared a heretic. Also, the writing of *The Dialogue* had been proposed by the pope himself. It was only that one view was proposed as far more likely than the other that was matter for censure. The Inquisition was confused, and also the Thirty Years War was raging, pitting Spanish and French cardinals against each other. But it could not lose face by freeing Galileo. He was shown the instruments of torture (perhaps told about them), and the Inquisition told him he was 'vehemently' suspected of heresy. They were trying to show him how hard they could press. Would he be prepared to rewrite *The Dialogue*?

Galileo made a public confession that he may have made the case for Copernicus too forcefully and offered to refute it in his next book. Was this perjury? Maybe he was terrified. Maybe he was saying he knew of no deductive proof, that induction was never totally conclusive, so how could he believe it? It is hard for us to place ourselves in his position at that time. Galileo officially retracted his views in 1633 and was placed under house arrest where he began to write *Discourse on Two New Sciences*.

Galileo was condemned for rocking the boat politically, and for disobeying orders, but never was officially charged with heresy; nor was he ever tortured or excommunicated.

Galileo lost the battle but won the war on the question of the heavens. More importantly perhaps, he changed the rules of science. Science hereafter was not bound to deduction, but could operate through induction. A scientific system is acceptable if it is coherent, and

---

13. Gingerich, *The Great Copernican Chase*, 111.

if it hangs together. The scientific method itself was effectively begun by Galileo. Much of Newton's synthesis stems from Galileo.

In 1998, the Pope apologised for the treatment of Galileo. John Paul II said Galileo was a better theologian than those he had contended with. In Galileo's words, 'Theology does not tell us about how the heavens move, but how to go to heaven'. Galileo has become a symbol of the relationship between the church and science:

> The Galileo affair has long become a symbol, concentrating in itself all the incompatibility between science and the church and marking the official break between faith and reason. Like any symbol it has been exaggerated, simplified, taken out of context, and given a universal and timeless value. A first-class component of the anti-clerical arsenal, it has scarred the Catholic conscience, at worst like a second original sin, at best an extremely embarrassing blackspot.[14]

Question: What is the church's present attitude towards science?

Revision questions
Give an account of the scientific thought of Aristotle.

---

14. Jean-Pierre Lonchamp, *Science and Belief* (Middlegreen: St Pauls, 1993), 78.

Describe how the scientific thought of Aristotle was gradually eroded by [a] the theory of Copernicus, [b] the observations of Galileo, and [c] the mathematical work of Kepler.

Describe the confrontation between Galileo and the church. Why did the church react so vehemently despite asking for Galileo's versions of both the geocentric and heliocentric models of the universe?

In the Galileo case, the church won the battle and lost the war.

Further reading

Bill Bryson, *A Short History of Nearly Everything* (Reading: Black Swan, 2004).

James A Connor, *Kepler's Witch: An Astronomer's Discovery of Cosmic Order Amid Religious War, Political Intrigue, and the Heresy Trial of His Mother* (San Francisco: Harper, 2004).

Annibale Fantoli, *Galileo, for Copernicism and for the Church* (Vatican City State: Vatican Observatory Publications, 1996).

Owen Gingerich, *The Great Copernican Chase* (Cambridge, Massachusetts: Sky Publishing Corporation, 1992).

Owen Gingerich, *The Eye of Heaven: Ptolemy, Copernicus, Kepler* (New York: The American Institute of Physics, 1993).

Owen Gingerich, *The Book Nobody Read: In Pursuit of the Revolutions of Nicolaus Copernicus* (London: Heinemann, 2004).

Michael Hoskin, editor, *The Cambridge Concise History of Astronomy* (Cambridge: Cambridge University Press, 1999).

Dava Sobel, *Galileo's Daughter: A Drama of Science, Faith and Love* (London: Fourth Estate, 1999).

Christopher Walker, editor, *Astronomy before the Telescope* (London: British Museum Press, 1999).

Margaret Wertheim, *The Pearly Gates of Cyberspace: A History of Space from Dante to the Internet* (Milson's Point, NSW: Transworld Publishers, 1999).

5

The Development of Cosmology: The Discovery of a Vast and Dynamic Universe

Chapter overview

- Early twentieth century: the universe is thought of as the Milky Way galaxy
- The troubling enigma of the nebulae
- Hubble provides a surprising solution: the nebulae are other galaxies
- Hubble provides a new problem: the red shift and runaway galaxies
- Runaway galaxies confirmed: further evidence for an expanding universe
- Most scientists opt for the *status quo* of an eternal unchanging static universe
    - Einstein's greatest mistake
    - Fred Hoyle's steady state
- Clinching evidence of the expansion of the universe: the cosmic microwave background radiation

The big bang that allegedly began the universe is now the standard and well-accepted theory. In the 1920s and 1930s its acceptance was resisted, and the idea was even ridiculed. Albert Einstein rewrote part of his ground-breaking general relativity theory in an effort to counteract the idea of a beginning. Renowned astrophysicist Fred Hoyle championed an alternative theory—steady state—and was even still advocating it in the 1980s. Now hugely advanced instruments and dedicated experimentation have delivered to us an amazing picture of the known universe: it is huge, expanding, and had a beginning.

Religion must reflect on reality. It cannot take its basic stand on the seven days of Genesis. When speaking of creation theology now takes this into account:

> An improved and more 'down to earth' appreciation of the laws of nature
> . . . provides a more fruitful scientific and philosophical context within which
> to discuss God's action in the world.[1]

It is now agreed the universe is huge and expanding; that it began at a specific moment and self-constructed; that it will end. While reading this sentence, the Virgo cluster of 2000 galaxies has slipped a further 750 kilometres away from the Milky Way. How did we come to know this?

---

1. William Stoeger, SJ, 'Contemporary Physics, and the Ontological Status of the Laws of Nature', in *Quantum Cosmology and the Laws of Nature*, edited by Robert John Russell, Nancey Murphy, and CJ Isham (Vatican City State: Vatican Observatory Publications, 1999), 231.

Question: How wide is the Milky Way galaxy? How long will it take to cross from the solar system to the other side? Will there ever be a 'Galactic Empire'?

....

....

....

....

....

....

....

....

....

....

1. Riddle of the nebulae

After Galileo's observations of stars at very different distances, it was assumed stars would be distributed evenly to infinity. But towards the end of the eighteenth century it was realised that the universe did not so extend, but that the stars were clumped together in a gigantic pancake.

Discovery: universe = Milky Way

- Contrary to expectations in the late 18th and early 19th centuries, it was found, using ever-improving telescopes that the stars seemed to be clumped into a structure whose diameter was about 10 times its thickness.
- There was thus a limit beyond which there were no more stars.
- This was said to be the universe.
- Nebulae?

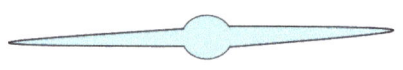

Then the universe was thought of as all the stars in the Milky Way, plus some other features called nebulae. These were seen as extended, unstarlike and seemingly gaseous regions.

These nebulae however presented a problem.[2] Many of these regions of extended light, seemingly luminescent clouds, had been detected before 1800. There was debate as to what they were and as to whether they were within or outside the Milky Way. The philosopher Immanuel Kant suggested that some of them were outside the galaxy, and were independent

---

2. Marcia Bartusiak, *Archives of the Universe* (New York: Vintage Books, 2006), 189–95.

groups of stars. By 1900 thousands more nebulae had been detected, and one at least was seen to have a spiral structure.

The universe circa 1900

Sun+planets= solar system
Solar system+stars= Milky Way Galaxy

What are the nebulae? Where are they?

1.1 Two theories about the nebulae
Were the nebulae inside the Milky Way or were they outside it? If they were outside the Milky Way, this could involve a paradigm shift in cosmology: a total revision of the theory. The accepted view in 1920 was that the Milky Way was the universe and hence the nebulae were inside it. A few maintained they were outside the galaxy, and hence could be other Milky Ways. There was not enough evidence to decide one way of the other. In 1920 Harlow Shapley, championing the view they were part of the Milky Way, debated the issue with Heber Curtis in what was known as 'the great debate'.[3] The issues were clearly presented, but as there was not enough evidence to decide one way or the other, the result of the debate was inconclusive.

1.2 Hubble found evidence to resolve the question of the nebulae
In 1924 Edwin Hubble (1889–1953) found that the Andromeda nebula was so far away that it had to be another complete star system,[4] and because it could be seen with the naked eye, it must have contained an enormous number of stars to be visible from so far away: about a million light years was Hubble's estimate. The evidence was a feature of variable stars called Cepheids whose brightness could be linked with their variation rate. The rate of Cepheids' variations in the Andromeda nebula meant they had to have a certain definite brightness. They were actually perceived as much less bright. This meant they were a great distance away. In this way, almost all—and there were many—of the nebulae were confirmed to be too far from the Earth to be part of the Milky Way, as Hubble recorded in his landmark paper in 1924. The universe was now very different from merely the Milky Way galaxy with its billions of stars. There were now thousands of galaxies within the distance as far as Hubble's telescope could reach. (This instrument is not the 'Hubble telescope'.)

Question: What is the Hubble telescope? Where is it? What has it revealed to us?

....

....

---

3. Bartusiak, *Archives of the Universe*, 409.
4. Bartusiak, *Archives of the Universe*, 409–10.

Hubble's universe

The universe is not seen as one huge group of stars but as very many similar groups of stars, as far as the latest telescope could see.

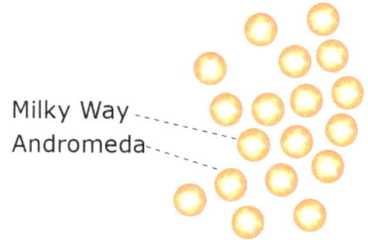

2. The expanding universe

Further work by Edwin Hubble, and other considerations, indicated that the universe did not consist of galaxies in fixed positions, but that they were all moving. It appeared that almost all galaxies were moving away from each other.

2.1 The red-shift

Having solved the problem of the nebulae, Hubble began work on the wavelengths of the light coming from the galaxies. He found nearly all of them had longer wavelengths than they should have if they were stationary. Therefore all of the galaxies were receding from us. He also found that the further they were from us, the longer were the wavelengths and hence, the faster they were receding.

The 'Doppler effect' is a well-known everyday experience. When a police car or fire truck with siren on is approaching you, its note, the pitch of the sound, is noticeably different from when it is receding from you. Approaching you, the sound is higher; receding from you the sound has a lower pitch. The waves making up the sound when the source is approaching become compressed. The waves when the car is receding become stretched apart. Technically, the wavelength of the sound becomes shorter on approach while the wavelength on recession becomes longer. The faster the car is going away from you, the lower the note will be. Larger wavelength and more stretching mean a lower note. Not only is sound a wave, but light is also a wave. If light is a wave it should show a similar Doppler effect. If a galaxy is receding from us, its light has a longer wavelength—it becomes redder. If a galaxy is approaching us, its light has a shorter wavelength—it become bluer.

The effect of stretching of the wavelength of the light from galaxies not only results from their motion away from us, but also on how fast they are receding from us. The faster is the velocity of recession, the larger the wavelength of the light becomes, the redder is the light.

Using this fact, Hubble found that the further a galaxy was distant from us, the faster it was moving. This is illustrated by the following sketch graph.

Recession speed versus distance from Milky Way

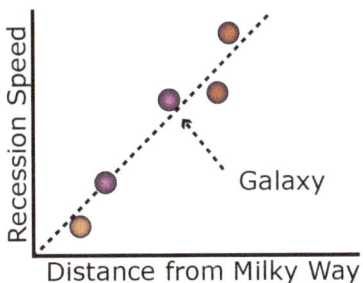

This was evidence, seemingly, of an expanding universe. This is not a constant speed expansion, but an expansion in which whatever is the most distant is moving away faster. And as is shown by the above sketch-graph (not an actual plot), there is a clear mathematical law linking the distance away with the speed of recession. The same spread of waves is being radiated from typical stars but shifted to a longer pattern as the next diagram shows.

The clear mathematical law led to the conclusion that all the galaxies now rushing away from each other were at one time together. The implication of their rushing away, and their having been together was that there was an initial explosion, the big bang which initiated them and set them on their way. This implication ran counter to the accepted cosmological picture that the universe was eternal.

The red shift

- 'Doppler effect':
    - luminous galaxies moving away
    - wavelength patterns the same but shifted: longer wavelengths
    - the greater the recession speed the greater the shift in wavelengths
- Galaxies seem to be moving away
- The further away the greater the shift, the faster they are going

- Stationary wavelength pattern
- High recession speed pattern

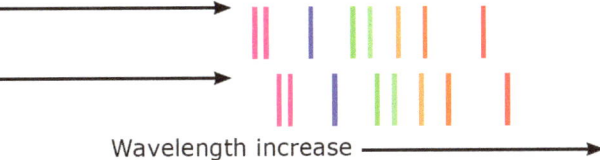

2.2 The argument from the force of gravity
Gravity would ultimately collapse a universe in which everything was stationary. Just as the sun exerts a force of gravity on earth to keep it in orbit, and the moon exerts gravitational forces on the ocean to cause the tides, so all the galaxies exert gravitational forces of attraction on each other. This means they should all move towards each other, eventually causing collisions and bringing great quantities of matter to the same spot, all still exerting attractive forces on each other and finally all colliding and perhaps causing an enormous black hole. This would happen according to the laws of nature unless the galaxies were actually moving apart, resisting this inward pull.

The force of gravity

Gravity forces: ➤

If the universe were stationary gravity forces would contract it and create an implosion

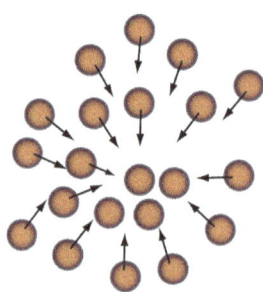

So the universe could not be stationary. If it were, it must begin to contract and finally to implode.

Question: Summarise the arguments in favour of the expanding universe.

....

....

....

....

....

....

....

....

2.3 Einstein's solution to the implosion

In the 1930s the majority of scientists resisted the expanding universe. The universe was and always will be as it is. But the expansion theory indicated the universe was always changing, and that it might have had a beginning. Even Einstein opted against expansion. Einstein's very successful gravitational theory, the general theory of relativity, had actually predicted a changing universe; this theory accounts for all everyday examples, like falling off a log, and in addition explains observations in high gravity fields, black holes and gravity's effect on light. For example in high gravity fields, not only does Mercury spin on its axis, and travel round the sun along an elliptical path, but also the whole ellipse (oval shape) itself rotates. It would be just like a football oval rotating. Its goals initially are north and south and, some time later, are east and west. This details of the precession of Mercury's orbit were well explained by Einstein's theory of general relativity.

Einstein was aware his theory predicted a dynamic universe—either expanding or contracting—and this clashed with his conviction that the universe was static, unchanging, eternal and infinite. Furthermore, the expansion, a conclusion from Hubble's data, could be traced back to a beginning, and so to a universe which was not eternal. Contraction also meant the universe would end. With much of the scientific establishment, Einstein believed the universe to be eternal, infinite and unchanging. He was unhappy with the direction in which his successful theory seemed to be pointing.

Einstein's universe

- Einstein's *general relativity*: initial assumptions:
   That the universe is homogenous: it looks the same wherever you happen to be.
   That the universe is isotropic: looks the same in every direction.

- **But *unstable: destined to destroy itself***

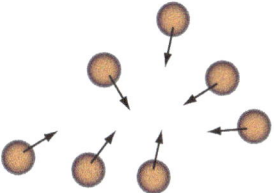

In response, Einstein proposed there was, in addition to gravity, a force permeating the whole universe, which was repulsive—like two north poles of a magnet. It was just the right strength to negate the gravitational attractive force pulling everything together.

Thus Einstein introduced his oft-quoted greatest mistake. He introduced an artificial force into the universe. The force was an artificial anti-gravity, a force that would just balance the gravitational impulse of the cosmos to implode, and render it static and stationary. He said that to admit the possibility of instability on a cosmic scale seemed senseless. This meant that empty space is imbued with an inherent pressure that pushed the universe apart. It indicated a repulsive force acting against gravity's attraction. He carefully selected the magnitude of the force so that the repulsive force equalled gravity's attraction, but was directed the other way. His force cancelled the pull of gravity and thus he retained a static eternal universe.

Technically, he introduced an artificial constant (lambda, Λ) into his equations so that this factor would enable his otherwise brilliant equations to predict a static universe. The constant (Λ) stood for an artificial anti-gravity, a force that would just balance the gravitational impulse of the cosmos to implode, and thus render it static or stationary. Thus he secured an unchanging universe. He said afterwards this was his greatest mistake. Recently the cosmological constant has been revived to explain the acceleration in the universe's rate of expansion.

The steady state universe of Einstein

-----> = Gravitational force : implosion

⟵ = Equal cosmological repulsion, Λ

Question: Why do you think scientists resisted the idea of a dynamic universe? Would a beginning lead to a question difficult for science to deal with?

....

....

....

....

....

....

....

....

....

2.4 Hoyle's 'steady state' resists the expanding universe

People endeavoured to get around further evidence of expansion, and Einstein was adamant. When priest-astrophysicist Georges Lemaitre's mathematical reasoning pointed to an expansion model, Einstein responded: 'your calculations are correct, but your physics is abominable'.[5] Einstein was won over by 1931, but astronomers were not, and there were big names who were much against the expanding finite universe.

Fred Hoyle, an illustrious cosmologist who later developed a convincing theory of the creation of the elements, led the charge against the expansion of the universe. The idea of an expanding universe, with its implication of a beginning, was not endorsed by many scientists for some, or all, of these reasons:

- The belief of an eternal changeless universe stretched back into the distant past. For the philosophic Greeks, there was no theory of creation as the universe was thought to be eternal. Up until 1900 generally scientists assumed an eternal universe.

- Newton's gravity implied a collapsing universe, but Newton himself had imagined God intervened to prevent it.

- Hubble's evidence was not considered conclusive.

- Einstein invented his cosmological constant for the same end. Einstein's constant produced a steady-state cosmos.

- The age of the expanding universe seemed less than the age of the stars.

- How could the higher elements have been created?

---
5. Simon Singh, *Big Bang*, 160.

Fred Hoyle became the campaigner for a rival model, the *steady-state* model.[6] He maintained that the universe is infinite; he accepted that the galaxies are moving away but new matter is being continually created to fill the gaps caused by expansion, so that the universe is always the same.

The difference between the expanding model beginning with a big bang and his model is illustrated in the following diagram. In Hoyle's model the universe is infinite and unchanging, because of the new matter being created to make it always look the same. Thus the need for a beginning was eliminated. Hoyle was the one who invented the term 'big bang', as a sarcastic turn of phrase. In the meantime, its derisive implications have disappeared.

Expanding vs steady-state universe

Expanding universe: ⟶ Gaps increase

Steady-state universe: Matter is being continually created to fill the gaps.
The universe always has had the same density.
It will always have the same density.
Continual creation ensures this.

The universe was thus eternal, and always the same.

Question: Hoyle's *steady state* model escapes the question of origin but the same question arises as a result of continuous creation. Discuss.

....

....

....

....

....

....

....

....

---

6. Bartusiak, *Archives of The Universe*, 320–6.

3. Microwave background radiation: the compelling evidence

In 1960 about one third of scientists supported the theory of the big bang; in the early 1980s this had become over two-thirds. Today, almost all accept some version of the big bang. What caused this change in sentiment? Again it was down to more accurate technology and the discovery of the cosmic microwave background radiation (CMB). This was an echo of the big bang bathing the entire universe at three degrees Kelvin, which is $-270°$ Celsius. (Zero degrees Kelvin, that is $-273°C$, means there is no heat at all). It was known that this radiation was predicted by the big bang theory and hence implied by the expanding model. But scientists did not look for it following its prediction because the theory was doubted and unfashionable.

3.1 The discovery of the cosmic microwave background radiation (CMB)

There are many accounts of the accidental discovery of the CMB. Two scientists were taken by the idea against the trend, and were searching for it experimentally in 1963. But it was discovered accidentally in 1964 by another two scientists, Arno Penzias and Robert Wilson.[7] They were calibrating a large microwave antenna, their project being to investigate radiation from space. They kept finding a troublesome background 'noise' which they could not eliminate. The noise remained the same irrespective of the direction in which they pointed the antenna. They heard of the search for the background radiation and, after consultation, realised they had found it. For their discovery they were awarded the Nobel Prize in 1978.

3.2 The origin of the background radiation

Explosions have two effects: they affect matter, sending pieces everywhere, and they are accompanied by heat and sometimes by light. Light and heat are both types of radiation. Big bang theory indicated that the appearance and outward propulsion of all the matter of the universe should have been accompanied by an enormous amount of radiation. Radiation does not cease to exist—it keeps on going forever. Theory predicted that this radiation should be still permeating the whole universe, giving all of space a temperature of three degrees Kelvin ($-270°C$). Big bang theory also predicts that the CMB should be the same from every direction. This is what Penzias and Wilson accidentally discovered.

This radiation has since been analysed with increasingly precise equipment. In 1992 a satellite, Cosmic Background Explorer (COBE), found the radiation to be extremely isotropic—almost the same from all directions and at all times. It has been shown to give all space a temperature of 2.725 degrees Kelvin—very close to the predicted three degrees. The discovery and qualities of this radiation was the convincing evidence needed to swing the bulk of the scientific community behind the big bang model.

3.3 Features of the CMB

- The cosmic background radiation is microwave radiation.

- The radiation is very smooth: it is almost the same coming from all directions at all times. The smoothness of the radiation is evidence of a smooth very early universe.

- There are slight variations in intensity. The COBE satellite found variations of one in a hundred thousand (1/100000) and less in the intensity of the radiation. But the small variations are highly significant. As the radiation originated from the big bang,

---

7. Bartusiak, *Archives of the Universe*, 509–10.

these variations today show there was enough variation in the initial event to give rise to the structures we see.

- The radiation reveals much about the early universe. The CMB carries fossil imprints of the early universe's density and temperature as a pattern of brightness variations. The early universe's density variations can explain how galaxies formed.

Question: Scientists have shown themselves reluctant to accept new paradigms: the sun-centred universe, the big bang. Is this out of regard for truth, or are they not open to change?

....
....
....
....
....
....
....
....
....
....

Question: On encountering the big bang does science reach its limits?

....
....
....
....
....
....
....

Question: Does the big bang demand a creative power?

Question: Theology should take into account the beliefs of science but on the other hand should hesitate about wedding itself to any current cosmological model Discuss.

4. Extension: Chaos

4.1 Billiard table thought experiment to illustrate chaos[8]

Billiard table thought experiment to illustrate chaos

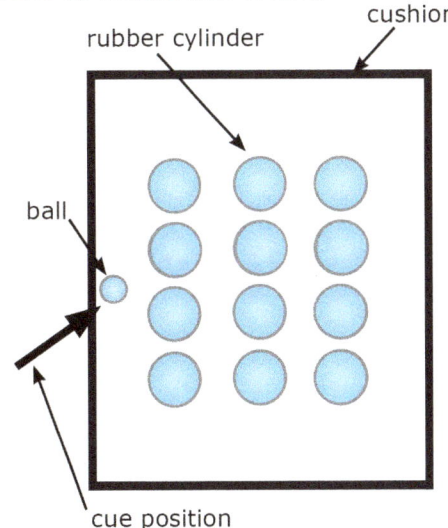

Imagine a billiard table in the middle of which are rubber cylinders of accurately known dimensions, and whose elasticity is known well. Same for the cushions. The ball's dimensions and elasticity are known accurately. The ball is struck with a highly accurate stroke at a very definite angle, measured to a millionth of a degree. The position of the ball 15 minutes later is calculated. The observed cue position will bear no relationship to the result of this calculation.

Why? The initial conditions cannot be known with sufficient precision. Very slight differences in these conditions will prevent any accurate forecast. The degree of precision needed is unattainable

4.2 Chaos in small systems

Two systems which are seemingly the same at one point of time will evolve differently in the long term. Their situations some time later will be very different. They are acutely sensitive to seemingly immeasurable differences in the initial conditions. Two billiard balls released in exactly the same way in the example above would not be following the same paths minutes after their release, even if the initial conditions of angle, force and elasticity are known to six decimal places. The laws operating on a system are deterministic laws but their activity is so dependent on the initial conditions that their applications in individual situations are *de facto* unpredictable.

4.3 Chaos in systems of innumerable particles

Pierre-Simon Laplace (1749–1827) maintained that if we knew accurately all the parameters involving the earth—pressure, temperature, velocities of particles—we would be able to predict infallibly the state of the earth any time in the future. This is not possible, because among other things, the degree of precision to which these parameters would have to be known would be ludicrously large. Any slight billionth of a per cent imprecision would result in a very different future for the world.

Large disordered systems are those involving innumerable particles moving randomly. Examples would be air masses, oceans and the pattern of water flow in a stream. We cannot predict the weather with certainty. We cannot know at the start of summer when a cyclone will develop. As it is developing we cannot predict its precise future activity. The history of a disordered system, is greatly affected by the initial conditions.

4.4 Uncertainty deriving from chaos

The uncertainty in chaos is not the uncertainty resulting from quantum theory. In both these above cases of chaos, the laws of nature are determined. The forces produce the results they should. But we cannot know them with enough precision to forecast the future. Such

---

8. Paul Davies, *The Cosmic Blueprint* (Heinemann: London, 1987), 30.

chaos is called, therefore, *deterministic chaos*. Given the causes, the results are necessarily determined. But we cannot know the causes precisely enough to calculate the result.

Quantum uncertainty is different. It means you cannot predict the result of a particular specified micro-world event; you can only assign the result a probability. You may know the initial conditions well enough, but the well-known initial conditions can give rise to different outcomes. The result of huge numbers of identical trials can be predicted. The percentage of trials finishing up in a certain way is known accurately. Also there are pairs of quantities that cannot be measured simultaneously with unlimited precision.

Further reading

Amir D Aczel, *God's Equation: Einstein, Relativity, and the Expanding Universe* (New York: Four Walls Eight Windows, 1999).

Steven J Dick, *Life on Other Worlds: The 20th Century Extraterrestrial Life Debate* (Cambridge: Cambridge University Press, 1998).

John Gribbin, *In the Beginning: The Birth of the Living Universe* (London: Viking, 1993).

Michael D Lemonick, *Echo of the Big Bang* (Princeton: Princeton University Press, 2003).

Mario Livio, *The Accelerating Universe: Infinite Expansion, the Cosmological Constant, and the Beauty of the Cosmos* (New York: John Wiley & Sons, 2000).

Martin Rees, *Our Cosmic Habitat* (London: Weidenfeld and Nicolson, 2002).

Michael Rowan-Robinson, *Ripples in the Cosmos: A View Behind the Scenes of the New Cosmology* (New York: WH Freeman and Co, 1993).

John Scalzi, *The Rough Guide to The Universe* (London: Rough Guides, 2003).

George Smoot and Keay Davidson, *Wrinkles in Time: The Imprint of Creation* (London: Little, Brown and Company, 1993).

6
The Big Bang:
Another Revolution in the Skies

Chapter overview

- Science is forced to face that the expanding universe implies a beginning
- The fascinating first three minutes
- 380,000 years after the big bang: the formation of atoms
- Further transitions: the increasingly structured cosmos
- The paradox of an explosion that engendered ongoing creativity
- Philosophical speculations
- Extensions:
    - Inflation
    - Dark matter

1. The big bang

1.1 The theory of an expanding universe leads back to a beginning

The model of an expanding universe leads back to an idea of a beginning. If we calculate the speeds and distances of the galaxies, and if we then explore what gave rise to these speeds and distances, we find that all the galaxies were once together. However, they were not pre-formed stars and galaxies waiting to be propelled outwards.

If you start from today's universe and extrapolate backwards in time you find all the galaxies converging towards each other. Then everything seems to coalesce together in a smaller and smaller volume, until we get to a point of almost infinite density and almost zero volume. Everything was to emerge from this point: there was an enormous explosion propelling matter outwards, accompanied by radiation.

The consensus among cosmologists is that the universe we know erupted out of a singular event. There is however now a small group beginning to doubt the present model.

Question: Do you think the big bang suggests the idea of a creation?

....

....

....

....

....

1.2 The explosion which began the universe

Scientists are now able to make precise statements about the first moments of the universe:

- It was not an explosion of something pre-existing.

- It was the appearance of space and enormous energy.

- Some of the energy condensed into matter.

- This matter dispersed as the space expanded.

- The big bang was not an explosion into a pre-existing void.

- It was the very beginning of space.

- It was the very beginning of time ('spacetime').

Question: The Book of Genesis proposes an unimaginable Being effortlessly bringing Creation into being. Is not this credible in the light of science?

....

....

....

....

....

....

....

....

2. After the bang

Various stages in the development of the universe from have been delineated.

2.1 The first three minutes
- 10^{-43} seconds after the big bang: This is the earliest time at which known physics can be applied. Between time zero and this time, highly speculative and theoretically demanding scenarios have been proposed. (10^{-43} is a decimal point followed by forty-two zeros and a one: 0.0000000000000000000000000000000000000000001 seconds.)

- Up to 10^{-34} seconds after the big bang: This is the time period known as *inflation*,[1] as the fledgling universe allegedly doubles in size many times. It expands from the size of a trillionth of a nucleus to the size of a grapefruit. There are many theories covering this time, and again the theories are very demanding theoretically. Inflation is a theoretical invention deemed necessary to account for certain features of the present day universe.

- The first microsecond (10^{-6} seconds) after the big bang: The universe is now a hot soup of quarks, electrons and other exotic particles and radiation particles (photons).

- One second after the big bang: The quarks have combined to form protons and neutrons so that there are now protons, neutrons and neutrinos, as well as electrons and photons (units of radiation).

- From one second to three minutes after the big bang: The temperature is high enough for one proton and one neutron to link up (to *fuse*) to form a nucleus of heavy hydrogen (deuterium), and more importantly, two protons and two neutrons could combine, and stick together to form a helium nucleus. In this way, large amounts of helium were formed in the first three minutes. One quarter of the universe's ordinary matter in the stars, galaxies, and intervening space is now helium and the rest is hydrogen. One argument in favour of the big bang is that it predicts the ratio of hydrogen to helium to be 3:1, and this is the composition found today. No other theories predict this ratio.

Primordial nucleosynthesis

neutron + proton
⟶ heavy hydrogen

2 protons + 2 neutrons
⟶ helium nucleus

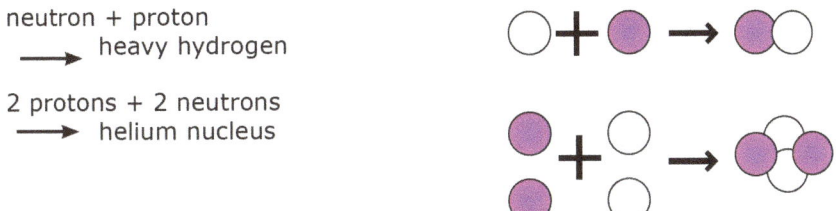

Small amounts of lithium, beryllium (Be) and helium 3 were also synthesised.

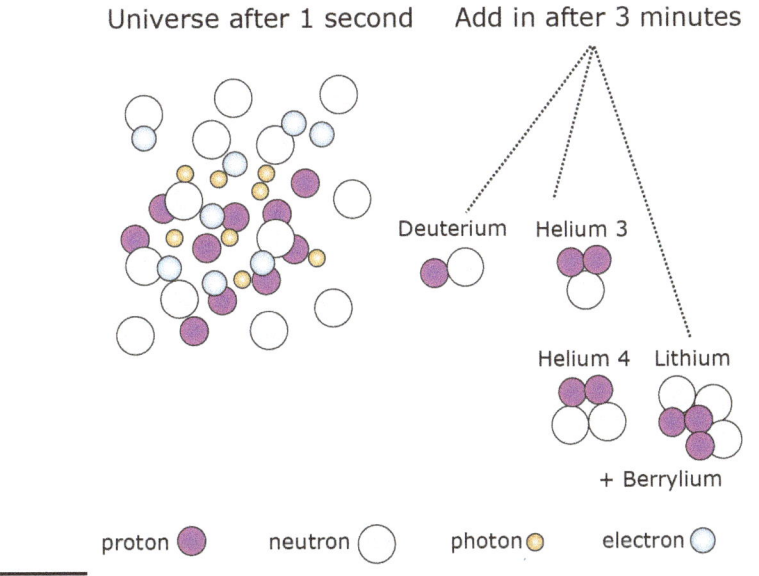

1. For more information, see Extension at end of this chapter.

2.2 From three minutes to about 380,000 years after the big bang:
This was the time during which the universe expanded as a chaotic mixture of sub-atomic particles, mainly positive protons, neutral neutrons and negative electrons. Radiation (photons) was continually and randomly reacting with all the charged particles.

- The temperature is now not hot enough for any more combining of protons and neutrons to form helium.

- Thus the proportion of all the particles remains the same: the ratio of the numbers of protons (hydrogen), neutrons, electrons, deuterium (heavy hydrogen), lithium, beryllium and photons (radiation) remains constant during this period.

- The temperature is falling rapidly.

- The space containing all this continues to expand strongly.

- Sound waves ripple through the hot dense chaotic swirling mass like ripples in a lake.

- There is a dense swarm of negative electrons pulled by the positive protons. They cannot join up because everything is travelling too fast. The electrons' motion accompanies the chaotic and vigorous ebb and flow of the protons, neutrons, deuterium nuclei and helium (nuclei).

- Photons (the smallest bits of radiation) are herded along by all this and are continually being captured and re-emitted by the nuclei (like frogs capturing and then spitting out flies).

- The space has expanded to about 1/1000 of the size of the present universe.

Question: How would you incorporate this chaotic scenario from time zero to 380,000 years into the religious doctrine of creation?

....

....

....

....

....

....

2.3 380,000 years after the big bang: a creative step, the formation of atoms
The universe does not remain chaotic. With the continual cooling the temperature reaches the point where electrons (negative) can now combine with protons or other nuclei (positive) to form atoms. Positive charges and negative charges always attract. Before this time, there were always forces between the protons (+) and the electrons (-), but the electrons were

moving too fast for the protons to capture the electrons. (Imagine a herd of wildly stampeding cattle. The herdsman manages to lasso a prize bull with a rope which had lost most of its strength through weathering. The rope snaps because the bull's force on the rope is beyond its breaking strain.) The speed of the electrons up to this time is so great that it snaps the force the protons exert on them. As the temperature falls, the speed of the electrons falls so that when the temperature has become low enough, the force between proton and electron is enough to capture the electron. The universe now, instead of being a mix of chaotically moving particles, becomes a mass dominated by atoms. The photons are free to move off unimpeded, because they only react with charged particles. These photons are the cosmic background radiation.

380,000 years after the big bang

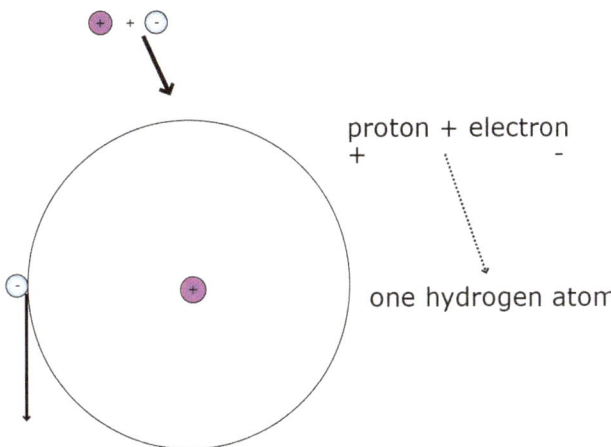

The speed of the electrons has decreased. They can now be captured by the protons.

2.4 Structure begins to form

The universe today is not smooth: it consists of stars, galaxies, clusters of galaxies and often rings of clusters surrounding voids. How could these features develop out of a smooth early universe?

Cosmology

Universe (totality of everything that is)

units = galaxy = 100,000,000,000 stars

total number of galaxies = 100,000,000,000

total stars = 100,000,000,000,000,000,000,000

+ clusters, superclusters and voids

How did the originally even distribution of matter arrange itself into clumps of matter out of which galaxies were to form?

The initial fireball was almost, but not totally uniform. Its searing heat and energy were almost the same in intensity everywhere. But there were regions where the energy density was slightly more and regions where it was slightly less. The factor by which they were more or less was less than one in one hundred thousand ($1/10^5$). These differences remained as the universe expanded.

As the temperature fell, and the motion of atoms became less and less, the particles accumulated preferentially (through gravity) in the regions of higher energy density, and less in regions of lower density. Once a region had a higher density of matter—even slightly higher—it attracted matter away from other regions, so that its density grew. As the density grew more and more, its ability to attract more and more to its region grew exponentially. So matter became unevenly distributed and more ordered. The whole universe has kept expanding, but instead of being an expanding chaos, it is now an expanding mix of clumps of matter and voids.

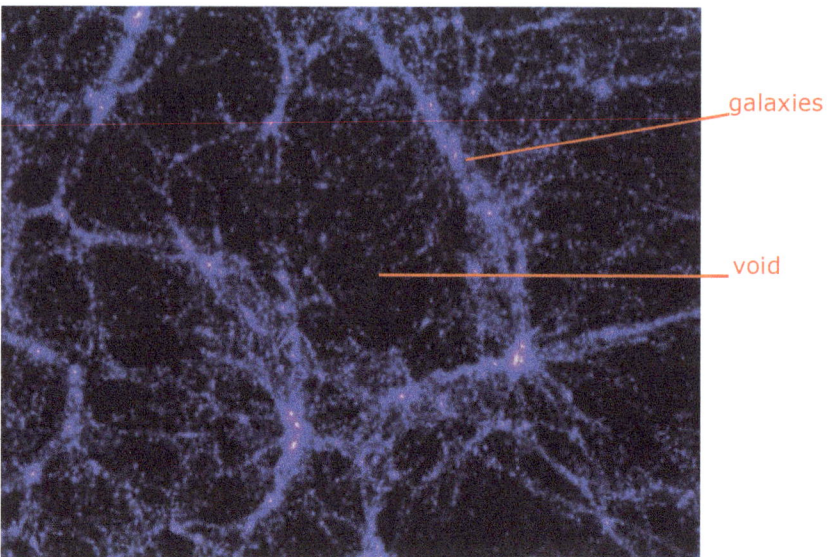

3. Reflections

3.1 Scientific: The big bang theory presents problems

The expansion model certainly leads to a big bang scenario. However, a simple picture of the primordial explosion has presented scientists with theoretical problems.

- Ultra-uniformity: The initial entity had to be incredibly uniform, ultra-homogeneous with the very slight irregularities necessary for the formation of galaxies. But there seemed to be no reason why it did not appear in a tempestuously irregular state, which would have resulted in a universe without clear structures, and hence not bio-friendly. There was an enormous number of other possibilities besides ultra-uniformity. But these would not have allowed a fruitful universe to evolve, nor were any of these in accord with the data provided by the cosmic microwave background, which predicted a very uniform early state.

- Incredible exactness: Not only did the entity have to be the same all through, but its density had to be orchestrated to a very particular value—to one part in 10^{60}. Had its features of energy, explosiveness and gravity been slightly different by this miniscule amount, it would either have exploded towards infinity, with such force as to prevent any clumping to form galaxies, or would have contracted back to nothingness, or to a black hole.

- There is a small group of serious cosmologists who now doubt the big bang scenario. They doubt it because since the initial promulgation of the theory so many new features have been added to the theory to explain theoretical difficulties that have emerged as the theory has been elaborated and developed over the decades. These features include cold dark matter, whose nature we do not know, dark energy of the vacuum again whose nature we are ignorant of. These two are said to account for ninety-five per cent of the matter/energy of the universe. Some theorists feel that a theory that has become overladen with *ad hoc* features is one waiting for a paradigm change, a complete replacement by a new vision. However they have been unable to provide a replacement plan. The problems of ultra-uniformity and incredible homogeneity are dealt with by the theory of inflation. (See section 4, extension.)

Question: What difficulties do you see for the big bang theory?

....

....

....

....

....

....

....

3.2 Philosophical
Science leads us to a point where something seems to be coming from nothing. This seems to be materially impossible. Does it not need another sort of being, perhaps in another dimension of existence? At first glance one would say here is the creation event, because something cannot come from nothing. This argument is encapsulated in the following form (a deductive syllogism):

> Whatever begins to exist must have a cause.
> The universe began to exist.
> Therefore, the universe must have a cause.
> An infinite series of causes does not explain itself.
> So ultimately there must be an uncaused cause,
> which is God.

Science must continue looking for natural explanations for every situation and there are speculative theories concerning the early moment.[2] In the 1600s, the church found it had wedded its creation doctrine to the geocentric model, the earth as the unmoving centre of everything else (see chapter 4). This led to the rearguard action on preserving this model, and people still use this historic stand to accuse the church of being anti-science. Clearly the earth-centred universe was the science of the time, not deducible from creation accounts in the Old Testament, which leave the *how* as an open question. The Old Testament delivers at least three different solutions to the *how* question (see chapter 7).

---

2. Paul Davies, *The Goldilocks Enigma* (London: Penguin, 2006), 172–216.

While being aware of the big bang scenario, and speculating philosophically on this, it would be unwise to say that the big bang is the last scientific word. Models come and go. Nevertheless the scenario pointing to a beginning makes for interesting speculation.

Perhaps ultimately it is more profitable to ask the question *Why is there anything at all?* The universe did not have to be and the universe did not have to be as it is. Whatever does not have to be does not have a reason for itself within its own existence. Therefore it owes existence to something other which *must* exist. Whatever scientific model comes to be, this question always remains.

Scientist-mathematician Roger Penrose reflects on the current situation:

> There's an extraordinary degree of precision in the way the universe began. A profound puzzle. Is the solution answerable in the future? It's beyond the present understanding.[3]

Question: 'Either the big-bang *or* creation' is not a valid disjunction. Discuss.

Question: One can believe in creation without being a creationist. Discuss.

---

3. Roger Penrose, *The Road to Reality* (London: Random House, 2004), 754.

4. Extension 1: Inflation: a solution to the big bang problems

4.1 The meaning of inflation

The initial speck which came into existence at the big bang doubled in size many times from 10^{-37} seconds to 10^{-32} seconds, so that it increased in size by a factor of 10^{50}; from the dimensions trillions of times less than that of a nucleus, to the dimensions of a basketball.

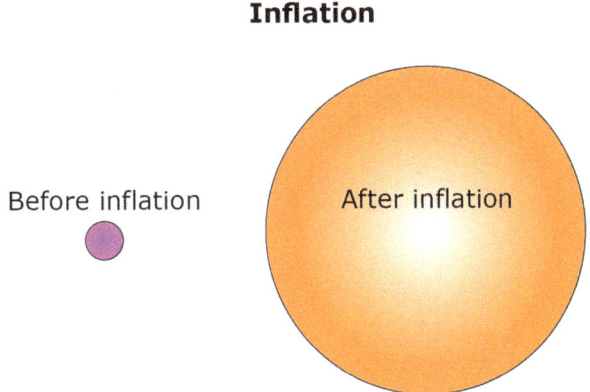

Curvature much less. Multiply the expansion shown here by 1000, and any local section would appear flat.

Theoretical considerations show that this inflation overcomes the first two problems for big bang cosmology outlined in this chapter.

No matter how non-uniform the primordial speck is initially, it would have become almost perfectly uniform. And no matter how dense at the start, it would be at the required degree of precision to set the universe on a fruitful expansion. An analogy is inflating a spherical balloon again and again until it acquires a surface very close to flat (presuming its material is infinitely elastic).

> Inflation does not explain how the universe began nor does it set out to do this. But it does provide a physical mechanism for taking a subatomic speck and producing a vast region of space-time filled with matter.[4]

The pioneer of Inflation was Alan Guth. The main points of his original theory are:

- The antigravity scalar field dominated the universe at 10^{-35} seconds.

- Smaller than a proton, the universe expanded faster than light.

- In a trillion, trillion trillionth of a second, it doubled 100 times.

- Inflation stopped suddenly due to antigravity-causing material becoming unstable.

- This released energy transformed during the expansion into radiation and matter.

- The universe continued to expand at a much more moderate pace.

---

4. Steve Nadis, 'Inflation comes of age', *Astronomy, Origin and Fate of the Universe* (November 2004): 33.

There are now many different inflationary theories, and it is thought that the Planck satellite (2007) will provide important information.

4.2 Big bang problems addressed by inflation

To end up with the highly structured present time universe, the initial entity would have to have been orchestrated in its composition to 1 in 10^{60}. Error one way would mean the bang was not energetic enough, and the speck would quickly collapse. Error in another way would mean everything would be dispersed so fast that matter could not come together to form stars and galaxies. Such ultra-fine tuning seemed too unlikely to be possible. The inflation theory allows an initial entity of any composition which then inflates to an identical state no matter how it started. This post-inflation state is just what was required for the universe to evolve.

> The big bang was not, evidently, any old big bang, but an explosion of exquisitely arranged magnitude. In the traditional version of the big bang theory we are asked to accept not only that the explosion just happened, but that it happened in an exceedingly contrived fashion. The initial conditions had to be very special indeed.[5]

The cosmic background radiation is identical no matter from which direction it is coming. But most of these regions could not have been in contact early on to produce this identity.

> Even today, when we observe the cosmic heat radiation coming from opposite sides of the sky, we are receiving identical thumbprints from regions of the universe that are separated from each other by ninety times the distance light could have travelled at the time the heat radiation was emitted towards us. (The universe then) must have been made up of some 10^{27} causally separate regions.[6]

Why is the radiation which emanates from trillions of causally separated regions so uniform? This is solved by inflation. All the regions were causally connected before inflation. Inflation then blew them apart, but they were identical before this, and because they had been subject to the same process, remained identical.

4.3 The limitations of the inflation theory

There is more in inflation itself that needs explaining, and these features are well beyond the scope of this extension: quantum tunnelling, true vacua, false vacua, negative pressure, the process's being fuelled by an exotic energy field called the inflaton (sic) field.[7] Many cosmologists are in favour of some version of the model.[8] And some of its predictions are in accord with more recent observations. After the big bang model grew in stature, theoretical problems arose in its connection some of which were solved by inflation.

Distinguished theorist and mathematician Roger Penrose is out of step with the rest of the scientific community in not being supportive of inflation. In fact he throws considerable doubt on the whole idea:

---

5. Paul Davies, 'A Naturalist Account of the Universe', *Philosophy of Religion*, edited by Michael Peterson, William Hasker, Bruce Reichenbach and David Basinger (Oxford: Oxford University Press, 1996), 212.
6. Paul Davies, 'A Naturalist Account of the Universe', 213.
7. Alan Guth, *The Inflationary Universe* (London: Jonathan Cape, 1997), 211.
8. Nadis, 'Inflation Comes of Age', views of Linde, Steinhardt, Vilenkin, 36, 38, 40.

> There's an extraordinary degree of precision in the way the universe began in the Big Bang, and this presents what is undoubtedly a profound puzzle. Is the solution of this puzzle of the Big Bang's precision something that may be answerable by a future scientific theory, even though it is still beyond our present-day scientific understanding? The view of inflationists is that this puzzle is essentially 'solved' by their theory, and this belief provides a powerful driving force behind the inflationary position.[9]

Penrose questions the introduction of a scalar field (or several) with very specific properties designed only for the purpose of making the inflation model work.

- He asks if its fashionable status is justified.[10]

- He says there are powerful reasons to doubt inflation, especially regarding the Second Law of Thermodynamics.

- He feels that speculative thought is presented as fact: 'In my opinion, this picture must be regarded as very speculative . . . although it is often presented as virtually established fact!'[11]

- He is sceptical about additional fields that have to be 'conjured' to explain inflation: 'To achieve the inflationary period, it is necessary to introduce a new scalar field into the menagerie of known and conjectured physical particle/fields—not directly related to any of the other known fields, but solely to produce inflation in the early universe'.[12]

5. Extension 2: The role played by dark matter in cosmic evolution

Dark matter is a concept which has been developed to help in the explanation of certain cosmic phenomena. It helps to explain why spiral galaxies do not fly apart, and gives a more detailed explanation of how ordinary matter clumped together to form structures of galaxies, clusters and stars. It helps explain present day cosmic phenomena, and how the universe developed structure. Although it seems that dark matter[13] is there, no one knows what it is. People have been searching for it for a few decades, but we still know little. It is not any of the particles such as protons and electrons we are familiar with. Its presence has been indirectly detected by its gravitational effect on light beams. Dark matter is called *cold* dark matter as it seems to consist of slowly moving particles.

5.1 Dark matter in spiral galaxies
If you put a block of wood on a merry-go-round, and start to spin the merry-go-round faster and faster, a point will be reached when the block of wood will fly off; the force of friction will no longer be capable of holding it in circular motion. Similarly the huge collection of stars making up a spiral galaxy is rotating, and is rotating so fast that the stars in the collection should not be held in their fixed positions. The forces of gravity are not strong enough to hold them in circular motion. They should be flying off into space. Given Newton's and Einstein's

---

9. Penrose, *The Road to Reality*, 754.
10. Penrose, *The Road to Reality*, 754.
11. Penrose, *The Road to Reality*, 752.
12. Penrose, *The Road to Reality*, 751.
13. Martin Rees, *Our Cosmic Habitat* (Princeton: Princeton University Press, 2001), 70–5.

well-accepted theories of gravity, there must be additional matter in each spiral galaxy to hold the galaxy together as it spins. Dark matter—whatever it is—is highly unsociable. It will not play games with the other particles, except to interact gravitationally. It will not combine with anything. While the other particles are colliding relentlessly with each other dark matter remains aloof and untouchable as if it is not there. It is not simply theoretical; its effect has been measured on light beams which are deflected as they pass by galaxies.

Huge quantities of this unknown type of matter were thought to be formed in the first few seconds.

5.2 The role of dark matter in shaping the cosmos

At the big bang, huge quantities of dark matter came to be as well as huge quantities of the matter we are familiar with. In fact, theory demands about ten times as much dark matter as ordinary matter. Dark matter does not have collisions with atoms even though it is there in greater numbers than atoms. Its particles do not collide with anything even though they are moving among themselves and among other particles. They only act on each other or on ordinary atoms by gravitational forces. Shortly after the big bang they could be construed to have formed a regular pattern, on the average equally spaced.

Cold dark matter

However, there are very slight density differences factored into the big bang theory. The dark matter, slowly interacting gravitationally with its own kind, moved into regions of higher density, leaving behind regions of lower dark matter density. These higher density regions exerted greater gravitational tug on the surrounding dark matter, so that more dark matter trickled in from the other regions leaving these regions less gravitationally strong. This was happening while the protons and helium and photons were swirling chaotically, unaffected at all by the dark matter. The dark matter itself seemed oblivious to what was going on, playing its own game behind the scenes.

The clumps of dark matter laid in wait for the events of 380,000 years later. At this time two events occurred. Firstly atoms formed: the electrons and protons combined to form atoms. Secondly photons of radiation ceased interacting with the newly formed atoms. Up until this point the photons had ceaselessly interacted with the charged protons and electrons. As they outnumbered the protons one billion to one, this interaction was very significant. When the photons ceased colliding with atoms, a great calm descended on the universe of ordinary matter. The denser regions of dark matter, therefore, were waiting for the time when the protons and electrons combined. With the removal from action of the photons, the number of interacting particles was reduced by a factor approaching a billion.

This allowed the atoms to be gravitationally attracted to the dark matter. Where there was more dark matter, more atoms were attracted.

Clumps of dark matter after mutual gravitational interaction

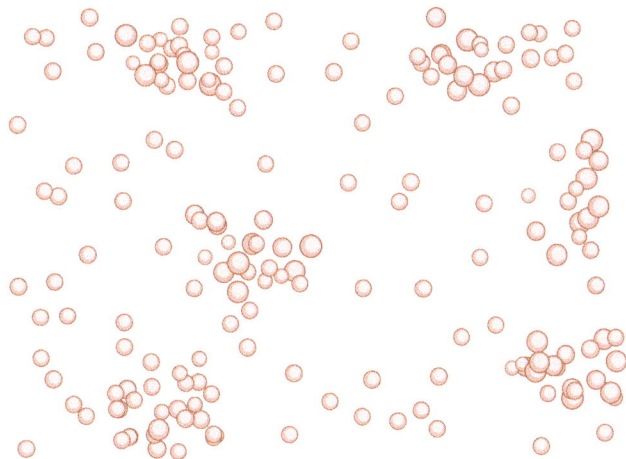

Hydrogen and helium attracted to dark matter

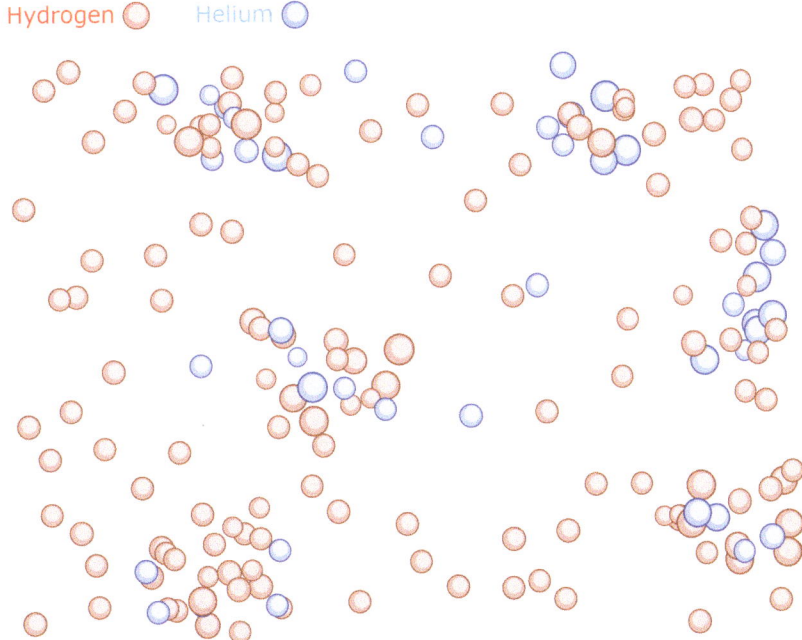

As soon as a region had a greater amount of matter attracted to it, the region would exert greater gravity and so attract more and more matter to itself, giving it larger gravity still. Such a process escalates exponentially. So after 380,000 years, atoms began to congregate around regions of dark matter.

But why was dark matter not uniformly distributed at the start? Why was it initially a little bit denser here than it was there? Quantum fluctuations in the initial fireball led to a slightly uneven distribution of dark matter, which then increased the unevenness because of the greater gravity it would exert. Quantum fluctuations created higher density regions in otherwise uniform space-time and inflation blew them out to cosmic proportion.

While ordinary matter was behaving chaotically and randomly, dark matter was clumping together and these clumps would eventually force a pattern on the 380,000-year chaos.

Further reading

ABC Video, *Universe*, Part 1, 2000.

John Gribbin, *In Search of the Big Bang* (Guernsey: Corgi Books, 1988).

Alan Guth, *The Inflationary Universe* (London: Jonathan Cape, 1997).

Janna Levin, *How the Universe Got its Spots: Diary of a Finite Time in a Finite Space* (London: Phoenix, 2003).

T Padmanabhan, *After the First Three Minutes: The Story of Our Universe* (Cambridge: Cambridge University Press, 1998).

Martin Rees, *Before the Beginning: Our Universe and Others* (London: Touchstone, 1997).

Steven Weinberg, *The First Three Minutes* (London: André Deutsch, 1977).

7

The Book of Genesis: Modern Scholarship

Chapter overview

- Literary myth is a story reaching out for a truth
- The difference between biblical and non-biblical myths
- Some amazing non-biblical myths
- An analysis of three creation myths in the Old Testament
- The essence of the biblical creation stories
- How can the Bible, a scientifically naïve document, be the word of God?

The church had gradually accommodated itself to the heliocentric universe of Copernicus and allowed this to be taught. However over the next centuries it was to be continually challenged:

- The revered biblical account of creation clashed with the picture of the universe that science was revealing.

- The biblical account of the immediate creation of the individual species by God and of the creation of the first human individuals, Adam and Eve, clashed with the evidence accumulating for evolution, and later for the evolution of populations.

- The discovery of many non-biblical creation and flood stories throughout the world pointed to Genesis as being another example of ancient pre-scientific myths.

1. The meaning of myth

Poetry, history, drama, fable, legend, story and myth are all literary forms. The Old Testament abounds in literary forms. There is history in the books of *Kings;* there is poetry in the *Song of Songs;* Jonah is a fable; and throughout the whole there are many prophetic utterances and prayers. Whether myth, fable or song they all have a message. The first eleven chapters of the book of Genesis are not history. There is more than an element of drama in them, but they are not plays. They are certainly stories. But ultimately these chapters are classed as myths. They fall into the class of cosmic myth. Does this mean they are simply untrue? William O'Malley provides a clear answer to this question:

> A great many not-yet-convinced Christians are harmed by well-meaning instructors who leave them with the false impression the Bible is nothing but a bunch of myths. The teachers have not realised—or been able to convey—

that there are two quite different (in fact contrary) meanings of the word myth. In the negative sense myth means a false belief uncritically accepted. In the positive sense, myth means a story that attempts to express or explain a basic truth, as in Aesop's tale of the turtle and the hare; neither Aesop nor his audience believed turtles and hares at one time spoke and made wagers on a race, but they saw within the story a real truth: slow and steady wins the race. This is the sense in which a great deal of Scripture is myth: stories trying to embody truths. The author of Genesis, writing about the same time as Aesop, did not expect his audience to believe snakes used to talk to naked ladies in the park, but he was trying to capture a very real truth: only humans go against God's will.[1]

1.1 Cosmic myths
Cosmic myths are stories about origins: the origin of the world, human origin, the source of good and evil, reasons for catastrophes such as floods and earthquakes, the birth and death of gods. Myth has come to mean fictitious, but this is doing cosmic myths an injustice. A politician may claim a statement of an opponent is a myth, meaning it has no substance at all. On the other hand, there is a sort of substance to cosmic myth.

Cosmic myth assumes there is a reality which lies beyond observation and simple deduction but which is recognised as existing and operative. This reality is perceived in events and not in abstractions, and the event is portrayed in the form of a story. Its language is consciously inadequate, being simply the nearest we can come to a formulation of that which we cannot adequately formulate. In particular, myth is the recognition that there is more to reality than what is observable. Myth-making asserts that there is a deeper explanation for natural events, and so in this sense is a search for truth.

Myths serve many purposes. They confront ignorance and deal with fear. They can express an underlying truth, a value, or they can be used to mould a people together. 'They are the truth to the people who believe in them and live by them. They give the people guidance and spiritual strength.'[2]

Deep explanations for the cosmic and natural realities humans experience have gone through three phases: myth, philosophy and science. A cosmic myth is the search for an explanation, admission of something operating, but unknown. Two thousand five hundred years ago, the scientific method was unknown, and explanations were in terms of divine beings, modelled somewhat on humans or even animals. In Greek philosophy reason supplanted myth as a path into the unknown. Philosophy and/or religion still need to be employed at the deepest level. When empirical observation and ever-improving instruments were added to the power of reason, the scientific method was born. The cosmic myths of Genesis deal with the transcendent, but they differ from pagan myths in many ways.

1.2 The prevalence of non-biblical myths and their polytheistic background
Cosmic myths are found in many ancient cultures, for example, Egypt, Greece, Rome and in contemporary cultures such as American Indians, Pacific Islanders and Australian Aborigines. In lands surrounding Israel, the diversity of gods was associated with diversities of tribes and nations. Over the East was a patchwork quilt of gods, tribal gods fashioned after the image and likeness of the tribes, a duplicate of the world itself, each with its own sphere and group of worshippers. Deeper explanations of the world and evil were given in terms of the origins, powers and adventures of deities. Gods of a people were often associated with expressions

---
1. William J O'Malley, 'Scripture and Myth', *America* 171/3 (1994): 6.
2. Virginia Hamilton, *In the Beginning* (London: Pavilion Books, 1992), ix.

of self-assertion, pride and sentiment. Magic and mechanical ritualism provided a means of manipulating the gods. Many of the gods were perceived as capricious in their dealings with humans.

1.3 The unique character of biblical myths
The world of the Old Testament was deeply influenced by these ideas. But this world did not adopt them; it reacted strongly against them. It declared there was one God unable to be depicted in any image; the sun, moon, stars were therefore not gods. Yahweh was not capricious; rather Yahweh was the God who saved. Primarily the Israelites asserted Yahweh had intervened to become the centre of the lives of the people. There was always the necessity to react against the popular tendency to drift back into paganism, and its seemingly more attractive practices. So biblical doctrine was intolerant of anything else.

Non-biblical mythic stories relate to the births, lives and activities of gods, seemingly outside of time. They go back beyond anything that ever was and begin before anything in the world had happened. Biblical myths are different. They place the mythic past within history. They do this by connecting Adam and Eve with history by means of genealogies reaching from them to Abraham (*Genesis*, chapters 10 and 11)

1.4 Differences between biblical and pagan myths: a summary

Differences between biblical and pagan myths: a summary

Pagan myths	**Biblical myths**
1. Polytheism	Monotheism
2. The gods are born and die	Yahweh was not born and will not die
3. Origin of world and gods often intertwined.	Eternal Yahweh created world
4. Gods often fight among themselves	One God
5. Creation is often a struggle	Creation is not a struggle
6. Chaos often pre-exists: a resistant entity	There is no resistance to creation
7. Gods' capriciousness towards human beings	God saves
8. Gods can be manipulated by magic, ritual, or by a person with power	God is supreme
9. Universal nature is swamped by national character.	God of the whole world: others false Will become the God of all
10. Preceded history	Within history

2. Examples of pagan myths[3]

2.1 Creation
- Mawa-Lisa, the Creators (Republic of Benin): A mother goddess gave birth to twins. One twin, Lisa, became the sun and the other, Mawa, became the moon. During an eclipse they came together and eventually their union produced seven pairs of twins. Each of the twin pairs was given a task: sky, lightning, forests, sea, humans, birds and other beasts. They were to remain hidden, but to report to their progenitors about everything that was to happen on earth and in the sky.

---
3. Hamilton, *In the Beginning*, material taken from this collection.

- Phan Ku, the Creator (China): There was originally space in the shape of a hen's egg, within which was a sort of something called *no thing*. *No thing* housed within itself something undeveloped, which was to be the creator and this creator, Phan Ku, finally broke out from the egg. Phan Ku was grotesque: he was hairy all over, had horns and tusks, and was a giant, growing another three metres every day and finally filling the region between earth and the sky. With a great chisel Phan Ku made earth, rivers, and mountains. The sky itself was only properly formed when, after 18,000 years, he died. His skull became the sky, his hair became the plants, his voice the thunder, his sweat the rain. Humans originated from his fleas, indicating their lowly position. His death enabled pain and suffering to enter the lot of humans.

- Greeks: *Nothing* appeared first, followed by Earth and from Earth came Heaven and Sea. From Earth came mountains, with Mt Olympus becoming the dwelling place of the gods. Earth and Heaven begat the Titans, one of which was Ocean. The father, Heaven hated his children and imprisoned them. One Titan, Kronos, succeeded in breaking out, married Rhea and brought forth Zeus.

2.2 The battles of the gods

- Egypt: As a child Horus had narrowly escaped being destroyed by Set who had murdered Horus' father. He claimed the leadership of the gods when Ra the sun-god grew old.

- Babylon: Tiamat was the sea. Apsu was fresh water. From Apsu came Marduk who was a leader and seemed to rule the Ages. Like a dragon he breathed fire, and boasted four eyes and four ears. He was tall and strong. Another son of Apsu, slew his father Apsu, in response to which Tiamat grew very angry and so created eleven monsters to avenge Apsu's death. Marduk was commissioned to address this challenge and to kill Tiamat. Flanked by gods, he found Tiamat and severed her body in two. With one half, Marduk made the sky, and with the other half made the earth. With Tiamat's bones and blood, Marduk made humankind. So now, with the human race as slaves, the gods would have to work no more.

2.3 Manipulating and capricious gods

- Ulgen, the creator (Russian Altaic). When the god Ulgen saw the shape of a human face in muddy water, he put into it the spirit of a man, and so brought to birth the first man, whom he named Erlik. But Erlik tried to rival Ulgen so the god sent him to the underworld where he became the devil. After this Ulgen created the earth, and the seven men and put them under seven trees, and completed his work by making an eighth man called Maidere. But there were no women, so Ulgen commanded Maidere to make a woman. He could only fashion a lifeless body. He needed Ulgen to breathe life into the body. While Maidere was away looking for the god, Erlik arrived and played seven notes on a flute and nine-stringed instrument near the woman's body. She sprang to life having been given a mind. This was the origin of woman.

- The Sun-god (Aztecs). A great threat to the Aztec people was the thought of the sun staying in one place and setting the earth below on fire. The sun was a powerful god. The sun could be propitiated with offerings of human hearts. So young people were killed and their hearts extracted and offered to the sun-god. This was graphically represented in Mel Gibson's film *Appocalypto* but wrongly attributed to the Mayas.

2.4 The use of ritual and power to attain favour

Australian Aborigines: At the completion of the supernatural beings' labours in forming the earth's features they returned to beneath the earth or changed into rocks, trees or other natural phenomena. They sleep the eternal sleep they had slept before their work. Sacred sites are the places the beings emerged from. They became waterholes, soaks, claypans, caves.

Whenever they were correctly summoned by rites, the ancestors, though asleep, had the power to send down rain, to fill earth with plants and animals. Everything on earth is continued gift. The people did not have to work, only collect the gifts.

Firstly the ancestor would be implored to send the gifts. Corroborees are ceremonies in which these human re-incarnations intoned the sacred verses that the supernatural beings themselves had first sung during their own labours of creation.

Aborigines believe they enter into and continue the creative activity of their ancestors. Corroborees re-enact what had gone before so that the events became present again.[4]

2.5 The origin of death

Old Man Blackfoot (American Indian): Old Man the creator decided one day to create the human race. So he made a woman and child out of clay. And he spoke to them. He covered up the clay shapes and went away. Over a period of four days the clay shapes gradually came to life. They walked with the god Old Man to a river. The woman asked Old Man if they would live forever. He threw a buffalo chip into the river saying that if it floated people will die but come back to life after four days, but if it sank their lives would end. The chip floated. The woman however would not accept the result. She threw a stone into the river and said that if it floated humans would live forever, and if it sank we would die. The stone sank. 'So you have chosen', said Old Man. 'There will be an end to people.'

2.6 The origin of evil

Pandora came from heaven. As she was leaving to come to earth, Zeus gave here a box which was closed and which she was never to open. This made her curious, but she resisted the temptation. She went to stay at the house of Epimetheus. She arrived carrying the box, and he cautioned her not to trust Zeus, and not to open the box. Epimetheus took it from her and standing on a stool, put it on a high shelf. The box suddenly vibrated, so he quickly got down, leaving it out of harm's way. His brother Prometheus arrived and roundly condemned Epimetheus for having anything to do with the gift from Zeus. Some time later, the brothers went out, and Pandora's curiosity got the better of her. She climbed onto the stool, tried to grasp the box, but only succeeded in knocking it off the shelf. It flew to the ground and opened. Screams and groans came from the box. Darkness descended for a moment, then all manner of ugly and evil looking creatures flew and slithered from the box. They went through the house, out into the street, into the town and throughout the rest of the world. Thus evil entered the world: starvation, poverty, disasters and depression. One fragile beautiful little creature remained in the box. This was hope.

One version of the story has hope flying after the creatures and challenging their influence. Another version has Pandora locking up the little creature in the box forever.

---

4. Paul Albrecht, *Aboriginal Creation Story*, edited version of talk to Lutheran Youth of Australia Assembly, Canberra, 1 August 1988.

Question: What are some myths which penetrate and guide our own culture?

....

....

....

....

....

....

3. Biblical myths

3.1 The relationship between biblical and non-biblical myths

The material of the first chapters of the book of Genesis is classed as mythical. There are two creation myths, which are quite different in details and purpose. These are followed by stories concerned with men and women messing up human life, followed by God's efforts to save the human race in one way or another.

As pagan myths are efforts to tap into the powerful forces unknown in themselves but clearly operative, so too are the Genesis myths. The Genesis myths however take us further into the mystery of the unknown. As with pagan myths, they are not to be taken literally. They are typical of pre-scientific myths in that they refer to beginnings, the origin of evil, the reasons for catastrophes and the relationships of humans to the transcendent.

The main difference between pagan myths and those in the Bible is in the nature of the God proclaimed. The God of the Bible, Yahweh, is an unimaginable, benign and transcendent being, creating with ease with the words 'let there be', challenging but compassionate. Genealogies link God with history. The biblical myths were not foundational stories for the Jews. God was primarily known through the divine saving acts in Israel's history. In this way Yahweh revealed godself as supreme and as a saviour.

Because Judaism had to take into account the traditional stories of the world and formulate explicitly its attitude towards them, the creation narratives were the result. The stories include much well-known non-biblical material but it is reworked. As the religious element in Israel's vision was very original, the borrowed narrative material was treated in an original way. The Genesis creation stories are thus new and radically different.

Many of the stories in Genesis 1–12 are virtually a new series of narratives containing distant reminiscences of more ancient material. For example, the Adam and Eve story is new although some of its imagery, such as the tree of life, comes from older stories. While some of the stories come originally from pagan literatures—for example, the Flood—the meaning of these is changed: now there is only one God, Yahweh, who cannot be represented by images and has a true concern for the chosen people.

3.2 The Bible's first creation story: Genesis 1.1–2.4

In this story, there is no laborious struggle. Rather great ease and a single command is enough, and everything is made in the totality of its being (see diagram in chapter 4, section 1.1).

The Hebrew word used for this bringing into being is *bara*. The result of *bara* is something which exceeds the potential of the preceding situation. There is no mention of material out of which the making was done. The *bara* was done from *tohu*. *Tohu* means the absence of any definite form, the absence of life, the absence of any particular thing. It is formless disorder or chaos; it is nothing because there is nothing outside God's power, who made heaven and earth, who made all that exists.

Tohu is as much nothingness as anything can be in the Bible. The word is used elsewhere: 'All nations are as nothing before him, for him they count as nothingness and emptiness'.[5] And again: 'He reduces princes to nothing, the rulers of the world to mere emptiness'.[6]

3.3 The Bible's second creation story: Genesis 2.5–3.24

In this story, man is not created from nothing. Rather, God creates man from mud. It presumes an initial creation: 'When the Lord God made the universe. then the Lord took some soil from the ground and formed a man out of it'.[7]

The order of creating is irreconcilably different from that of the first story. God still transcends creation, and is the foundation of all existence, but the creator God seemingly unattainably far off, in this story is intimately close; God is not bound up in life in a crudely materialist fashion, but, nevertheless, God is concerned about the details of our existence. God's demands and love are real; and God's claims are total because God infinitely transcends those who are created.

This text, the 'paradise and fall' narrative, is an independent Israelite text included by the author just as it was found. The symbols in the paradise narrative are from older sources: man made out of clay, tree of life, serpent, cherubim. But the meaning given to these common symbols is unique. There is no hint of the real content of this narrative anywhere else.

The second creation account (verses 5 to 24) is a prelude to the main concern of this story, which is the fall.

3.4 The two Genesis creation stories compared

There are two distinct creation stories in Genesis which differ greatly in detail and in purpose. They are not open to being harmonised.

Two creation stories

Stage	Story 1 (chapter 1) God distant, with great power	Story 2 (chapter 2) God near, cooperative, intimate
1	Dark and wet	Barren dryness without plant, animal.
2	Light	Mist came up from land to water earth
3	Firmament	Man
4	Dry land	Planted a garden: plants and trees
5	Plants and trees	Put man into the garden
6	Sun, moon, stars	River to water the garden
7	Birds and fish	Commandment not to eat from tree of knowledge
8	Animals	Animals and birds
9	Man and woman	Woman

---

5. Isaiah 40:17.
6. Isaiah 40:23.
7. Genesis 2: 4b–5.

Question: Genesis is a book couched in the language and symbols of the times, exuding a mentality very different from our own. Yet its underlying affirmations retain a perennial value. Discuss.

....

....

....

....

....

Question: Evil abounds in the world today. Do you agree with the essence of the biblical account, that while created good, the human race is deeply flawed?

....

....

....

....

....

3.5 A third creation story: Psalms and the Book of Job
There is a third creation story in the Old Testament which may be seen as a reaction against some pagan narratives. In the Psalms, the Book of Job, and in Isaiah, God is pictured as overcoming the monsters of chaos: 'By his power he has whipped up the Sea, by his skill he has crushed Rahab'.[8]

A common background pagan narrative was this: the pagan gods had to struggle against chaos, and against the monsters which inhabited chaos in order to bring about a coherent world. The Sea itself was a legendary goddess held back from sweeping civilisation away. In contrast, these parts of the Old Testament picture God effortlessly quelling the fierce primeval monsters. This is an affirmation of the supreme jurisdiction of God.

> Rahab seems clearly to be associated with or identified with the monster of chaos which is slain by the creative deity in ancient Semitic myths of creation. In the Old Testament this victory is attributed to Yahweh. Yahweh hewed Rahab in pieces, pierced the dragon, dried up the sea (Is 51:9). He rules the raging sea, crushes Rahab (Ps 89:10). He stilled the sea, smote Rahab, slew the fleeing serpent (Job 26:12). The helpers of Rahab are bowed under his power (Job 9:13).[9]

---

8. Job 25:12.
9. John L McKenzie, *Dictionary of the Bible* (London: Geoffrey Chapman, 1966), 719.

And the Psalms speak of another legendary monster, Leviathan:

> By your power, you (Yahweh) split the sea in two,
> And smashed the heads of the monsters on the waters.
> You crushed Leviathan's heads,
> And gave him as food to the wild animals.[10]

Leviathan is:

> a monstrous being to be identified with the mythological monster of chaos, Lotan, 'the serpent slant, the serpent tortuous, Shalyat of the seven heads' slain by Baal. The victory of the creative deity is transferred to Yahweh.[11]

Rahab and Leviathan were legendary monsters representing the forces of chaos and evil, effortlessly disposed of by Yahweh. As the turtle and the hare were known by Aesop not to exist, so too neither did the monsters; the allusions refer to Yahweh's supremacy over creation.

3.6 Why are there three different creation stories?

Clearly the Israelites did not know how God created. Of course, no one was present at creation. Their foundational experience of God was not as creator, but as saviour. It was the facts of history that forced Israel to acknowledge its national God, Yahweh, was the utterly one unique God. Judaism knew this God first as redeemer. They had experienced God's self-revelation as a living reality. Other tribes had their gods, but this one was the living God.

With the common idea of God's mastery, the stories attest explicitly to monotheism, and to God's decisive role at the beginning. There is one God who stands over all else that exists. Through Jewish history this idea took shape. The idea began as a personal God and became then a family God. From this it evolved to a people's God and finally became the world God: 'You out of all peoples shall be my personal possession, for the whole world is mine'.[12] And this is not a god for a particular society. There was to be no graven image of Yahweh and Yahweh had definite views about the whole world.

Question: Imagine yourself born to a Bedouin family, being just as intelligent as you are today. What would you have believed?

....

....

....

....

....

....

---

10. Psalm 74: 13–14.
11. McKenzie, *Dictionary of the Bible*, 505.
12. Exodus 19:5.

3.7 A summary of what the biblical creation stories tell us

About God:
- There is one God unable to be represented.
- Everything that is, is ultimately due to this one God.
- God created from nothing, chaos, trackless waste.
- God saves.

About the world:
- It was good, until humans introduced evil.
- Any progress comes from humans—not from fate or the gods.

About humans:
- Humanity is the pinnacle of creation.
- We are created in the image and likeness of God.
- We have freedom.
- We can—and do—choose evil.

Against pagans (the Bible is a polemic against the contemporary worldviews):
- There is no mythological world of the gods.
- The sun, moon and stars are not gods.
- There was no prehistoric disconnected mythic era, in which great battles were fought. Hence God's work is connected to history by genealogies.
- Monsters of Chaos were deemed irrelevant. Creation was effortless.

Genesis was thus a radical document which released people from domination by myths, from fear of monsters and of anti-human capricious supernatural beings. But it must be seen in the context of its time: it is a cosmology still attached to pre-scientific views of the universe.

3.8 The philosophical view of creation
Creation not only means an initial act, but it means the continual absolute dependence of everything on God for its existence. No piece of reality explains its own existence, its own separation from nothing. It needs God's continual causal input. Thus creation is not necessarily the beginning of existence, but God's continual conferring of existence.

Question: The literal interpretation of Genesis is untenable today. Discuss how Genesis' underlying assertions sit well with the findings of modern science.

4. The Bible as the word of God

4.1 How was Genesis 1–12 written?

An extreme fundamentalist view would be that the actual text of Genesis is word for word, idea for idea, the work of God. This implies some sort of dictation, or a direct revelation. From this point of view nothing at all in it can be wrong.

The mainstream Christian view is that the first twelve chapters of Genesis are the work of one author. This person worked from three existing texts, constructing a coherent narrative around three central themes:

- God initiates,
- Man messes it up,
- God saves man from the mess.

Although it is a coherent narrative, the three previous strands from which the final writer worked can be easily identified.

In the Old Testament as a whole, some books bear traces of many different epochs and generations; they show different stages of Israel's spiritual development. They are not the outcome of the literary activity of any one writer or period. For example, the book of Isaiah comprises three books each written at different periods of Israel's history. So the three strands of Genesis mirror different times.

The three strands from which the Genesis chapters were formulated, are the work of many generations, editing and re-editing, and the final editing is in Genesis 1–12. The writer inherited the work of others, and the end product is the synthesis at the end of a long tradition. It is the work of a single mind full of conviction. This last author of Genesis put together the first twelve chapters by arranging and manipulating already existing materials. The author took over some materials, adapted others. For example, chapter one is a liturgical hymn.

Thus Genesis 1–12 was composed very gradually in this way. But the final single author of the first twelve chapters had three documents in front of him. The writer, showing some synthetic and didactic talent, selected and combined together material into a coherent whole.

The biblical narrative is unique: there are no other texts dealing with its overall theme (though elements of it are in other texts).

Question: God revealed to intelligent people the idea of a creation, expressed in the rudimentary science of the time. Should we thus expect advanced science in the Book of Genesis?

4.2 How are these chapters the word of God?

The geography, history, cosmology and anthropology of the Old Testament are what was known at the time. It is very rudimentary without any scientific exactitude. The scientific age did not begin for another two millennia. Over time God's dealing with humans emerged as a radical departure from how other gods were envisaged to relate to people.

These ideas grew up gradually, during centuries, among the people inspired by the prophets, who are certain of God's influence in history, meditating on triumphs and setbacks. They were honed and perfected by the centuries of reflection, and the rewriting, re-editing by people of prayer. God was guiding them.

4.3 What the Bible teaches

The Bible is a religious testimony. The Bible sets out to teach:

- Who God is
- Who we are
- God's purpose for us
- God as master whom we must freely acknowledge
- God's love for us
- What God expects of us—our part of the Covenant
- What we can expect of God—God's part of the Covenant
- God's intervention in history

The Bible does not make any claims to teach science or be authoritative about what happened in human society in the past, about the positions of cities, lands and mountains.

Thus the bible does *not* set out to teach:

- History
- Geography
- Cosmology (the structure and evolution of the universe)
- Anthropology
- Biology

Question: How is it possible to link biblical creation with the scientific story? Science has discovered that the universe began and it did not have to be. Although the details of Genesis are mythical, this finding sits well with the idea of a transcendent creator.

Question:
Can one believe in Creation without being a Creationist?

Further reading

Lloyd R Bailey, *Genesis, Creation, and Creationism* (New York: Paulist Press, 1993).

John D Barrow, *The Book of Nothing* (London: Vintage 2000).

Anthony F Campbell, SJ, Mark A O'Brien, OP, *Rethinking the Pentateuch* (Louisville: Westminster John Knox Press, 2005).

Virginia Hamilton, *In the beginning* (London: Pavilion Books, 1992).

David Leeming with Margaret Leeming, *A Dictionary of Creation Myths* (Oxford: Oxford University Press, 1994).

H Renckens, SJ, *Israel's Concept of The Beginning: The Theology of Genesis I–III* (New York: Herder and Herder, 1964).

Eugenie C Scott, *Evolution vs Creationism* (Berkeley: University of California Press, 2005).

Claus Westerman, *Genesis: An Introduction* (Minneapolis: Fortress, 1992).

8

The Stars:

Instruments of Creation

Chapter overview

> Stars are not eternal: they are born, have a life, grow old and die
> - The source of life, the sun, is a cosmic balancing act
> - Stars and suns are the manufacturing centres of the universe
> - The death of a star: a supernova
> - The death of the sun
> - Extension: The neutrino coincidence: the threefold luck that gave us carbon

1. Two gigantic leaps forward

1.1 The skies appear static
Looking up at the stars night after night we see the stars in the same positions, and to all intents and purposes they are in the same positions as they were during the time of Galileo, Ptolemy and Aristotle. There are a few changes: the dissipating remnants of the Crab Nebula are the result of a giant explosion four centuries ago; there are other similar remnants from exploding stars; and comets come and go and temporarily change the sky. But overall things have not changed. As we have seen, this has led humankind to conclude they were always there as they are now; in the old days, the stars were said to be clinging to the inside of the celestial sphere; in later times, given that it is the earth that is rotating, they were deemed to have been eternally stable in their allotted positions in space.

1.2 The cycle of life and death in the skies
Cosmology, however, has revealed three facts about stars:

- Stars were not always there. The forces of nature fashioned them from clouds of hydrogen gas.

- The stars are not idle. In fact, as well as shining, they are cosmic factories. It is the stars that have created all the elements above helium. Our sun is at present creating more helium. In a later stage it will manufacture carbon.

- Stars die. A star undergoes a series of processes ending in death. Large stars have short lives (some millions of years), medium sized stars like the sun have a long life (ten billion years), while small stars burn for much longer.[1]

---
1. T Padmanabhan, *After the First Three Minutes* (Cambridge: Cambridge University Press, 1998), 69–79.

After the big bang, how did stars form? And how did the elements essential for the formation of planets, life on earth and the matter of the human brain come about? We must explore how the fertile laws of nature have led to the formation of stars, and how within stars the laws have brought about the synthesis of the other ninety elements.

1.3 Creationism is not the answer

Creationism is the doctrine that all things were created substantially as they now exist by the fiat of an omnipotent creator and did not gradually evolve or develop. These developmental events fly in the face of fundamentalist creationism. Mainstream Christianity teaches creation, but not creationism. Christianity is open to the scientific understanding of stellar processes, and sees God's hand marvellously at work in the cosmic processes through laws imparted to nature.

The media does not reflect the reality of the interface between religion and science, rarely reporting non-fundamentalist Christian scholars. Most Christian theologians are opposed to creationism. Yet so often, 'Christian' is taken to mean some version of the seven days of creation, thus positing science and religion in unresolvable conflict, and downgrading the acceptableness of Christianity. Educated Christian scholarship marvels at the way the laws of nature have brought about order from chaos. From the point of view of religion, God maintains everything in existence, and has given to creation the capacity to develop itself. Creation has been endowed with very special laws to bring about order in the cosmos, the manufacture of the other ninety elements in the stars, and finally to bring about life forms and the complexity of the human brain from inanimate matter.

Question: Do you believe Christianity must adhere to the simple creation story? Do you believe that any other interpretation risks compromise?

2. The stars

Stars, other suns, were not there from the beginning. There are stars which have been and gone; there are the countless trillions visible today through telescopes; there are stars at this moment coming to birth. The world followed the death throes of a star in 1987, and witnesses the formation of new stars in fiery clouds in the spiral arms of the Milky Way.

Question: Why are there so many stars? Are they all there for us?

....

....

....

....

....

....

....

....

2.1 How did the stars form?

After millions of years of cosmic expansion, the universe consisted of clouds of hydrogen and helium. Within a cosmic cloud of hydrogen and helium there are regions of dark matter which are denser than others.[2] These denser regions of dark matter preferentially attract hydrogen and helium to themselves. These still more dense regions exert greater force still on the surrounding gases which are attracted to the region, adding their mass to the region and thereby causing greater forces still, which in turn causes accelerated migration of hydrogen and helium to the region. The pressure in the region builds up exponentially. As the pressure builds up, so does the temperature.

The relationship between pressure and temperature may be seen in the simple process of pumping air into a bicycle tyre, which heats up through the pumping. More matter (air) in the restricted volume of the tyre means greater pressure, which means higher temperature. It is this principle in evidence cosmically in the pressurised hydrogen cloud—its temperature rises.

The pressure in the ever-denser region of the hydrogen cloud keeps on increasing at an ever-increasing rate, and with it the temperature rises constantly, and both would do so limitlessly except for another effect which halts the process putting an end to this runaway heating and unstoppable implosion.

The temperature becomes so great—millions of degrees—that the hydrogen ions (protons) join together and fuse to make helium, with the emission of light, heat, and other radiation. It needs great energy to make the hydrogens (protons) fuse, and this is supplied by the increasing heat due to pressure. Once a certain temperature is reached, the fusions take place and the whole cloud ignites. This nuclear explosion reverses the implosion of the massive gas cloud. The mass of gas now contains a continuous giant hydrogen-bomb-type explosion. The additional heat, caused by the nuclear explosion, enables more of the hydrogens to join together, and the process goes on; it is self-perpetuating. A star is born. This is what is happening now in the sun, and has been happening there for five billion years, and will continue to do so for some billions of years to come.

---

2. Extension, section 5, this chapter.

A star is born

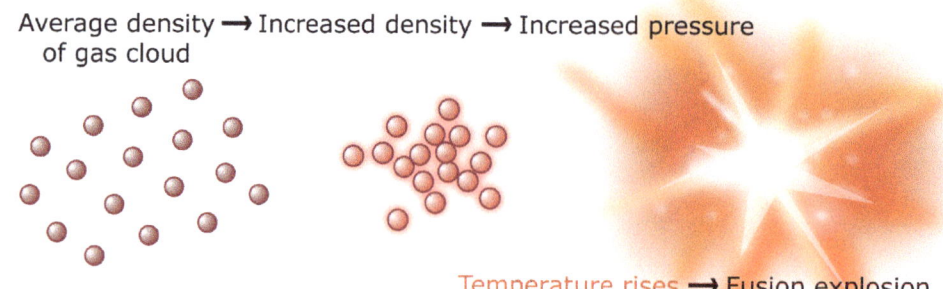

Although the ancients thought the universe eternal and unchanging, and the conviction of the scientific community up until the 1930s was that the universe was static, eternal and unchanging, all stars have now been shown to have a life cycle: a birth, different stages of life, degeneration and death. Examples of all these stages in stellar evolution are visible through telescopes. Looking around the Milky Way, we can see new stars, stars like the sun, red dwarfs, red giants (dying suns) and bright giant blue stars.

Our sun's life is marked by these stages:

Birth ⊠ Present stage ⊠ **Red Giant** ⊠ White dwarf ⊠ **Black dwarf** (see section 4)

The red giant phase will probably occur in about 4 billion years time.

2.2 A balancing act between implosion and explosion
The present constant shape and heat of the sun is the result of an equilibrium, a balance between two natural effects. All the trillions of tonnes of highly concentrated matter deep within the star are pulling on all the matter above it, trying to make the star implode. It does not implode. How does the sun resist the deadly forces of implosion? Deep within, the sun houses a continuous violent explosion. An explosion catapults matter out in all directions. Thus the fires of nuclear fusion propel the matter of the star outwards. So the explosions occurring continually in the sun are spreading the matter out continually, resisting the implosion.

So why does the sun not blow itself apart? The tremendous gravity of all the matter in the sun pulls the products of the explosions continually back into the sun. Nothing can escape the sun's gravitational grasp. If you throw a ball up into the air, it comes back. Rocks hurled at great speed from volcanoes may rise a thousand metres, but they are eventually drawn back by the earth's gravity. So, all the matter sent on its way by the sun is drawn back into the sun by the sun's gravitational force of attraction.

Implosion - explosion

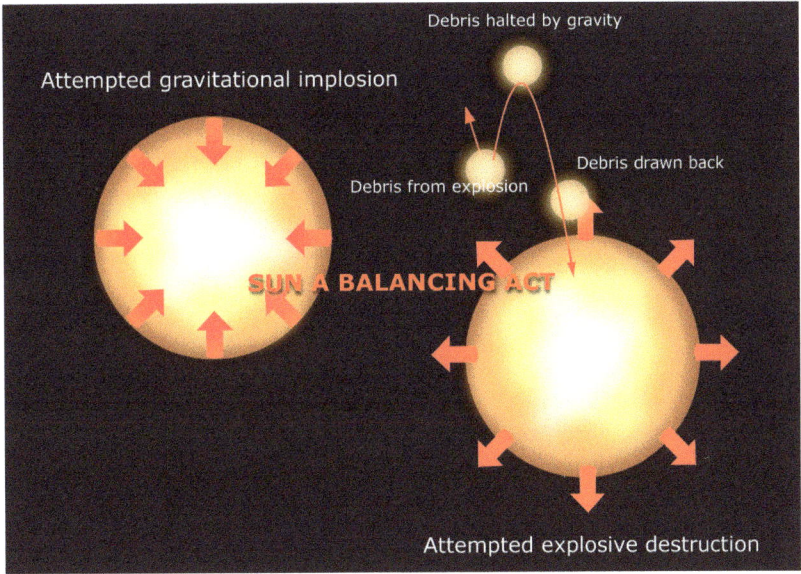

The fact that the sun can be just as it is, is due to a coincidental relationship between the gravitational and the explosive impulses, pulling in opposite directions. If gravity were only slightly larger as a force, the sun would contract to a slow burning weak red dwarf. If gravity were slightly less, the explosive outrush would increase the sun's diameter significantly. Stars with large volumes burn much more quickly. The star would exhaust its fuel in about one tenth of the time of the sun's projected lifetime. Evolution of life then could not have occurred. It would not have a long-lived constant phase like our sun, which is to have a steady phase for approximately eight billion years. A long constant phase is needed for life-forming processes. Any shorter and it would burn out too quickly to produce a habitable earth. Evolution would be impossible because of a lack of time. The possibility of human life depends on this fine-tuning between gravity (imploding) and the nuclear-fired explosion.

Question: Is this example of fine-tuning explainable by chance?

....

....

....

....

....

....

3. Formation of the elements

The elements present within the chaotic clouds of the early universe were hydrogen (75%) and helium (23%), with small amounts of heavy hydrogen (deuterium), lithium and beryllium.

The first stars were formed from these clouds and thus were mainly hydrogen and helium. Big bang theory accurately predicts the amounts of these elements present in old stars. But there are ninety other elements which occur in nature; some such as carbon, nitrogen and oxygen are vital for life, and silicon which is vital for the formation of rocks. Our sun contains all of these. And the earth was originally formed out of material from the sun. When and how did these elements arise? Our sun is a third generation star. It contains not only early universe elements, but the whole ninety-two elements of the periodic table. Ninety of these elements were cooked up in large early stars, and sent into space to mix with the ubiquitous hydrogen and helium with which they formed new stars.

3.1 A large star: a stellar cooker
A large star begins its life as a mixture of hydrogen and helium in the ratio of three to one. As described before, when the pressure builds up inside the chaotic mass of hydrogen and helium, as it contracts under its own gravity, the temperature reaches a point which enables hydrogens to fuse, releasing large amounts of energy. The heat generated by these fusions enables more fusions to keep occurring and to produce heat to generate still further fusions and so the process goes on. The helium produced tends to fall to the centre of the star and become inert—for the moment.

Large star after a long time burning hydrogen

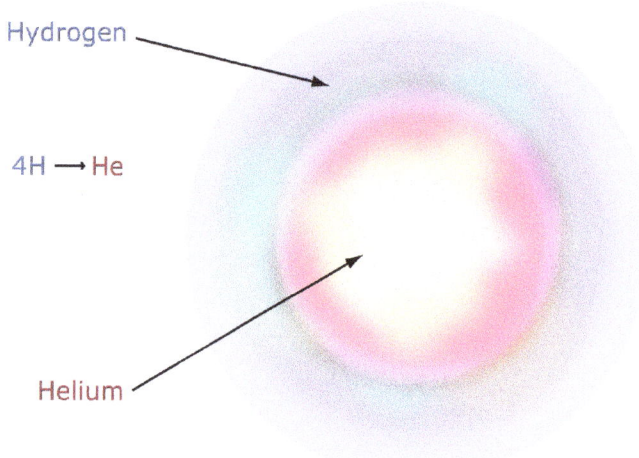

(The initial step in the fusion process actually is low in probability. Relatively few of the hydrogens take the fusion path. But as there are such a large number of atoms, despite the low probability, enough fusions take place to trigger the next steps. Thus, the whole mass of hydrogens does not go up at once. Because the rate of fusions is controlled by the initial slow step, the sun can glow on for billions of years enabling time for planetary formation, and evolution.)

Question: Could this control of the star processes be a lucky accident?

....

....

....

....

....

....

....

....

As time passes, a lot of helium builds up in the centre, and its gravity leads to the contraction of its volume, increasing its density. Its pressure increases, and so does its temperature. Thus the pressure and the temperature within the helium increase, just as they did in the initial hydrogen cloud. Eventually the temperature reaches the point at which the helium nuclei can fuse together. The fusing of three heliums produces carbon. Carbon, the element essential for life, is thus manufactured inside the star.

The carbon formed tends to fall to the centre of the star where it builds up gradually, with the hydrogen layer still contributing to the helium layer.

Helium atoms fuse to form carbon

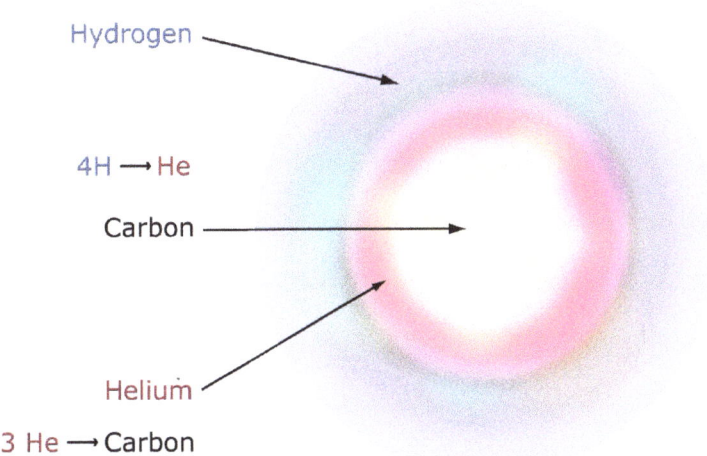

3.2 The syntheses of the remaining elements
The same thing happens to the carbon dumped in the centre of the star. The pressure and the temperature increase and the carbon fuses to form neon, and silicon. Then the atoms in the silicon layer fuse to form iron.

But this is where the process ends. Iron cannot fuse to form higher elements. The iron builds up and the gravitational pull on all the layers builds up. But iron will not provide a counter blast. Imploding forces build up. For a while the explosive outrush keeps the star from collapsing. But as gravity forces increase and the various explosive fires gradually die down, the whole star suddenly collapses.

A series or further fusions makes all the elements as far as iron

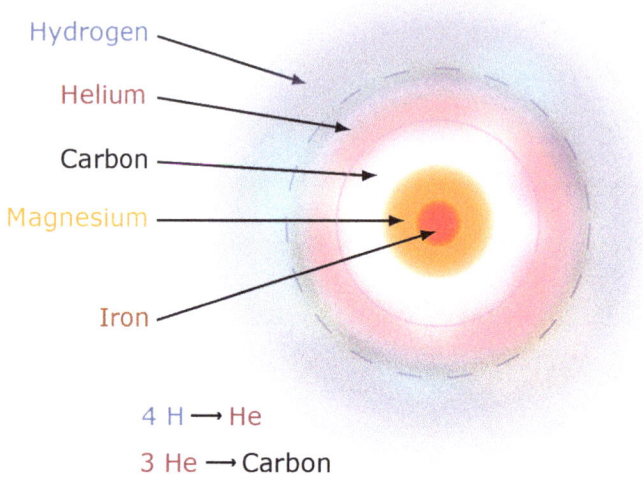

4 H ⟶ He
3 He ⟶ Carbon

Question: A creation given the ability to then create itself gives rise to thoughts of the God of whom Einstein said 'subtle is the Lord'. Discuss.

3.3 The death of a large star: supernova

As the nuclear fusion and its explosive results die down, there is nothing left to resist the implosive impulse of gravity. All the matter implodes towards the iron, with nothing to stop it. The core of the star is crushed.

Having crushed the core, the matter bounces back up again, accompanied by a gigantic shockwave, which propels a tremendous mix of newly manufactured elements into space, never to return to its source.

The supernova bounce

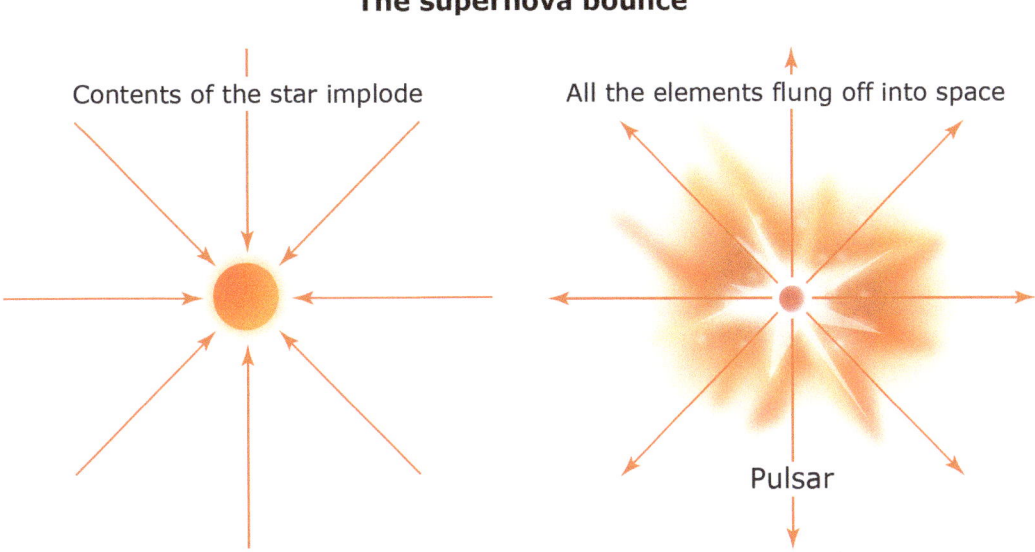

Contents of the star implode

All the elements flung off into space

Pulsar

The elements have been cooked up and distributed through space. These elements form part of later generations of stars like the sun. The crushed former core of the giant star is what is known as a pulsar. The force of the impact is so great that not only is the matter crushed (as a car would be with a giant rock landing on it) but the atoms themselves are crushed. A core of tremendous density is left, which is called a pulsar.

The electrons are forced into the nucleus. This has three consequences:

- The volume of the atom is reduced to $1/10^{15}$ of what it was (10^{15} is a one with fifteen zeros).

- The electron/nucleus combination becomes a neutron.

- The pulsar is thus a spinning mass of neutrons. A teaspoon full of pulsar material would weigh a billion tonnes.

Pulsars, thousands of them, have now been detected. They spin up to a thousand times per second. And every time they spin, they emit a radio wave. These radio sources were known decades ago. It was thought they may have been alien civilisations, and hence they were called 'LGMs', short for 'little green men'. However, it was soon realised that the signals were too repetitive to be from an intelligent source.

In 1987, in the Large Magellanic Cloud (a satellite galaxy), a star transformed into a supernova. From being invisible, it became clearly visible. It shone with the brightness of a billion suns, fading gradually during the next months. The debris has been tracked ever since. The debris contains all the elements cooked up within the star during its life. Lots of the theory about supernovas has been vindicated by these observations. The event actually happened 160,000 years ago. The light has taken that long to reach us.

Supernova 1987, in the Large Magellanic Cloud

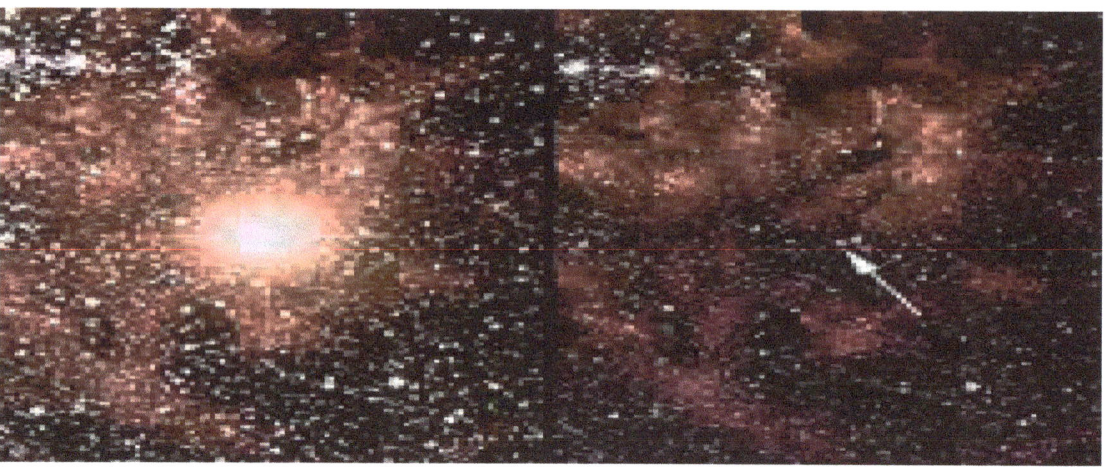

Star after collapse.   Star before implosion.

3.4 The formation of solar systems

The trillions of tonnes of elements expelled from a dead star wander the universe. Some enter other clouds of hydrogen and helium. These clouds of gas, laced with carbon, oxygen, nitrogen, silicon and so on, contract, ignite and form second and third generation stars. The sun is one like these. The pre-sun cloud contained mostly hydrogen and helium, but also contained the other ninety elements released in previous supernovae explosions.

The enriched cloud contracted under its own gravity as the earlier stars had done. At various stages of the contracting process, rings of these cooked up elements separated out. The swirling rocks and dust grains in the rings then eventually came together and formed the planets. The exception was the asteroids; these remained individual rocks because of the huge gravity of nearby monster planet Jupiter.

At the temperatures during the supernova explosion higher elements, such as uranium, were formed by various fusion processes. Uranium is essential deep within the earth to supply heat for geological processes necessary for life.

The sun is a later generation star, a hydrogen/helium fusion bomb, perpetually exploding, laced with quantities of every known element, some of which were left behind as the cloud contracted, and so formed the planets, one of which we are standing on.

Our sun is born from a gas cloud

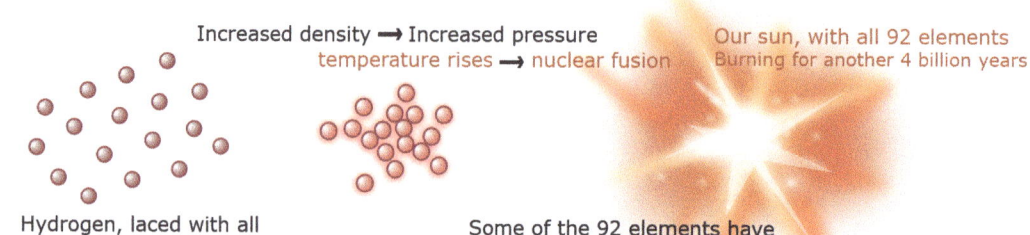

Hydrogen, laced with all the 92 elements from supernovae

Increased density → Increased pressure
temperature rises → nuclear fusion

Some of the 92 elements have become planets, Earth, us

Our sun, with all 92 elements
Burning for another 4 billion years

3.5 Life-giving carbon

All life is based on the element carbon. Human bodies involve long chains of carbon atoms as the basis for their structure. The formation of carbon is the fortunate outcome of an extremely tenuous and improbable process. Two helium atoms fuse to make beryllium and in an almost miraculous chance process (and within a fraction of a fraction of a second) this beryllium, which has an ultra-short life, is struck by another helium to form carbon. This has to happen within a billion billionth of a second, otherwise the beryllium would cease to exist, destroying itself from within.

It is well known that Fred Hoyle, who proposed the whole scenario of the manufacture of the elements inside stars, remarked that the emergence of complex structures was as likely as a whirlwind blowing through a junkyard and in the process assembling, by chance, a 747 airliner.

The element carbon is the basis of all life. DNA, the chemical of life, is a string of carbon atoms three billion units long, like an enormous string of beads. There are important attachments all the way along the chain. No other element can form chains like this, chains which are essential for DNA to exist. Without carbon there is no life.

The stellar manufacture of carbon and distribution nearly did not happen at three stages:

- Its formation (see above).

- Its perseverance in being. Calculations show all carbon produced inside stars just misses being destroyed.

- Its dissemination to new clouds so that in solar systems like our own, life can emerge given the right conditions.[3]

Paul Davies is concerned with the seemingly fortuitous emergence of life in *The Goldilocks Enigma*. He says, 'A really big question is why the universe is fit for life; it looks like it has been fixed up'.[4]

Question: God said to Job: 'Who fixed the earth on its foundations?' God said to Fred Hoyle: 'Fred, who fixed those resonances?' ('Resonances' are the fortuitous conditions promoting the formation of carbon). Discuss.

....

....

....

....

....

....

....

---

3. Extension, section 6.
4. Paul Davies, *The Goldilocks Enigma* (London: Penguin, 2006), 18.

Question: No carbon would mean no life, which would mean no humans. Is chance having a dominant influence? Or is there a deeper purpose operating?

....

....

....

....

....

....

4. The death of the sun

The sun is continually giving out light and heat. To do this it continually turns hydrogen into helium. The helium gathers in the centre of the sun. As the quantity of helium builds up so does the pressure. As the pressure increases, so does the temperature until it is finally so great that the helium fuses to beryllium and carbon. This blows the sun outward. It will engulf the earth and even stretch as far as Mars. At this stage it will become a red giant.[5]

Explosion to red giant

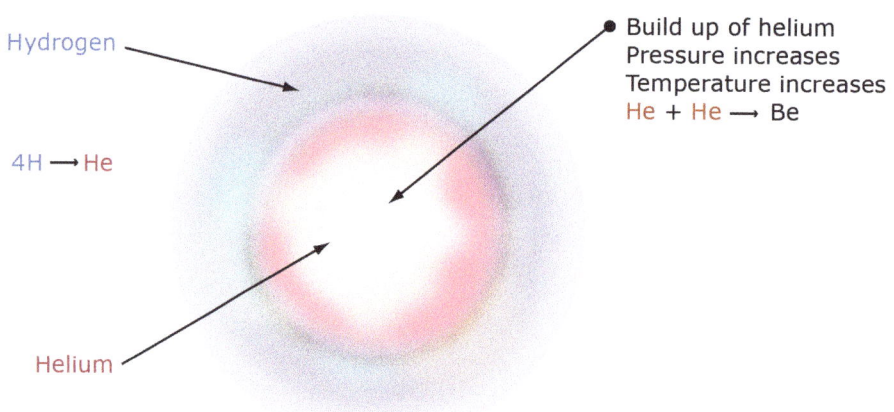

High temperature causes helium fusion
Result: enormous expansion

The sun, not being a large star, does not synthesise any more elements. There will be no manufacture of magnesium, silicon, iron and other elements. It does not go to the supernova stage. The red giant phase is the beginning of the end. The huge outer layers, of carbon, helium and hydrogen, gradually drift away leaving behind an incandescent ball of highly compressed matter called a white dwarf. The Helix Nebula is the expelled contents of a dead star. The white dwarf is nowhere near as dense as the pulsar, but a lot denser than the

---

5. Peter Ward and Donald Brownlee, *The Life and Death of Planet Earth* (London: Piatkus, 2003) 149–65

matter we are accustomed to. In a pulsar one cubic centimetre weighs a billion tonnes. In a white dwarf, the same amount weighs a paltry hundred kilograms.

Stages in the death of the sun

The huge volume of matter gradually drifts off into space, leaving behind a white dwarf.

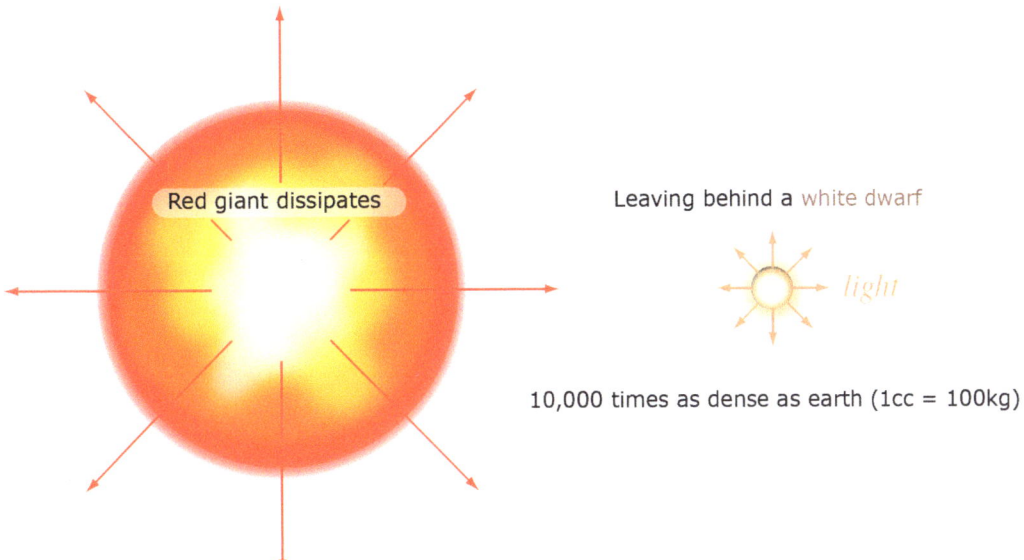

10,000 times as dense as earth (1cc = 100kg)

Over the aeons, the white dwarf loses its light and heat and becomes a black dwarf, the size of the earth, but 100,000 times as dense. (This is not a black hole.)

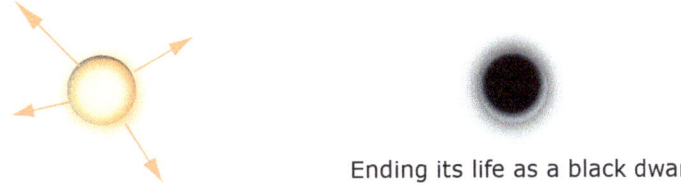

Question: All the signs of humanity will be vaporised by the sun as it expands. Humanity vanishes. Has our existence been meaningless?

....

....

....

....

....

....

....

....

....

....

....

Question: 'The whole creation until this time has been groaning in labour pains'.[6] Does this sum up what has happened, what is happening? Is it eventually to give birth to a new heaven and a new earth?

....

....

....

....

....

....

....

....

---

6. Paul, *Romans*, 8:22.

5. The end of a superstar: a black hole

A black hole occurs when a very large star implodes. Any star which is about ten times the size of the sun will finish its life as a black hole. When all the air is let out of a balloon it implodes to a much smaller volume. When a star's explosive processes wind down, the gravity of the inner core pulls on the outer matter forcing it towards the centre. When there is a lot of matter in the core, it pulls on all the outer matter with such a force that it all implodes to almost a point. When a very large star goes supernova, the core collapses as already described, but it collapses beyond the pulsar stage. Gravity is so great that the pulsar collapses completely so that all its mass is at one point. This point is called the singularity.

Black Hole

- a hole in space
- with a definite edge
- into which anything can fall
- out of which nothing can escape
- not even light
- curves space and warps time
- in centre space and time end

In a black hole all the matter of the former star becomes crushed to a point. Its sucking power, its gravity, remains just the same a long distance from it: if you are watching its collapse from thousands of kilometres, you will not be suddenly drawn in. There is a region around it called the event horizon, which is just a line in space. Anything venturing over the line can never emerge—not even light. The hole is called black because any light radiated from within is sucked immediately back into it.

It is said that if you fall into a black hole, when you have passed the event horizon, you can see all reality outside it, but nothing out there can touch or see you. Your fate would be 'spagettification'. The gravity difference between your head and toes would be so great you would be stretched into a thin strand before entering the singularity.

Many black holes have been allegedly detected in space.[7] There is no direct evidence: they themselves are not visible, but they are observable by their effects. For example, a star Cygnus XI seems to be orbiting around nothing. Calculations show the centre of the orbit to have the mass of black hole.

What would happen to a robot, dropped from a spacecraft towards a black hole, approaching the event horizon?

Drop a robot

time after fall (seconds)	distance fallen (km)	speed (km/second)
10	2600	550
20	10,500	1060
60	135,000	9700
61	150,000	14,000
61.7	158,000	39,000

Through the event horizon at light speed.
0.0002 seconds later: disintegrated: tidal forces
61.8 seconds: into the singularity

---

7. Steve Nadis, 'Black Holes: Seeing the Unseeable', *Astronomy* 35/4 (April 2007): 26–31.

Question: A universe comes into existence, then goes out of existence, leaving not a trace of itself. Is this futile and meaningless? 'The more the universe seems comprehensible, the more it seems pointless'.[8]

....
....
....
....
....
....
....

6. Extension: The neutrino coincidence

The manufactured elements, bursting from the star shattered by the supernova explosion, would not get out except for the help of trillions of ghostly neutrinos. The gravity of the pulsar slows the escaping elements, and would stop them and pull them back to be forever part of the neutron star (pulsar). And so all the carbon in the universe would be locked up forever—life would not happen.

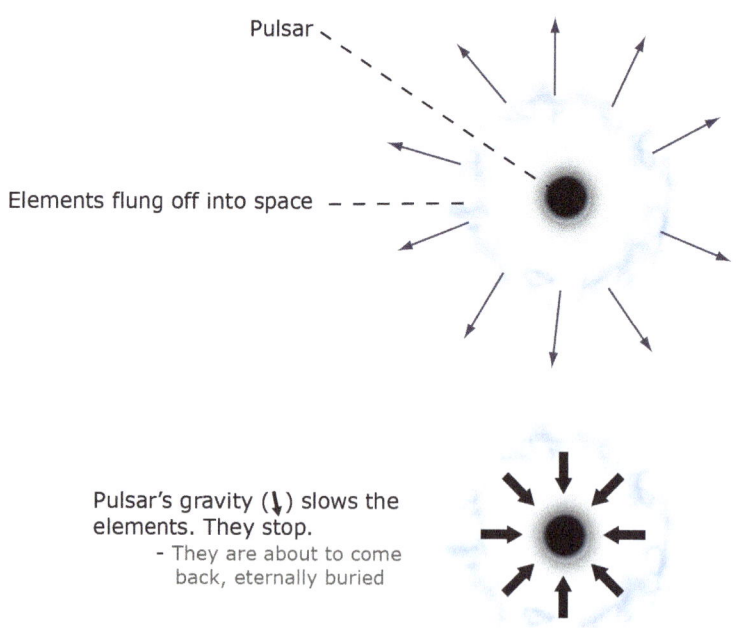

Manufactured elements expelled

Pulsar

Elements flung off into space – – – – –

Pulsar's gravity (↓) slows the elements. They stop.
- They are about to come back, eternally buried

---

8. Steven Weinberg, *The First Three Minutes* (London: André Deutsch, 1977) 149.

But floods of neutrinos have also been released from the pulsar, a little later. These follow the expelled elements and enable them to escape. Just as a multi-stage spacecraft would fall back to earth if the second stage did not ignite, so the elements would fall back to the crushed core were it not for the extra impulse given them by the neutrinos.

Neutrinos to the rescue

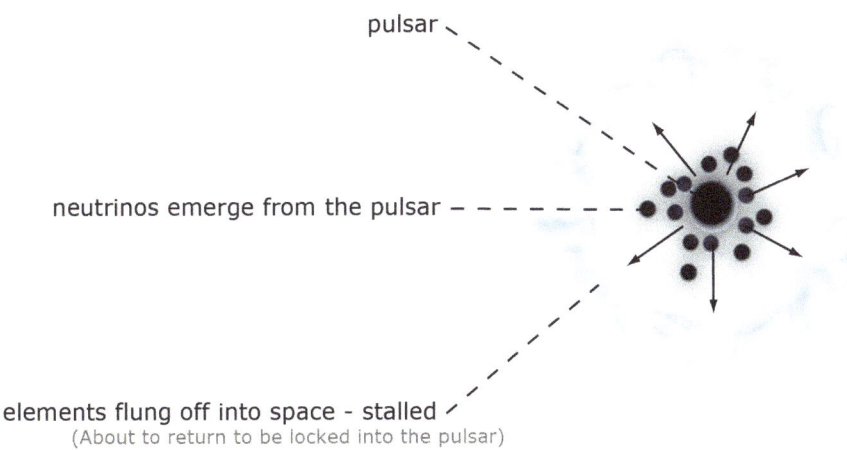

The neutrinos overtake and interact with the slowing mass, giving the elements an extra kick, enabling them to escape forever.

Neutrinos interact

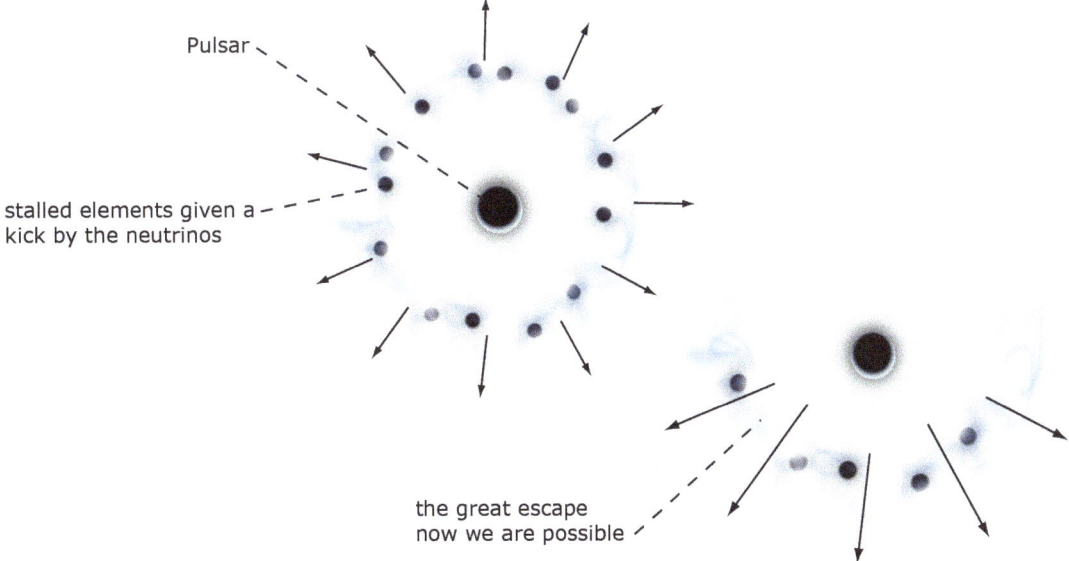

The neutrino is a sub-atomic particle with a mass less than a thousandth of the mass of an electron and with no electric charge. It moves at near-light speed. It was postulated in the early 1930s and its existence experimentally proved in 1956.

The fine-tuning of the force between neutrinos and ordinary matter:

- If the force between neutrinos and other matter were slightly greater, the neutrinos themselves would be stopped by the pulsar's gravity, and fall back to whence they came, before they reached the stalled elements. Hence the neutrinos could not interact with the expelled elements. Hence the elements would not receive the extra little kick to propel them away from the dead star. They would fall back into the pulsar, and so the carbon would not get out to fertilise later generation stars. Life would not happen.

- If the force between neutrinos and other matter were slightly smaller, the neutrinos would not interact sufficiently with the manufactured elements to enable them to escape. They would pass through the elements almost unnoticed. Hence the elements would again fall back into the pulsar and be locked in there forever.

Thus the force between neutrinos and visible matter is *just right* to enable the outwardly propelled matter to escape to the void, and be available for the formation of planets and even perhaps life if the conditions are suitable. Either a little bit more or a little bit less, and life would never have happened. All the carbon and all the other elements would have been imprisoned forever in the pulsar.

Further reading

ABC Video, *Universe*, Part 2, 2000.

Fred Adams and Greg Laughlin, *The Five Ages of the Universe: Inside the Physics of Eternity* (New York: The Free Press, 1999).

John L Casti, *Complexification: Explaining a Paradoxical World Through the Science of Surprise* (London: Abacus, 1994).

Paul Davies, *The Last Three Minutes: Conjectures about the Ultimate Fate of the Universe* (London: Weidenfeld and Nicolson, 1994).

Armand Delsemme, *Our Cosmic Origins: From the Big Bang to the Emergence of Life and Intelligence* (Cambridge: Cambridge University Press 1998).

Nigel Henbest and Heather Couper, *The Guide to the Galaxy* (Cambridge: Cambridge University Press, 1994).

Malcolm S Longair, *Our Evolving Universe* (Cambridge: Cambridge University Press, 1996).

Harold J Morowitz, *The Emergence of Everything: How the World became Complex* (Oxford: Oxford University Press, 2002).

T Padmanabhan, *After the First Three Minutes: The Story of Our Universe* (Cambridge: Cambridge University Press, 1998).

Clifford A Pickover, *Black Holes: A Traveller's Guide* (New York, John Riley, 1996).

Kip S Thorne, *Black Holes and Time Warps: Einstein's Outrageous Legacy* (London: Picador, 1994).

9

The Anthropic Universe: Science at its Limits

Chapter overview

- The slowness of science to accept that the universe was not unchanging
- The amazing evolution: from featureless chaos to structure and order
- The pessimistic arrow of time and the purposeless end of everything
- The optimistic arrow of time: purposeful progression
- The *anthropic* principle: science at its limits
- Finely tuned laws of nature have directed the purposeful progression
- Specialised catalysts of cosmic progression:
    - Is it chance? One in a trillion upon trillion?
    - Does everything possible exist? The multiverse solution
    - Does an ultimate designer fit the case?
    - Other approaches
- Extensions:
    - Multiverse theory: arguments for and against
    - String theory
    - Intelligent design theory

1. The universe

As we have already discussed, until the mid-1950s there was little thought of cosmic evolution. The universe was seen as changeless, static, infinite in extent and eternal. When Einstein himself could not accept relativity theory pointing to a changing universe, he postulated a cosmic repulsive force (lambda, Λ) which would keep the universe from succumbing to an unstoppable implosion.

A Catholic priest-scientist, Georges Lemaitre, broke ranks and argued for an expanding universe which had a beginning: if it was expanding, it must have had a beginning, a small compact region (primeval atom[1]). At a conference he explained it to Einstein who replied: 'your calculations are correct, but your physics is abominable'.[2] A year or two after this Einstein realised Lemaitre was right, and said his cosmic repulsive force was his 'greatest mistake'. The recent discovery that the universe's expansion rate is increasing has renewed interest in Einstein's lambda force.

In 1998, against all expectations, it was discovered that the expansion rate of the universe was actually increasing. Whether or not the universe expands forever, it was always taken for granted that the expansion rate would slow down because of the braking force of gravity.

---

1. Bill Bryson, *A Short History of Nearly Everything* (London: Transworld Publishers, 2004), 173.
2. Simon Singh, *Big Bang* (Netley: Griffin Press, 2004), 276.

The 1998 finding, independently from two different research teams, has resulted in the proposition of dark energy to explain it:

> What is behind the mysterious force we call dark energy? One way or another it will overturn our ideas about how the universe works. It is beginning to sink in that there is no easy way to understand what dark energy might be. The problem has become so intractable that many now see it as the greatest challenge facing physics.[3]

Stuart Clark outlines four possible theories concerning dark energy: it is a new force of nature; it is a modification of an old force; it is a new idea altogether which denies a previous dogma that on a large enough scale the universe is the same everywhere; and finally that it is a revival of Einstein's cosmological repulsive constant.[4]

Question: Find information of the 'phlogiston' theory of combustion. Is 'dark energy' the modern day 'phlogiston'?

....

....

....

....

....

....

....

1.1 General possibilities for a universe
There are four general possibilities for a universe:

- A universe in which no processes take place and which never changes.

- A universe which is totally chaotic: no fruitful processes take place, because there are no laws.

- A universe in which there is chaotic randomness, but out of the chaos comes law and order. Laws impact on the chaos to produce fruitful results.

- The multiverse: a boundless number of universes, one of which happens to exist.

1.2 Evolution of the universe
The universe has evolved, seemingly from a superdense, microscopic, extremely hot seed of space-time and energy, which was without structure and uniform throughout. It has

---

3. Stuart Clark, 'Heart of Darkness', *New Scientist* 193/2591 (2007): 28.
4. Stuart Clark, 'Heart of Darkness': 30–3.

gradually become what we see around us now. Many of the ninety-two elements make up our particular environment. The element carbon is the basis for billions of different combinations which give rise to the huge variety of animals and other life forms, and finally the most complex device in the universe—the human brain.

We can observe results of cosmic evolution through telescopes: 100 billion stars per galaxy and 100 billion galaxies in the observable universe. Theory points to regions beyond this.

We can even observe stages of the universe at earlier times as we intercept light beams that began their journey to us millions and billions of years ago.

Cosmologist Bill Stoeger schematised cosmic evolution from then to now thus:[5]

Cosmic evolution

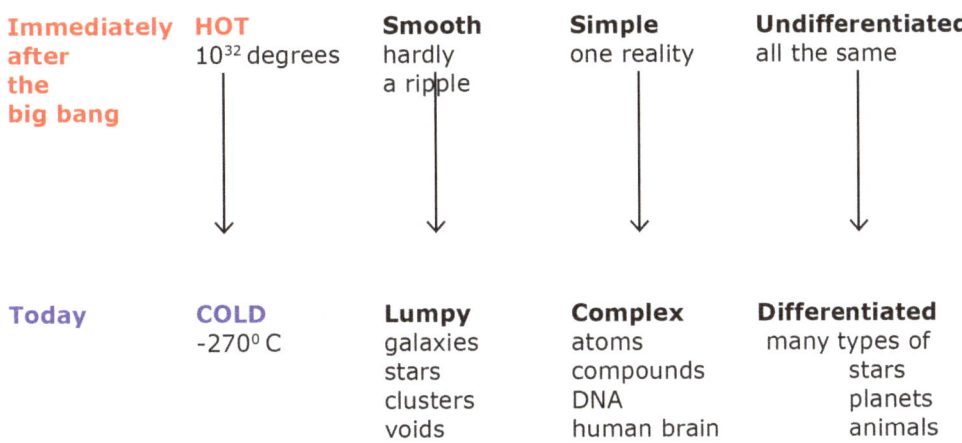

Immediately after the big bang	**HOT** 10^{32} degrees	**Smooth** hardly a ripple	**Simple** one reality	**Undifferentiated** all the same
Today	**COLD** -270° C	**Lumpy** galaxies stars clusters voids	**Complex** atoms compounds DNA human brain	**Differentiated** many types of stars planets animals

1.3 The anthropic question

Has this non-boring universe been so constructed that the arrival of intelligent beings is no accident, but was prewritten into the laws? Or is our arrival the end point of a very lucky series of accidents? To attempt an answer to this question, it is necessary first of all to look once again at the currently accepted picture of the evolution of the universe.

2. The arrow of time

Question: Can you define time? Write down your definition.

....

....

....

....

---

5. William Stoeger, at a lecture at the *Science and Religion Conference*, Adelaide, 2001.

Is time some sort of background entity which flows forward? Has it been going forever? Can we theorise back as far as we like? Will time keep going forever into the future? Did time begin? Will time end? These are philosophic questions. Scientifically and more practically we can discern two forward arrows of time, the pessimistic arrow, and the optimistic arrow of time.

2.1 The pessimistic arrow of time
Although earth dwellers are assured of up to a billion more years of time circling around a virtually unchanged sun, the future beyond that is bleak indeed[6]:

- The sun's output of heat increases with time. This is a long term effect having nothing to do with today's alleged global warming. It is very gradual but inexorable: it will eventually make life impossible, even to the point of boiling away the oceans.

- Much later, the sun will run out of hydrogen and begin to burn helium and in the process expand to a red giant[7] whose radius will extend beyond the earth, thus incinerating the earth.

- The luminous stars we observe will eventually burn out, new ones will form, go through life cycles and burning out. Eventually all the hydrogen in the universe will run out.

- Either galaxies of dead stars will, over the aeons, form black holes, which will then very gradually evaporate or dark energy will end up destroying structures and matter itself.

So what happens if the universe expands forever?

- stars die (10^{25} years)
- black holes assimilate galaxies (10^{30} years)
- protons decay (10^{31} years)
- black holes disappear (10^{64} years)

Pessimistic arrow of time in an accelerating universe

- Sun expands to Mars - Red Giant - in approximately 4 billion years
- Incinerates earth
- Stars burn out ⟶ new ones form, until
- All hydrogen used up ⟶ no more new stars
- Either dead stars unite as black holes
    - Black holes evaporate ⟶ **finish**
- Or all strutures disintegrated by dark energy   **Big Rip**

---

6. Peter Ward and Donald Brownlee, *The Life and Death of Planet Earth* (London: Judy Piatkus, 2002), 129–89.
7. Chapter 7, section 4.

In the light of this depressing scenario, cosmologist Steven Weinberg wrote: 'The more the universe seems comprehensible, the more it seems pointless'.[8] Paul Davies recently reworked this to 'The more the universe seems pointless, the more that it also seems incomprehensible'.[9]

Question: What do you think Davies means in saying: 'The more the universe seems pointless, the more that it also seems incomprehensible'?

....

....

....

....

....

Optimistic arrow of time

Energy ⟶ protons/neutrons ⟶ nuclei ⟶ atoms ⟶ gas clouds

Stars (cook up elements) ⟵ denser spots ⟵ dense spot

(Supernovae) ⟶ elements seed gas clouds ⟶ starts (2nd generation)

more complex molecules ⟵ molecules ⟵ water ⟵ planets

DNA ⟶ single cell ⟶ multi-celled life ⟶ fish ⟶ amphibians

hominids ⟵ australopithecines ⟵ mammals ⟵ reptiles

humans ⟶ ecstasy

2.2 Optimistic arrow of time
Wedged in between the beginning and the end, there is the series of life generating processes. By looking backwards we can discern another arrow of time, one in which elements, molecules, life and conscious awareness appear successively on the scene, by virtue of creative processes which build on each other.

---

8. Steven Weinberg, *The First Three Minutes*, (London: André Deutsch, 1977) 149.
9. Paul Davies, *The Goldilocks Enigma*, 18.

Over the 13.7 billion years of the universe's existence various processes have taken place; these processes have built on one another and finally have resulted in intelligent beings (see previous chapters).

The series of creative processes are ones which have resulted in progressively increasing complexity:

- Energy gave rise to sub-atomic particles protons and neutrons.

- Giant gas clouds contracted and gave rise to stars.

- Giant stars manufactured all the elements. Protons and neutrons fused in various ways inside giant stars, and became the nuclei of the ninety-two elements.

- Planets formed around later generation stars.

- Elements joined up in various ways and became molecules. Hydrogen and oxygen link up to form water, for example. This happened in space.

- Simple molecules joined in various ways and became more complex molecules. This happened especially on earth.

- The end of this process was the complex molecule of life, DNA.
- More and more complex life forms gradually emerged: bacteria, multi-celled organisms, fish, amphibians, reptiles and primates.

- The final product is the human being, whose brain is the most complex entity in the universe.

All this happened because the laws of nature, interacting with trillions of trillions of particles, were just right to bring all this about. These laws encompass and describe: the well-known forces of gravity, magnetism, electricity; the less well-known nuclear forces; the masses and charges of the particles; the strength of the initial bang; and the contents of what resulted from the bang.

The values of the parameters that govern the physical world, especially those with a role in particle physics and in cosmology, are incredibly fine-tuned in enabling life to evolve. This is so at every stage of the above processes. Paul Davies says:

> It is sometimes objected that if the laws of physics were different, that would only mean the structures would be different, and that while life as we know it might be impossible, some other form of life could well emerge. However, no attempt has been made to demonstrate that complex structures in general are an inevitable, or even probable, products of physical laws, and all the evidence so far indicates that many complex structures depend most delicately on the existing form of the laws.[10]

---

10. Paul Davies, *Superforce* (London: Heinemann, 1985), 243.

Question: Imagine a class of twenty students. They all toss coins together for ten minutes. What is the chance of everyone in the class tossing 'heads' at the same time in one of the throws?

....

....

....

....

....

Question: Does the time and space between the big bang and the death of the universe reveal another purpose for the intelligent creatures it has spawned?

....

....

....

....

....

....

....

....

3. The fine-tuning of the laws of nature

Nature has been endowed with many laws. The law of gravity accounts for things falling. Newton's first law of motion says if something is moving, it will keep on moving unless something or someone tries to stop it. A beam of light when it hits a surface will reflect in a certain way. Mass can be converted to energy, $E = mc^2$, and we can generate nuclear power using this law.

There are many other laws. Careful examination of the laws of nature shows the laws are just the ones needed to usher in the optimistic arrow of time. Structure, life and the human brain emerge given the laws of the universe. Paul Davies observes: 'A really big question is why the universe is fit for life; it looks like it has been "fixed up"'.[11]

3.1 Some examples of the fine-tuning needed for life to emerge

These are a few of the thirty identified fine-tunings. Many of these cannot stray by more than 0.1% of their measured value for life to be possible.

---

11. Paul Davies, *The Goldilocks Enigma* (London: Penguin, 2006), 18.

- The strength of the big bang: If the big bang had been very slightly less forceful, the universe would have collapsed back quickly to a black hole or nothing. If the big bang had been slightly greater, all the matter would have exploded away so fast that it could never have got together to form stars and planets.

- The smoothness of the big bang: There were tiny variations in the initial fireball. If the initial tiny fluctuations had been a bit smaller, the universe would be dark and featureless. If the fluctuations were a bit larger, the universe would have been dominated by black holes.

- The masses of particles: The masses of sub atomic particles have to be just what they are to within 0.1% for matter to be possible. The neutron is slightly heavier than the proton (1.675 units versus 1.673 units), making hydrogen possible. If it were the other way around (the proton 1.675, and the neutron 1.673), matter would be impossible; the proton would decay into a neutron. But it is the proton which determines the element. Why iron is different to carbon is that iron has twenty-six protons in the nucleus, carbon has six. There would be no periodic table, no elements and no stars. The proton's mass is 2000 times that of the electron; this imbalance allows molecules to take on well-defined shapes. Well-defined shapes are essential for DNA and proteins, and hence for life.

- The strong nuclear force: The force which holds the nucleus together is called the strong force. It has to be just what it is for matter to exist; it cannot be any stronger or any weaker. And it has to be what it is to enable stars to shine.

    The actual existence of atomic hydrogen depends on a finely tuned strong nuclear force. If the nuclear force were slightly stronger relative to electromagnetism, atomic hydrogen would not exist (because the extra force would cause hydrogens to stick together). Stars would not be possible. All the other elements are built up starting with atomic hydrogen (chapter 8).

    If the nuclear forces were slightly weaker no chemical elements, apart from hydrogen, would be stable. Also elements such as iron would be radioactive. More technically, had the nuclear force been a bit weaker, the early universe would have had only simple hydrogen, and no heavy hydrogen. The first step in 'starshine' involves small amounts of heavy hydrogen, deuterium. The stars would form but would not shine.

- There is a finely tuned relationship between the gravitational and explosive impulses in stars making energetic long-lived stars possible. Such stars, like the sun, are essential for the evolution of life (see chapter 8, section 2.2).

- Carbon is essential for life: Carbon's production, its non-destruction, its distribution to space, so it could be used to make life, all depend on features of laws which are exact. It is worth repeating Fred Hoyle's reminder that the chances of the formation of carbon is like that of a tornado going through a junkyard and leaving behind a 747. The very synthesis of life-dependent carbon is a fluke (see chapter 8, sections 3.2 and 3.5). Then it just misses destruction. Finally carbon's availability to new stars depends on the neutrino coincidence (see chapter 8, section 6).

- The strength of gravity: If gravity were a bit stronger the universe would have quickly collapsed in a big crunch with no time for structures, let alone life, to evolve.

If gravity had been a bit weaker then matter would never have coalesced into stars and galaxies. Gravity would not have been able to force matter into close proximity. All the particles would have raced off independently into the distance.

3.2 Is the fine-tuning a chance occurrence?
It is often said that life has emerged from the universe simply through chance. Imagine the possibility for the formation of life on earth as equivalent to thirty gambling wheels ('wheels of fortune'), each with a million divisions. For life to occur in this context these wheels, when spun randomly, must all end up at very precise places. Unless each of these incredibly precise places are achieved, the universe would not proceed through the stages that end with life.

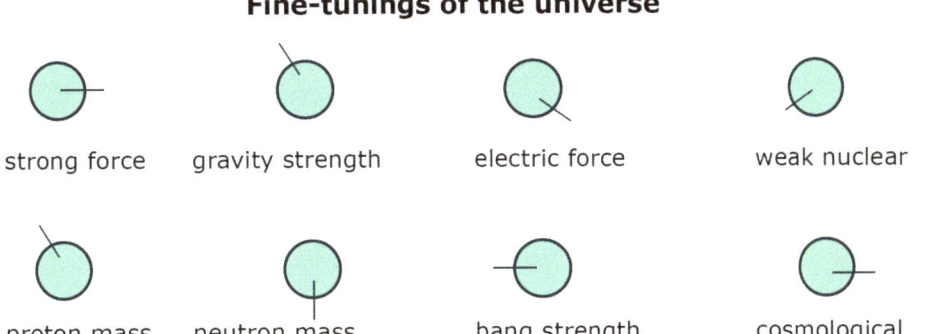

Cosmologist Lee Smolin in his book *Life of the Cosmos* estimates the chance of life's emergence as a purely random occurrence to be $1/10^{229}$. There are about 10^{78} atoms in the observable universe. If one atom in the universe had your name written on it, your chance of grabbing it would be $1/10^{78}$. So $1/10^{229}$ is unfathomably high odds. It is a billion times less probable than $1/10^{220}$. Lee Smolin continues:

> In my opinion, a probability this tiny is not something we can let go unexplained. Luck will certainly not do here; we need some rational explanation of how something this unlikely turned out to be the case.[12]

Paul Davies, writing to both science and theology, says:

> The universe is fit for life and had some of the laws of physics or the initial conditions of the universe differed by even a tiny amount, then life—at least as we know it—would almost certainly be impossible.[13]

Question: The laws of the universe seem to have been prearranged to produce conscious life. Is it legitimate to inquire for a reason, even though it seems to be beyond science?

....

....

---

12. Lee Smolin, *The Life of the Cosmos* (London: The Orion Publishing Group, 1997). For Smolin's solution, see pages 90–106.
13. Paul Davies, *Science and Theology News*, April 2006.

4. The anthropic principle

Anthropos is the Greek word for man. In this context, *man* is a generic term for the human race. The anthropic principle was developed to take account of the fine-tuning. Basically it means that the laws of nature are such as to promote the emergence of intelligent consciousness, such as is found in the human race. The principle does not explain the fine-tuning, but says something about it.

Generally, the principle means: *the cosmos has those properties that allow for the eventual existence of persons endowed with mind*. The principle has a strong version and a weak version.

4.1 The strong anthropic principle

The strong anthropic principle states that the universe is *designed* to produce intelligent life. The propensity of the universe to ripen in direction of conscious beings is best explained by its having been seeded so that this would happen.

The acorn's tendency to grow into an oak tree is best explained by the seed's having the right properties for this to occur. So the propensity of the universe to ripen in the direction of conscious beings is best explained by the universe's having the right initial properties for this to occur.

Thus mind is an inherent part of reality and not an accident. This is seen in matter's hospitality towards mind when things could have been otherwise. The physics of the universe is generously disposed to bring about mind. Paul Davies, speaking on this, says:

> Some biologists intimate that perhaps intelligence is some accident that just happened to be because of certain special conditions that by a total fluke happened to occur on Earth. But I question that. It seems to me it's actually a very basic phenomenon, and if we could rub out the universe and start again, something similar would have emerged somewhere else at some stage.[14]

4.2 The weak anthropic principle

The weak anthropic principle states that the conditions governing the universe *permit* intelligent life. The observed values of all physical and cosmological quantities are not equally probable but they take on values restricted by the requirement that there exist sites where carbon-based life can evolve and by the requirement that the universe be old enough for

---

14. Paul Davies, 'The 21c Interview', *21ºC* Winter-Spring (1991): 66.

it to have already done so. The causes operating in the universe must be such as to allow intelligent existence.

The weak version omits the necessity of the formation of conscious life; it does *not have to* occur, but it *could* happen. Thus the cosmos must have properties which allow this to happen. (The strong version says it *must* happen.)

Although the weak version seems to be a tautology, it can be used to explain mystifying features of the universe. Fred Hoyle used this to predict an excited state of C^{12}. Theoretical analysis showed that if this unknown state did not exist, nuclear reactions inside stars could not assemble carbon and all the heavier elements. Hence if the excited level did not exist, oxygen, nitrogen, phosphorous and so on would not have been formed, and life would not have happened. Life has happened, so this energy level must be there.

But examination of this phenomenon known as stellar nucleosynthesis was not a priority. (Stellar nucleosynthesis is the manufacture of elements inside stars.) No one was concerned with Hoyle's theory of the fashioning of higher elements inside stars, so it was not a priority for research. He eventually persuaded some researchers to look for this state, and they found it. The scientific community was thus enlightened. So the weak anthropic principle has had predictive value. It predicted the existence of an excited state of C^{12} and so his successful theory of stellar nucleosynthesis was launched.[15]

The weak principle is also expressed in a number of different ways:

- We can see in the cosmos only what the conditions that produced us allow us to see. An implication here is that there could be regions, even universes, where the conditions are otherwise. There might be different laws elsewhere.
- The universe is the way it is because if it were not we would not be here to see it. This places constraints on laws and constants of nature. Formulation of the laws of nature must take our existence into account.

5. The multiverse solution to the fine-tuning

The multiverse means an ensemble of separate universes. According to this hypothesis, our universe, unimaginably vast though it is, is one of many universes. There is a large number of universes; perhaps a huge unimaginable number, perhaps even an infinity. Each universe has its own laws and so its own constants associated with the laws. Going back to the image of the wheels, every possible setting for every wheel has been realised, and every possible combination of settings. At least one of these universes by accident would be fit to develop life and human beings with their incredibly complex brains. The more universes there are the greater the probability of there being one fitted for this. Our existence is best explained as a result of unimaginably long and vast, essentially random, processes of trial and error.

Multiverse theory proposes the laws of physics are very different in different universes. There are regions of space-time that are and always will be completely cut off from our own universe. We happen to live in the one (one of the ones?) in which the laws are just right.

Question: Does the multiverse invoke too much to be a plausible explanation?

....

....

---

15. See Davies, *The Goldilocks Enigma*. 151-7.

5.1 Different styles of multiverse speculation
Different versions of the multiverse have been worked out. Some of these are as follows:

- Many separate parts of our universe emerged in the one big bang—enough to have sufficient variation in the constants to make the fine-tuning combination certain.

- There have been many separate big bangs generating universes separate in time and space.

- The propositions of string theory (Extension 2, this chapter) say that other universes are allowable. In fact, string theory allows for 10^{500} universes. This number is beyond imagination. It is a million times greater the 10^{493} which in turn is a billion times greater than 10^{484}.

- There is an eternal inflation with 'bubble universes' which emerge in an endless series of big bangs. A bubble universe may break off from a parent universe, and eventually also become a parent universe. Cosmologist Andrei Linde remarked: 'The universe is a self-producing fractal. We live in but one of the bubbles that has properties conducive to life, while other bubbles may be entirely different from ours'.[16]

5.2 Some reflections on the multiverse
Questions that could be asked are: Assuming a multiverse, why is there one set of constants that is fruitful? Why isn't matter altogether useless? Why are there any laws at all? Paul Davies again:

> Take the seemingly arbitrary form of the laws of nature. The laws of nature marvellously permit the universe to create itself. Not possible with any old laws. It turns out in order to permit such (cosmic) evolution the laws of physics need to have a special form. If the various fundamental forces of nature such as gravity and electromagnetism had differed even slightly, it is doubtful if life of any sort would have been possible.[17]

There are laws, not chaos, and the laws are not 'any old laws'.

Can the multiverse be the final solution? Proposing a multiverse may give an explanation of why one universe is capable of producing life. But this ultimately merely postpones the problem. Pre-existing laws dictate the formation and the evolution of the universe. What is the origin of the laws that dictate the existence and form of the multiverse? What is the origin of the law which results in eternal inflation? Why are there any laws at all?

---

16. Steve Nadis, 'Inflation Comes of Age', *Astronomy, Origin and Fate of the Universe:* 37.
17. Paul Davies, 'God Must Not Flee From Science', *The Age*, 22 August 1997.

One can even ask is the multiverse a scientific theory? We are causally disconnected from other universes. Can we ever observe them? Can a test be devised to establish the existence or non-existence of other universes?

On the other hand, multiverse theory seems to follow naturally from various efforts to pin down the properties of the big bang, and so is somewhat widely accepted.

Theologically, religiously, the theory proposes no objection. Given the extravagant graciousness of God, God easily brings about an abundance of worlds. This mirrors the divine infinity.

Question: Other universes are not the object of scientific investigation. We can neither prove nor disprove their existence. Does this detract from their usefulness as an explanation of the fine-tuning?

....

....

....

....

....

....

....

6. The design solution

(This is not the creationist theory called *intelligent design*, according to which God acts alongside natural causes as another natural cause so that cosmic and animal evolution will proceed fruitfully. Intelligent design theory maintains that the laws of nature by themselves can never be sufficient to bring about key advances in evolution).

> The creation was subjected to futility, not of its own will but by the will of him who subjected it in hope; because the creation itself will be set free from its bondage to decay and obtain the glorious liberty of the children of God. We know the whole of creation is groaning in one gigantic act of giving birth, unable of itself to achieve its purpose.[18]

There seems to be a purpose in the way the universe has developed. The increasing complexification has resulted in beings who can understand the universe out of which they have emerged. Purpose inherent in the universe necessitates a giver, an implanter of the purpose. A universe developing because of intelligent mathematical laws demands ultimately an intelligent designer. The purpose was implanted from the very beginning, and does not need an intervention by God to bring about certain transitions. But God is always there, maintaining the laws, holding everything in existence.

Monotheistic religions—Judaism, Christianity and Islam—maintain that the universe was created by God out of nothing. God is responsible for the existence of reality. God had a

---

18. Paul, *Letter to the Romans*, 8:20-2.

purpose for the universe in creating it, and so implanted purpose within the laws and the particles so that intelligent life will be the result.

The laws of nature have inevitable effects. For example, the law of gravity combined with Newton's law of inertia describe how the moon must keep circling the earth. Things must fall to the ground. Magnets must attract pieces of iron. These laws, with their inevitable effects, interact with countless trillions of randomly moving particles. In the whole system are prewritten the laws of chance so that the laws must achieve their purpose given the bigness of the universe. Creation is seeded so that it creates itself.

God is not absent from creation: the divine causality is necessary at any instant to enable its continuance in existence, and to preserve the laws.

Laws of nature

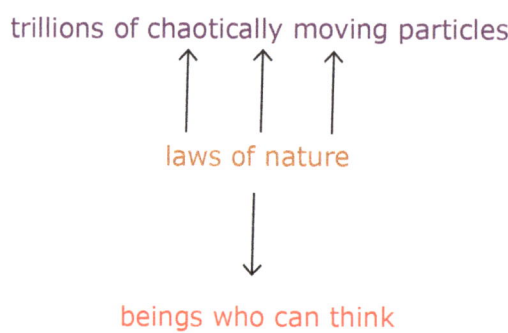

Question: The designer does not interfere in the processes of nature. But nature itself has been designed with a purpose. Is such design feasible? Can such a process achieve its purpose?

....

....

....

....

....

....

....

....

....

Question: Reality is intelligible, able to be understood. Does this demand an overriding intelligence?

Question: The universe does not have to exist. The same applies to other speculative universes. Why does anything exist at all?

7. Other approaches to fine-tuning

Exact mathematical constants associated with the forces of nature and some basic masses are fundamental to the possibility of matter as we know it. The very existence of any stable atoms depends on these. Even small changes in quark and electron masses would make the proton, and hydrogen unstable, and hence all other elements impossible. Even more so, the possibility of an interesting range of chemical elements depends on these. What other approaches are adopted to take account of the fine-tuning?

7.1 A fluke

Will the gambling wheels end up at the right values if spun randomly? Astrophysicist Lee Smolin's estimate, in *The Life of the Cosmos*,[19] of the chances of this happening were quoted as $1/10^{229}$. In theories of chance it is widely held that given enough time, anything that could possibly happen will happen. Given the utter smallness of the chance, the time to be allowed for this to occur would be a huge number of times the age of the universe. To overcome this difficulty, Smolin proposed an evolution of the constants of nature through survival of the fittest. This is not popular with physicists. The theory necessitates the coming to life again of the deadest of dead matter: black holes. Perhaps also Smolin's interesting theory is an unjustifiable extension of Darwin's survival of the fittest mechanism, so successful in biology.

7.2 A given

Philosophers, such as David Hume, who are sceptical of any reasoning beyond the facts, would say you cannot speculate beyond the data of experience. Any non-scientific speculation on what has been delivered by experience and observation would therefore be forbidden. The universe, the fine-tuning, is a fact of experience; end of story.

The proponents of *scientism* would say that the only form of knowledge which leads to truth is scientific knowledge. Knowledge deals with the material universe as it is given. Speculation on the totality of material existence to anything else is forbidden. Metaphysical speculation on the fine-tuning would not be a path to truth.

Other protagonists of *a given,* pragmatists, would say not to worry about impractical speculation. Get on with the work.

Paul Davies reacts against such a view. We apply reasoning everywhere. It is illogical to deny the application of reason to, what he called in an early book of his, 'the accidental universe'. His views in writings and on the ABC's *Lateline*[20] are summarised below.

Alternatives - Paul Davies

- Cosmic determinism
  - Only one logically consistent set of laws
- No evidence
- Easy to write alternative sets

- Cosmic proliferation
  - An infinity of universes with every possible value of constants
  - In one, laws are just right - ours
- Overkill
- Untestable. May as well believe in God
- Why any laws anywhere?
- Why one set of laws so fruitful?
- Why isn't reality useless clods?

- Package of marvels that happens to be:
  - There's no explanation
  - Beyond the powers of human minds
  - Luck
- No reason? Absurd!
- Logic all through Science, why not about the laws?

- A deeper level to reality
- Purpose: intelligent life intended
- Probably in many other places
- I'll leave it to theologians, philosophers

---

19. Smolin, *Life of the Cosmos*, 105–6.
20. Paul Davies, Tony Kelly and Peter Slezak, *ABC Lateline,* 1993.

Recently Davies has explored the question in great detail in a new book, *The Goldilocks Enigma*. He examines the above views exhaustively, and presents a slightly different solution to 'a deeper level of reality' based on time.

7.3 A necessity

This explanation of the fine-tuning proposes there is some fundamental theory which has determined all the constants uniquely. There seems to be no *a priori* reason why the constants are what they are. They seem to be like numbers arbitrarily chosen. A scientific task is to find a theory of everything from which the values of the constants would automatically fall out. This is how they would have to be. There is no other way the constants could be. One view is that this ultimate theory of everything would not be string theory (Extension 2, this chapter), because this theory is open to many (that is 10^{500}) sets of constants.

Question: What is the origin of the laws of nature? Do they pre-exist the universe? Do they begin to begin to exist with matter itself?

....

....

....

....

....

....

....

....

....

8. Extension 1: Reasons for and against the multiverse theory

8.1 Reasons against the multiverse theory

- This hypothesis flies in the face of Ockham's razor, which in Latin says *entia non sun multiplicanda absque necessitate*. It means don't apply any more reasons to the explanation of any phenomenon than is necessary to explain the phenomenon. Entities should not be invented without their being necessary to do so. Put another way, among competing hypotheses, the simplest is most often correct.

- A theory postulating that *everything possible actually exists* is unreasonable.

- The multiverse is by definition scientifically unverifiable. Different universes are in their own space and time, or different parts of the universe are too far away to be ever encountered in any way by us. Thus it is a metaphysical conclusion.

- For a theory to be a scientific theory it has to be falsifiable. That is an experiment has to be envisaged which can test it. An experimental verification cannot prove the theory beyond doubt, but it can show if the theory is wrong. This theory does not seem to be falsifiable. Can anyone think of an experiment whose result could be *there is no multiverse*?

8.2 Reasons for the multiverse theory

- It flows naturally out of some of the current explanations for the big bang and the evolving universe. Thus eternal inflation is a natural extension of Alan Guth's successful inflationary theory;[21] this for some makes it a good bet. Inflation hints the observable universe may simply be one bubble among very very many others in a vast ocean of space.

- It gives an immediate explanation for the fine-tuning. Further questions can then be asked about the multiverse. Paul Davies summarises:

    > Although a strong motivation for introducing the multiverse concept is to get rid of the need for design, this bid is only partially successful . . . The popular multiverse models merely shift the problem elsewhere—up a level from universe to multiverse. To appreciate this, one only has to list the many assumptions that underpin the multiverse theory.[22]

    The assumptions underpinning the multiverse are:

    - Universe generating machine.
    - Source of quantum laws that permit inflation.
    - Why do some sort of laws exist in every universe?
    - If predicted by string theory, the origin of this theory needs explanation.
    - Why is multiverse explainable by mathematics?[23]

- It is a conclusion from string theory. Leonard Susskind, a Stanford physicist, accepts the multiple universes proposed by this theory: 10^{500}.[24]

- It conforms with the principle of maximum diversity, which would seem to be a law in the universe: the cosmos has always been intent on diversifying into as many experiments with form as possible. Consider the variety of star forms, galaxy types, the great numbers and varieties of life forms.

---

21. Extension, chapter 5.
22. Paul Davies, *The Goldilocks Enigma* (London: Penguin, 2006), 231.
23. Davies, *The Goldilocks Enigma*, 232.
24. Steve Nadis, 'Making Multiverses', *Astronomy* 33/10: 37.

- It has the support of some notable authorities. Martin Rees, Astronomer Royale, asserts we do not know whether there a many universes or not, but he would stake his dog's life on it. Andrei Linde (Stanford) would stake his own life on it. Max Tegmark (MIT) and Alexander Valenkin (Tufts University) are some others in favour.[25]

9. Extension 2: String theory

The first sub-atomic particle, the electron, was discovered by Thomson in 1897. Within ten years Ernest Rutherford had found the proton. It was not until the early 1930s that Chadwick discovered the neutron. Now the number of sub-atomic particles runs into hundreds. Just as the atomic theory makes sense of chemistry, and sub-atomic theory (protons, neutrons and electrons) make sense of the atomic theory, so string theory is designed to make sense of the families of sub-atomic particles and units of radiation (photons).

The basic physical entity is not a particle but a string, a quantum mechanical string, 10^{20} times smaller than a nucleus. Each particle is said to be a variation of a tiny *string*. Just as different notes can be caused by plucking guitar strings, so all the fundamental entities are different vibrations of the one unique minute string.

- The unique string is unbelievably small—trillions of times smaller than a nucleus.

- These strings vibrate in nine or ten dimensional space. (The guitar string vibrates in one dimension in three-dimensional space).

- Each particle—proton, neutron, electron, photon—is a different vibration of the unique string.

- The string can be closed (like a thin rubber band) or open with both ends free.

9.1 Michio Kaku

Michio Kaku is at the forefront of string theory development.[26] He likens his work to that of Mozart. Mozart, he says, must have spent hours staring out the window as random fragments of melodies ran through his head, seemingly in a dream. Eventually fragments began to gather into themes, and he began to play on the piano. Then he would begin to fill the music paper. Then he would go back to the window and at length a great symphony would be there.

Kaku spends most of his time staring out a window seeing blocks of equations dancing in his head, trying to fit them together. 'I get out a scratch pad, jot down formulae, then another pad and fill it with dense equations, sometimes a hundred pages to prove a hunch correct or not'.[27]

Kaku also thinks of himself as a detective. Sherlock Holmes comes to a ransacked museum with its treasures shattered. He thinks and tries to piece it together, work back to what happened and why. So Kaku thinks of the crime as the big bang when the universe was shattered into fragments.

The subatomic particles, electrons, quarks and neutrinos, are all different resonances of a string vibrating much like a rubber band. Each note on the string represents a different particle. Physics is the harmonies from the strings and chemistry is the melodies we play

---

25. Nadis, 'Making Multiverses': 37.
26. Michio Kaku 'Unifying the Universe', *New Scientist* 16 April (2005).
27. Kaku 'Unifying the Universe'.

on the strings. The whole universe is a symphony of strings, and the mind of god is cosmic music resonating through nine or ten dimensional hyperspace.

Kaku maintains its direct proof may be possible. When the Large Hadron Collider now under construction is working it might be powerful enough to create super-particles predicted by the theory. Four years after this, the laser interferometry space antenna (LISA) may be sensitive enough to at least rule out many string cosmologies.

9.2 Arguments in favour of string theory

- Mathematically the theory shows possibilities. String theory already has given insights into maths, black holes and field theory itself.

- The standard model, the highest version of quantum theory, tested to one part in 10^7 is *ugly*: thirty-six quarks and anti-quarks, eight gluons, three weak bosons, and so on; and there are nineteen arbitrary numbers which have to be added to make the theory work—and it does. String theory makes sense of this gaggle of disconnected entities, just as the periodic table makes sense of the hundred or so different elements. The subatomic particles (electrons, quarks and neutrinos) are all different resonances of a string vibrating. Each note on the string represents a different particle. The photon is a different frequency of the tiny string.

- After decades analysing fragments from the big bang, we have glued the debris into two large pieces: *relativity* theory which describes the world at large (gravity, the expanding universe, light deflected by a star) and *quantum* theory which caters for the world of the atom and particles. These two theories resist each other. General relativity fails (at the level of atoms) and quantum theory fails where relativity succeeds (at describing gravity). String theory promises to solve this major problem in theoretical physics, the reconciliation of general relativity and quantum theory: it actually predicts a particle that unifies these seemingly contradictory theories.

- A *beautiful* theory explains the largest amount of data with the simplest mathematical structures. String theory is a beautiful theory. It can swallow relativity and the quantum model, which otherwise seem to be at odds with each other. Some string theorists believe that the beauty of the equations point towards its being a true theory.

    Newton banished centuries of mysticism with forces. Faraday's concept was *fields* that can permeate space. Einstein's relativity threw light on gravity. Is string theory following the lead of Newton, Faraday and Einstein? Is it a new insight of the mind leading us deeper into reality?

- The magnitude of the cosmological constant: its astronomically measured value is a very, very small fraction of the value predicted by particle physics. (This predicted value would prevent galaxy formation). The observed value is absurdly improbable according to present particle theory. String theory helps with the problem of the finite but very small value of the cosmological constant.

- String theory gives many different solutions for universes. String theory leads to a multiverse. 10^{500} is the number of different situations, vacua, from which the universe could evolve, each with different values of the constants, including the cosmological constant. Thus it solves immediate problems involved with the fine-tuning.

- Why are the laws of nature just as they are? Scientists hoped some deep mathematical principle would reveal why the laws are as they are, why the mathematical constants have particular values. Do we need a unique mega-theory now, analogous to the scientists' dream of one theory yielding all the constants? Yes.

9.3 Arguments against string theory

- The strings are trillions of times smaller than nuclei, which are vastly small compared with atoms; millions of nuclei would fit on the head of a pin.

- The theory does not explain what the strings are made up of.

- For a theory to be a scientific theory it has to be falsifiable; that is an experiment has to be envisaged which can test it. An experimental verification cannot prove the theory beyond doubt, but it can show if the theory is wrong. No experiment can be thought up to try to prove string theory wrong. This theory is not falsifiable. Therefore it is not a scientific theory.

- How can something vibrate in ten dimensions?

- 10^{500} universes is an absurdly high number.

According to Sten Odenwald:

> String theory is based on three key ideas that remain experimentally unproven after 30 years of research; the principle of supersymmetry; additional spatial dimensions; and gravity as a force defined by the exchange particles.[28]

10. Extension 3: 'Intelligent design'

The approach called intelligent design has been a source of controversy especially in the United States. According to adherents of this approach, natural causes are insufficient to explain certain phenomena. Scientific investigation conclusively reveals this. Therefore, a concomitant supernatural cause in certain situations is the only possible explanation. So science has proved the existence of a designer.

The contention firstly is that the laws of nature cannot explain irreducible complexity, such as the structure of the eye. Secondly, the laws of nature cannot explain the evolution of life from non-life, nor the major stages of evolution: from fish to amphibians, from amphibians to reptiles, from reptiles to mammals, from mammals to humans.

A number of responses can be made to this view. For some evolutionary transitions the mechanism of the transition is not known. This does not mean it cannot be known. The intelligent design argument here is an example of the logical fallacy of the argument from ignorance: 'the claim that a statement is false because it hasn't been proven true'.[29] We have not uncovered the mechanism, therefore, there is no natural mechanism. Another example of this fallacy is the argument against aliens: Aliens do not exist because despite all human effort no evidence has been found for their existence.

Although God's creative activity upholds nature, God in the Christian view is not part of nature. Although one can submit the findings of science to philosophic analysis, God's

---

28. Sten Odenwald, 'What if String Theory is Wrong?', *Astronomy*, 35/ 2 (2007): 30-4.
29. C Stephen Layman, *The Power of Logic* (McGraw-Hill: Boston, 2002), 131.

presence or absence cannot be the conclusion of a scientific investigation. This theory places God's activity in nature on a par with the laws of nature. It makes God a creature.

Science has a history of shedding light on many phenomena deemed unexplainable, so that it must be concluded science has a chance of unravelling natural explanations for phenomena either as yet unexplained, or whose explanations 'Intelligent Designers' do not accept.

There has been an enormous progress from hydrogen to mammal. Scientists have unravelled a curious fine-tuning inherent in the laws of nature, adequate to explain the formation of stars, elements and planets. Natural selection is agreed to play a major role in evolution, again given fine-tuning, the right conditions, and plenty of time. There has been plenty of time. And we constantly are made aware of natural selection in action as bacteria adapt to combat antibiotics. There is ample evidence of evolution in the fossil record, though not exhaustive. Robert John Russell concludes:

> Intelligent design cannot be a competitor to neo-Darwinian evolution because it cannot in principle be an alternative scientific theory. Instead it is a misguided attempt by some conservatives to include a divine designer—God in disguise—into science. The lack of reference to God within a scientific theory does not mean the scientific theory claims there is no God. The existence of God and the workings of providence are simply beyond the competence of science to adjudicate. Christians must offer an alternative interpretation of neo-Darwinian evolution that recognizes it as the work of God.[30]

---

30. Robert John Russell, 'Evolution and Christian Faith', *America* 194/6 (20 February 2006).

Further reading

John D Barrow, *Theories of Everything: The Quest for Ultimate Explanation* (London: Vintage, 1992).

George V Coyne, SJ, and Alessandro Omizzolo, *Wayfarers in the Cosmos: The Human Quest for Meaning* (New York: Crossroad Publishing Company, 2002).

Paul Davies, *The Goldilocks Enigma: Why is the Universe Just Right for Life?* (London: Allen Lane, 2006).

Paul Davies, *The Cosmic Blueprint* (London: Heinemann, 1987)

Paul Davies and John Gribbin, *The Matter Myth: Towards 21st-century Science* (London: Viking, 1991).

Brian Greene, *The Fabric of the Cosmos: Space, Time, and the Texture of Reality* (New York: Alfred A Knopf, 2004).

John Gribben, *In Search of Susy: Supersymmetry and the Theory of Everything* (London: Penguin, 1998).

John Gribbin, *Deep Simplicity: Chaos, Complexity and the Emergence of Life* (London: Penguin, 2005).

Michio Kaku and Jennifer Thompson, *Beyond Einstein: The Cosmic Quest for the Theory of the Universe* (Oxford: Oxford University Press, 1997).

Mario Livio, *The Accelerating Universe: Infinite Expansion, the Cosmological Constant, and the Beauty of the Cosmos* (New York: John Wiley & Sons, 2000).

Abraham Pais, *Subtle is the Lord: The Science and the Life of Albert Einstein* (Oxford: Oxford University Press, 1997).

Corey S Powell, *God in the Equation: How Einstein Became the Prophet of the New Religious Era* (New York: Free Press, 2002).

Robert J Sawyer, *Calculating God* (New York: Tom Doherty Associates, 2000).

Steven Weinberg, *Dreams of a Final Theory* (London: Vintage, 1993).

Peter Woit, *Not Even Wrong: The Failure of String Theory and the Continuing Challenge to Unify the Laws of Physics* (London: Jonathan Cape, 2006).

10

Resurrection:

The Redemption of Creation

Chapter overview

> - The Jesus of faith and the Jesus of history
> - The drama of the empty tomb
> - The evidence:
>   - The earliest witness: 1 Corinthians 15
>   - The extraordinary transformation of the apostles
>   - Resurrection: the only plausible explanation for the apostles' turnaround
>   - The growth of the early church
> - The meaning:
>   - He is Lord of Creation
>   - A blueprint for life
>   - The final human purpose

1. The foundational belief

After examining the marvellous findings of science on the evolution and creative function of stars, and examining the fact of fine-tuning and its possible interpretations, it is time to look at the foundational experience of the Christian community, the resurrection of Jesus Christ.

The resurrection is a major issue for both science and religion. For a scientist, the resurrection cannot be demonstrated by the scientific method because it is on the other side of space and time. From the point of view of a theologian, there is evidence in so far as it affected many individuals who proclaimed they had had a life-changing of Christ and the effects of the belief in the resurrection have had an on-going witness in history.

1.1 The quest for the historical Jesus
The major source for knowledge of Jesus is the gospels which are not historical documents, though they contain links with historical events. A distinction has clearly emerged between the historical Jesus and the Jesus of faith. The historical Jesus is Jesus as he was born, lived, worked and died in Palestine. The Jesus of faith is the one we encounter in much of the New Testament. It is the Jesus of faith who is encountered in the church.

In the seventeenth century a distinction was first drawn between the Jesus of faith, and the historical Jesus, and from this time on, theologians have been on a quest for the historical Jesus. The first quest, issuing from the Enlightenment, rejected anything of miracles and resurrection, but clearly set the agenda for seeking the Jesus of history. In the 1950s there was a return to Jesus of faith, linking the risen and exalted one with the

Jesus of history. Efforts were made to unmask historical material from more faith-based statements in New Testament writings. Finally from the 1980s a study of the culture in which Jesus was immersed and of non-biblical sources about him and the society in which he lived served to shed light on who he was during his lifetime. Researchers during this era did not necessarily dismiss the miraculous, the resurrection, and the exaltation.

Over the years Jesus has been interpreted in many ways even to the point of a denial of his historical existence. The Jesus of history has been cast as a political revolutionary, a magician, a rabbi, an eschatological (end-time) prophet, a wandering philosopher, and the Son of God.[1]. Some do not accept his divinity, some say he knew he was God's only begotten Son while others highlight his divinity and in so doing diminish his humanity.

The Jesus of faith comes primarily from the New Testament in which there are many christologies. There are the many reported encounters of Jesus with different groups of people. These reports are often overlaid with the 'sequel', the after-death story—the one speaking in Galilee is the risen one, the Son of God. Then in John's gospel and in some of Paul's writings, we have the 'prequel', that is Jesus' pre-existence. 'In the beginning was the Word, the Word was with God, and the Word was God . . . and the Word was made flesh and dwelt among us'. The actual doctrine about Jesus, his nature and his pre-existence was established amid controversies in the first four centuries.

1.2 Christological controversies

Controversies in the first four centuries clarified the meaning and person of Jesus. Arius had proposed he was the incarnation of a superior spiritual being previously created by God, and so was not God. Nestorius had proposed the second person was God and had two natures, but that Mary was not the Mother of God, and hence the human nature of Christ was not substantially God. The church responded in creeds issuing statements such as 'God from God, light from light, true God from true God, one in being with the Father', and 'true God and true man'. As the gospels were written from the standpoint of faith to bring the faith to others, much of the risen Jesus is present in these writings.

1.3 Resurrection interpretations

There is a spectrum of views about the resurrection: from a purely subjective experience to a bodily presence, albeit different, but nevertheless eventually recognised to be the one who was crucified. The disciples were traumatised and terrified after the crucifixion, but soon after emerged transformed, confident about witnessing to Jesus. They say they changed because they experienced him again. It was he, but possessing a new life which was difficult to explain. Something happened to the disciples to change them to give them a total certainty, once they had come to terms with it. The gospel accounts cannot be harmonised, but the gospel stories plus statements in the *Letters* and the *Acts* testify to an experience which itself cannot be demonstrated historically but which has left an obvious mark on history. It is an event 'that takes place on the other side of space and time, death and history'.[2]

2. He is risen!

(The following is a dramatic reconstruction involving a coalescing of the empty tomb stories.)

The supper room is full of the disciples coming to terms with the trauma of Jesus' condemnation and execution. He had been their inspiration; their whole future they had committed to him.

---

1. Thomas P Rausch, *Who is Jesus? An Introduction to Christology* (Collegeville, Minnesota: Liturgical Press, Michael Glazier Book, 2003), 9–10.
2. Thomas P Rausch, *Who is Jesus?,* 120.

Now their immediate concern was that they would be next. They were gathered in the room, where they had recently had their last supper with him, hiding and in fear.

There are urgent running footsteps in the corridor; perhaps it's the lookout come to say get out and run. But a frantic knock on the door and women's excited voices reveal friends. 'That sounds like Mary Magdalene and Salome. What's up with them? Let them in.'

The door is unbarred, they rush in, frightened, agitated.

'The tomb, the tomb,' they say.

'What about the tomb?' retorts Peter.

'The tomb is empty.'

'How do you know? How did you get in?'

'The stone was already rolled back.'

'Come on, we're all upset, but this is too much—have some wine.'

'No, inside the tomb, we were told he's alive, and it's true, he's alive; Mag saw him.'

Peter muttered, 'Can't take this. I'm going for a walk.' He quietly left the room, leaving the others to deal with the problem.

The others continue to question.

'How could he be alive?'

'We saw his dead body, destroyed. Nicodemus embalmed it, and we saw Joseph of Arimathea roll the stone into place. Settle down, you're only making things worse. Mary, you were his mother, you cradled his body in your arms; you look after them.'

The women go apart accompanied by Mary, defiant at not being believed but sharing their joy with great enthusiasm.

An hour later, after much striding in the corridor, Peter re-enters, utterly agitated.

'You won't believe this. A man spoke to me. I didn't know it was him at first, but there's no doubt I've seen him. He spoke to me. He's alive, different, but alive'.

They discuss this, heatedly, as Peter sides with the women.

More quick footsteps are heard and a knock. It's Cleopas and his friend.

'What are you two doing back here? You said your final good-byes as you went back to your fishing lives in Emmaus'.

'We were. We were half-way there and this stranger joined us, had a meal with us, and suddenly we were shocked out of our daze. It was him. He's not dead. In fact he's more alive than ever. But he disappeared after breaking the bread'.

A lone voice, Thomas, said 'Disappeared? You mean your dream ceased, you came back to reality. You're as bad as the women, I'm going'. Thomas makes a dramatic exit and slams the door as he leaves.

But the room was hushed, as reality began to sink in. Someone broke the silence and said to Cleopas, 'It must be true—he's appeared to Simon'.

3. The Resurrection of Jesus

Although there is now devotion at a tomb where it is alleged Jesus was laid, for centuries after his death there was no worship at such a shrine. There are shrines of saints, of founders of other religions, even of secular leaders, like Lenin. Was the story of Jesus' tomb all made up?

Did the resurrection actually happen? Is this belief credible for us today? Philosopher David Hume would say any violation of the laws of nature is impossible, and so would physicist Paul Davies. However, do we know all the laws of nature? The door seems shut on the ultimate nature of matter itself, and present theories are our approximations to what nature is, not reality itself.

With faith in the resurrection stands or falls the Christian concept of God. Easter faith is not a supplement to belief in God and Christ. It encapsulates the entirety and essence of that belief. 'If Christ be not been raised your faith is futile . . . we are of all most to be pitied'.[3]

3.1 The belief

Christ was executed, and his lifeless body placed in a tomb. He came back to life again, not merely as a vision, but as a glorified human being who could be seen, heard, spoken to, touched, and who ate and drank. 'And suddenly coming to meet them was Jesus. And the women came up to him and, clasping his feet, they did him homage'.[4]

A boy was buried in the sand on the beach one summer. As he was constructing a tunnel through the sand, it fell on him and he was buried. A passer-by saw his legs protruding from the sand, and pulled him out. He had stopped breathing and was blue in the face. But artificial respiration resuscitated him.

In the gospel story, Lazarus was brought back to life after four days in the tomb. This is the resuscitation of a corpse.

The resurrection is not a resuscitation. People today are fascinated by such stories: Jesus may have been buried while in a coma, resuscitated in the tomb and escaped to the East; or maybe came back to lead his disciples again. But after the resurrection he was not the same; he was different, and his disciples did not immediately recognise him.

Paul said the risen body grows, emerges out of the mortal body as the oak tree does from the acorn. It is more than a spirit; it is a *spiritual body*.

> What you sow must die before it is given new life; and what you sow is not the body that is to be, but only a bare grain, of wheat I dare say, or some other kind . . . What is sown is perishable, but what is raised is imperishable . . . What is sown is a natural body, and what is raised is a spiritual body.[5]

Jesus entered an entirely new form of existence, one in which he shared the power of God. Jesus is raised to endless life, transmuted and glorified, possessing new abilities, yet bearing the scars.

3.2 The evidence for the belief

There is no evidence in material objects. Despite what they may have erected in Jerusalem, we cannot locate the tomb in which Christ lay. We therefore cannot have scientific tests made to determine if a man of Jesus' description lay in a tomb for three days. We cannot examine the rock to see if it was moved back miraculously or not. Of the finding of a tomb alleged to be that of Jesus, *Catholic News* had this say:

> Melbourne New Testament expert, Fr Brendan Byrne, has described as 'bizarre' claims in a new documentary that an ancient tomb unearthed in Jerusalem 27 years ago was the burial tomb of Jesus and his family.
> The James Cameron-produced documentary, *The Burial Cave of Jesus*, by the US Discovery Channel, says the crypt contains coffins with residue of the remains of Jesus and Mary Magdalene and their son Judah, *The Age* reports. But Fr Byrne says the claims are 'pretty bizarre', noting that the Bible said Jesus was buried in Joseph of Arimathea's tomb. 'If they found bones it would

---

3. Paul, *1 Corinthians* 15: 17, 19.
4. Matthew 28:9 (see also footnote 5).
5. Paul *1 Corinthians* 15: 36-7, 42, 44.

Resurrection: the Redemption of Creation

be problematic, because it would suggest Jesus didn't physically rise from the dead,' he added. 'But Jesus and Joseph and Miriam and Judah are four of the most common names of the time. To assert this group of names is the family of Jesus is a very remote possibility.[6]

Question: Why do stories such as this one, and 'The Da Vinci Code' create such interest?

....

....

....

....

....

....

....

We have no evidence from anybody who was not his friend. He was not seen by the Scribes and Pharisees, or by Pilate, or by any of the Romans, or by most of the people who had seen him during his preaching apostolate.

We have the word of his friends that he rose again and showed himself to them. These friends saw him several times after he had risen and they told their friends about it. Then Peter and the others passed on the news to those who had known Christ during his preaching apostolate—who were Jews. Finally the message was delivered to the Gentiles.

Question: Seeing that we only have the word of Christ's friends for the resurrection, do you think it a better explanation of the events of Easter that they plotted together, hid the body and then told the people that he had risen?

....

....

....

....

....

....

....

---

6. http://www.cathnews.com/news/702/155.php

The oldest resurrection text we have is from St Paul in 1 Corinthians 15. Here Paul incorporates an early creed (belief statement) into his text. This creed is a good deal older than the letter which is dated at about 50 CE. This is significant evidence of the resurrection, compiled within ten years of the events.

> The tradition I handed on to you in the first place, a tradition which I had myself received, was that Christ died for our sins, in accordance with the scriptures, and that he was buried; and that on the third day he was raised to life, in accordance with the scriptures; and that he appeared to Cephas (Peter); and later to the twelve; and next he appeared to more than five hundred of the brothers at the same time, most of whom are still with us, though some have fallen asleep; and then he appeared to James, and then to all the apostles. Last of all he appeared to me too, as though I was a child abnormally born.[7]

Question: How good a witness is a creed written within ten years of his death?

....

....

....

....

....

....

3.3 Inconsistencies in the evidence

If you compare the account of a sighting as recorded by one evangelist with the account of the same incident as recorded by another evangelist, many inconsistencies will be observed. In the details surrounding the story of the empty tomb, compare Luke 24:1–11 with Matthew 28:1–10, and Mark 16:1–8. Mark has one messenger; Luke has two; and Matthew has an angel sitting on the rolled-back stone. In Mark, the women were terrified and said nothing to anyone; in Luke, they were overjoyed and went back to tell the others; in Matthew, they rejoice and Magdalene meets Jesus outside the tomb.

In the places where appearances are said to have occurred, Luke has the appearances to all the disciples in Jerusalem while Matthew places them in Galilee. And the sequence of appearances related by one may be contradicted by one of the others.

Question: Do you think these inconsistencies decrease the credibility of the resurrection stories. Or do you think they increase their credibility?

....

....

....

---

7. Paul *1 Corinthians* 15:3–8.

....

....

....

....

3.4 The inconsistencies can be seen to increase credibility

That we have distinct variations of the same stories indicates separate traditions in which the same belief was held, each tradition performing the function of a separate witness. That the stories differ in many details—and differ greatly—means that we have a number of independent traditions all testifying to the same central fact: Christ rose from the dead.

Consider how the stories arose. They were passed on by preaching and teaching for over thirty years before they were committed finally to paper in a permanent form. There were not even any newspapers. Different communities in which converts were being taught were often secluded, so that in the course of being taught, the stories were gradually changed in each community. The details were various—but the central message was kept intact. It is likely that sometimes the details were deliberately altered to make better stories for the purposes of teaching.

The witnesses are unanimous about the central fact of their message: bodily resurrection. The stories of the evangelists differ in small and large details, but they agree in this: Christ was dead; Christ came back to life again; Christ then communicated with his friends. The four evangelists and St Paul tell us by their resurrection stories that the bodily resurrection of Christ was believed by the first generations of Christians.

Question: Have you ever experienced details of incidents being changed after telling and retelling? Explain.

....

....

....

....

....

3.5 The transformation of the apostles

During Christ's passion, the apostles fled. They were bewildered and shattered by the defeat and death of Christ, and did not expect him to rise. When the women came back and reported what the angel had said, the others scoffed and would not believe them. Their story seemed pure nonsense, and they did not believe the women. When Christ appeared to the whole group, they were alarmed:

> They were still talking about all this when he himself stood among them and said to them 'peace be with you'. In a state of alarm and fright they thought they were seeing a ghost. But he said 'look at my hands and my feet; yes, it

is indeed I. Touch me and see for yourselves; a ghost has no flesh and bones as you can see I have'.[8]

The apostles were depressed, had no concept of individual resurrection before the end time, were beginning to leave Jerusalem and return to their old occupations. Then they became full of great joy, and set out with tremendous conviction to tell the world about the resurrection of Christ. What caused this change? The unanimous witness of the early Christian community was his victory over death.

Question: He could have thus vindicated himself in front of the Romans. He could have thus triumphed over his enemies. Why didn't he show himself to anybody but his friends?

....

....

....

....

....

....

....

....

3.6 The birth of Christianity

If one is involved in a detailed examination of the gospel stories, the letters, the *Acts of the Apostles*, in a search for the early Jesus of faith, one can find what people believed close to the events. Why did they believe the resurrection? Why did this counter-intuitive idea make such progress? It is counter-intuitive: its leader was executed as a criminal; he was no mysterious ineffable guru who made the promise of ultimate earthly prosperity or bliss. Its upholders were ordinary folk. 'They (members of the Sanhedrin) were astonished at the fearlessness shown by Peter and John, considering that they were uneducated laymen; and they recognised them as associates of Jesus'.[9]

Christianity was born amidst a proud, stubborn Jewish faith which had survived the Exile, decades of slavery at the hands of the Egyptians, occupation by the Greeks, and then by the Romans. The leaders of the Jewish faith, who were considered representatives of God, condemned it and tried to stamp it out:

> Then the high priest intervened with all his supporters from the party of the Saducees. Filled with jealousy, they arrested the apostles and had them put in the public jail . . . The high priest demanded an explanation. We gave you a strong warning not to preach in this name.[10]

---

8. Luke 24:36–40.
9. *Acts of the Apostles* 4:13.
10. *Acts* 5:18, 27-8.

But a Pharisee, Gamaliel, cautioned the council:

> Men of Israel, be careful how you deal with these people. What I suggest is you leave these men alone and let them go. If this enterprise, this movement of theirs is of human origin, it will break up of its own accord; but if it does in fact come from God you will be unable to destroy them. Take care not to find yourselves fighting against God.[11]

The Roman power at various stages tried to discourage the apostles:

> Taking them before the magistrates they said, 'these people are causing disturbance in our city . . . the magistrates had them stripped and ordered them to be flogged. They were given many lashes and then thrown into prison, and the gaoler was told to keep close watch on them. So following such instructions, he threw them into the inner prison and fastened their feet in the stocks.[12]

The early Jewish Christian believers still regarded themselves as a branch of Judaism and attended the synagogue services in addition to their own *breaking of the bread*. The influx of Gentile believers, and there being excused from Jewish law practices meant an inevitable separation of Christianity from Israel. In 70 CE, all the Christian groups were expelled from the synagogues. This was a crisis point for Christianity.

4. Alternative explanations for the transformation of the apostles[13]

No one can deny that something happened. We have to account for the fact that a man living in a peripheral province of the Roman Empire, leaving virtually no trace in contemporary secular history, writing no book and dying an ignominious death, nevertheless has been dominant in human life and thought ever since. Something happened to reverse the natural reaction of the disciples. The demoralisation of the disciples caused by the arrest and execution of their master is understandable, even undeniable. Also undeniable is the fact that within a short space of time those same disciples were defying the authorities, who had previously seemed so threatening, and they were now proclaiming the one who had died disgraced and forsaken as being both Lord and Christ. The sole moving force of their new way of life had just been executed, had been discredited by a criminal's death, and his followers had been rendered useless by the removal of their leader. What happened?

Question: They said they believed he rose; therefore they believed he rose; therefore he rose. Is this good reasoning?

....

....

....

....

---

11. *Acts* 5:5, 38–9.
12. *Acts* 16:20, 22–4.
13. Gerald O'Collins, SJ, 'The Resurrection of Jesus: Four Contemporary Challenges', *Catholic Theological Review* 6 (1985): 5–10. The thought of O'Collins is presented here in this section.

4.1 The apostles deliberately made up stories in order to feel better
After Jesus' grim and grizzly death, what was the atmosphere in their meeting place next day? Did they all gather together in strength and rebellion? Was the following a possible scenario?

'Let's do something. Let's all go out and get the high priest, drive a mega-chariot into the temple and do some damage.'

'Yes', said Matthew, 'they have some great new catapults of mass-destruction over in Mesopotamia. We could get some and wipe out the Romans and string up Pontius Pilate.'

'Calm down,' said Peter. 'I've got another idea, one which will be better in the long term. Let's *pretend* he came back to life'.

'Good one,' said John. 'I've got some parchment here. Quick, let's get to work and write some stories before people forget about him. Luke and Mathew, you are educated and can read and write. That's your job. In fact, write the story of his life and put that coming back to life bit at the end'.

Mark said, 'I've got an idea about an empty tomb.'

'Great idea,' said Matthew. 'I'll try to make it good. I'll pretend the stone rolled itself away; no, better still, let's say an angel rolled it away, and there was a great earthquake'.

'That's a bit too far-fetched,' said Mark. 'You write your version, I'll write mine.'

Is such a scenario as this possible? They gathered in defiant strength? Remember, Peter denied him; they all ran into hiding fearing they'd be next. Some were already on their way back home, on the road to Emmaus.

Is it possible they manufactured the stories? The stories don't agree. You would think if they did this, they'd get the details right! One account, Matthew's, has all the appearances in Galilee, another, Luke's, all in Jerusalem. The empty tomb stories[14] differ in significant details (as outlined earlier in this chapter).

To have had such an effect and to have gained so many converts, the disciples must have convinced their hearers of the resurrection and they must have been convinced of it themselves. The early preaching recorded in the *Acts of the Apostles* continually cites the resurrection.

And in that male-dominated world women were chosen to be the discoverers of the empty tomb, the first conveyers of the message. If you chose to make up the stories and hope to fool the populace, you would not cite women as the first witnesses. Women were second-class citizens, and were not allowed to be witnesses in a court of law. A story based on women witnesses was hardly likely to convince anyone in those times.

4.2 The swoon theory: Jesus was not dead
Jesus did not die on the cross, but was taken down from the cross alive, buried and later revived in the tomb; he somehow got out and so 'appeared' to his followers. One story has Jesus buried with one of the co-executed thieves who was a doctor who not only was not dead, but also had some medicine. He treated Jesus' wounds. Meanwhile, the apostles, hiding around the tomb, seized upon a chance when the guards were distracted, rolled back the stone, led Jesus out, stayed with him while convalescing until he was fit enough to go to another country and marry Mary Magdalene—the last idea having been made much of in Dan Brown's hugely successful novel *The Da Vinci Code*.

The New Testament contains no evidence in favour of any version of swoon theory. The most primitive texts are in the letters of Paul and in the speeches found in the *Acts of the Apostles*. Texts from these works agree that Jesus died by crucifixion and was buried as a

---
14. Mark 16: 1–8; Luke 24:1–10; Matthew 28:1–8.

dead man. There are various testaments to his death in the New Testament,[15] while other sources also confirm this:

- In the *Antiquities* written by the Jewish historian Josephus, Jesus was said to be crucified on the orders of Pilate.

- The Roman historian Tacitus writes that Christ was put to death during the reign of Emperor Tiberius. His execution was ordered by Pilate:

    The author of this denomination, Christ, in the reign of Tiberius, had been condemned to death by Pontius Pilate; but though checked for the moment, the deadly superstition broke out afresh, not only throughout Judea, where this evil originated, but also throughout Rome.[16]

- The *Babylonian Talmud* has the words: 'Yeshu was hanged on the eve of the Passover'.

- David Friedrich Strauss over a century ago wrote:

    It is impossible that a being who had stolen half dead out of the sepulchre, who crept about weak and ill, wanting medical treatment, who required bandaging, strengthening and indulgence, could have given the disciples the impression that he was a conqueror over death and the grave, the prince of life, an impression which lay at the bottom of their future ministry. Such a resuscitation could by no possibility have changed their sorrow into enthusiasm, have elevated their reverence into worship.[17]

No source provides any evidence of an ordinary after-execution life. 'The swoon theory reduces the origin of Christianity to a story of a bungled execution, an incredibly lucky revival, an escape, later misrepresented as a glorious resurrection.'[18]

Question: What are the arguments for and against the 'swoon theory'?

---

15. Giuseppe Riciotti, *Life of Christ* (Cork: Mercier Press, 1955), 45–7.
16. Tacitus, *Annales*, XV, 44. Quoted in Riciotti, *Life of Christ*, 46.
17. David Strauss, *A New Life of Christ*, volume 1 (London: 1879), 412.
18. O'Collins, SJ, *Catholic Theological Review* 6: 6.

4.3 The story as an imitation of earlier dying and rising gods

Spring following winter in colder climates is new life being born. Gods such as Dionysius were believed to rise each spring, bringing the springtime of leaves on trees, birds, sunshine and growth. Is Jesus' resurrection another such story, of a god ushering in rebirth of nature?

The annual resurrection of Adonis was such a festival: the cycle of death gave way annually to the cycle of life.

Gerald O'Collins recounts the story of Adonis, and finds it not a good comparison:

> Adonis was a beautiful youth beloved by Aphrodite. While hunting a boar, he was gored to death, but each year was permitted to return from the underworld to his mistress for six months. Was Jesus' resurrection modelled on this?
>
> There is no reason to suspect Adonis actually existed. Adonis was not conceived as dying for sins, nor did the people hope for an afterlife through him. The blessings were those of health and prosperity for the next year, celebrating new organic life and tolerating sexual licence. This was an annual affair, not a once and for all final resurrection from the dead. In the legend, he died by accident, not by execution of one crucified as a blasphemer, and a threat to national security. In first century Palestine, there was no hint of cults borrowed from vegetation deities such as Adonis. [19]

Jesus' resurrection promised forgiveness of sins, and eternal life, not mere deliverance from biological death.

4.4 The story as symbol in the minds of the apostles

It is said that the resurrection was an event which affected the disciples, not Jesus himself. The disciples suddenly realised that God had lived among the human race through Jesus. What their new faith really meant was that the same God's presence and action continues in the midst of human life through the church. The resurrection was pre-eminently an event in the history of meaning. It was a symbol, not an actuality.

The story of a bodily resurrection is just a way of saying that the death of Christ is his great victory over sin. The apostles told the people the meaning of Christ's death. By the time this came to be written down, this message had taken the form of a bodily resurrection.

But how does such an interpretation sit with the texts which say that he was raised, that God raised him, that the Lord is risen indeed? This seems to mean more than some new idea: it seems rather to signify an event which gave rise to the new idea. These texts concern Jesus, not the disciples' minds. We must search for meaning here as we would with other ancient texts, not trying to make them conform to our own ideas. All the testimony declares it was the event itself that triggered the conversion.

4.5 The apostles were hallucinating

The hallucination theory says that Jesus' life was brim-full of meaning. After his death the disciples reflected on his life and found new insight into what he had said and done. But this interpretation does violence to the central and repeated affirmation of resurrection. Were resurrection events something that happened to them in their minds? Was it hallucinations that changed the disciples' consciousness? Peter first hallucinated and his excited telling of what he thought was real served to produce similar effects in the other disciples? Or perhaps it was a post-hypnotic suggestion of Jesus? Or did a mass gathering of all the disciples suffer the same hallucination together?

---

19. O'Collins, *Catholic Theological Review* 6: 6–7.

Again, this idea goes strikingly against the constant affirmation of actual resurrection. The apostles were ordinary tradespeople or professionals, not unbalanced visionaries. Jesus' death was an unexpected crisis, the trauma of total defeat, the total smashing of hope. They were not awaiting a return.

The idea of an executed Messiah was nowhere in the Jewish tradition. There was nothing in the tradition about a resurrection of a single individual.

How could hallucination theory be applied to the Pharisee Paul who experienced Jesus two years later on the road to Damascus? Paul's business was to hunt down and imprison members of the followers of Jesus when he abruptly changed.

Crowds can be persuaded by powerful oratory. Can the same effect happen as a mass hallucination? Is a mass hallucination possible? Although skilled orators may have powerful influences on crowds, this is not the same as a mass hallucination.

Question: Were the New Testament authors liars? Were they unskilled in committing their thoughts to paper? Or did they mean what they wrote?

5. The meaning

Friedrich Nietzsche proposed the famous *death of God* philosophy. In his book *Thus Spake Zarathustra*, he has the madman with the lantern searching in the morning everywhere for the god who cannot be found. Later that day he visits the churches in town and sings a requiem: 'what are these churches now if not the tombs and sepulchres of God?'[20]

Jesus rose. God is not dead. Christians do not speak about Jesus as some spoke after the death of South American political revolutionary and hero Che Guevara: 'Che lives because his cause goes on', the revolution goes on. Jesus is different. This is not simply a new insight, nor the subjective product of the overheated brain. He is not symbolically alive in his cause nor has he come back from the dead like Lazarus, but has gone from death into a transformed existence.

Yes, we might say, a great story and it ended up well, but what has this got to do with us today?

5.1 Jesus is the living Lord

Part of Christian testimony is that the church in every century has spoken of Jesus not as a revered past founder, but as its living Lord in the present. It treasures memories of his life as found in the gospels, but looks to him as present:

---

20. Friedrich Nietzsche: God is dead quote, www.csudh.edu/dearhabermas/goddead01bk.htm

> God raised him high, and gave him the name which is above all other names; so that all beings in the heavens, on earth, and in the underworld, should bend the knee at the name of Jesus, and that every tongue should acknowledge Jesus Christ as Lord, to the glory of God the father.[21]

He is experienced in the assembly of believers, declared in the word, encountered in the sacraments and addressed by prayers. Our faith is confirmed not so much by reference to the past as by the reality of Christ's power in the present. Christian faith is the response to the living God whom Christians declared is powerfully at work among them through the resurrected Jesus. He is not a long ago loved one who died and is treasured, but one who is treasured now and with whom a relationship grows and matures.

> Can anything cut us off from the love of Christ? I am certain of this: neither death nor life, nor angels, nor principalities, nothing already in existence and nothing still to come . . . will be able to come between us and the love of God, known to us in Christ Jesus our Lord.[22]

The news of the resurrection took a long time to spread, but when it did, it changed cultures and overwhelmed ancient civilisations. It established our own. The resurrection is the proclamation of an eternal hope.

5.2 Resurrection is the answer to life

Evil has been defeated: every evil was thrown at Christ and though destroyed he was not crushed. The heart of this despairing world has been changed into something good. In the midst of the worst tragedies people can find peace, meaning, hope and trust, and people can grow spiritually when affected as Jesus was. People help each other when tragedy strikes. We might be tempted to say 'sure he has done all things well, but we are still in the same predicament'. However, possessed by his risen spirit we know the forces of evil have ultimately been conquered. Everything that happens in the world no matter how painful and cross-filled is really already penetrated with the victory of Christ, the same Christ who rose from the dead and ascended to glory and remains with us as the Lord of history.

5.3 Resurrection is not earthly utopia

The resurrection does not render neutral the reality of the world. It is a critical corrective of utopia, because of its association with the life and death of Jesus. Utopia has many guises: the modern Western world in which we deserve to be fulfilled and get what we want; the workers' paradise of Marxist-Leninism; the world in which all people will see the light; the reappearance of the Messiah who will wave the magic wand; the scientific elimination of death itself.[23] The resurrection sets the Christian on the road of the cross, but with hope. There will always be people who fail, people who cannot cope, who do not understand themselves. Some choose evil and some have evil forced upon them.

5.4 The risen one: the spirit he released transforms us

It is the spirit of Jesus that sets us free, not only for a nirvana of soul, but free to care, to love, to trust, to pardon, to challenge, to respond to difference. Who is the risen one now? *Kyrios*, Lord (see footnote 22).

---

21. Paul, *Letter to the Philippians* 2:9–11.
22. Paul, *Letter to the Romans* 8:35, 38–9.
23. Karen McGhee, 'Living Forever', *Cosmos* 1: 58–67.

The risen one inspires us with faith, with the energy to work for justice as he did. Convinced of the resurrection, men and women risk their lives. Many working in the vast network of voluntary agencies throughout the world are motivated by religious ideals.

As he did not move every heart in his own time (far from it) so he will not move every heart today. There will be those, as we see today, who will take the path of violence, greed and exploitation. The resurrection has not ended war, cruelty or the miseries of the poor. But it ameliorates all these things as people have the courage to stand up and point out abuses and continually address wrongs that keep coming up. Jesus offers a continuing vision of our better purer selves, and of the better world we could create. Those with resurrection faith strive successfully to swim against the current.

5.5 The promise of personal resurrection

Death is news in the media. Two adventurous sky divers in their thirties; die one day; two teenagers die in a car crash on another; ultra wealthy John Paul Getty II dies at seventy and has the headlines 'Protein diet man slips over and dies'; a winner of a twenty million dollar United States lottery is struck fatally in the car-park after collecting his winnings; a minute virus slashes $18 billion from Asia's income, and kills hundreds; six thousand die in an earthquake; two hundred thousand die in a tsunami. Death lurks everywhere: on the battlefield, on the roads, in the hospitals and in our homes.

The resurrection of Christ is the victory over death. As for Christ, death is a birth. Resurrection is the end of death, as well as the beginning of lives empowered by the risen one. The dark hole of the grave is not the end. The final book of the Bible says: 'Do not be afraid; it is I, the first and the last; I am the living one, I was dead and look now I am to live for ever and ever, and I hold the keys of death and of the Hades'.[24]

5.6 The final revelation of God and God's purpose

If the past history of the universe is a guide, present speculations point beyond what we now believe about the cosmos. No previous state of the evolving universe, whether considering cosmic happenings, or animal evolution could predict what was to be the next stage. Could gigantic star factories be predicted from aggregations of dark matter, and accumulations of hydrogen? Could the human have been predicted from ancient fish? St Paul says 'all creation is groaning in one gigantic act of giving birth'.[25] Everything will follow Christ's resurrection into a new form of life.

In the resurrection of Jesus, it is finally revealed who God is. In this event God shows godself conclusively. God's power embraces life and death, existence and non-existence. God is creative love and faithfulness. God possesses potential far beyond existing reality, far beyond death:

> God raised him from the dead and made him sit at his right hand, far from every sovereignty, authority, power or domination, or any name that can be named, not only in this age, but also in the age to come. He has put all things under his feet.[26]

---

24. *Revelation* 1:17-8.
25. *Romans* 8:22
26. Paul, *Letter to the Ephesians* 1:20-2.

Further reading

Bruce Barber and David Neville, editors, *Theology and Eschatology* (Adelaide: ATF Press, 2005)

Marie-Emile Boismard, *Our Victory over Death: Resurrection?* (Collegeville: The Liturgical Press, 1995).

Marcus J Borg, *Meeting Jesus Again for the First Time: The Historical Jesus and the Heart of Contemporary Faith* (San Francisco, Harper, 1994).

Stephen Davis, Daniel Kendall, SJ, Gerald O'Collins, SJ, editors, The Resurrection: An Interdisciplinary Symposium on the Resurrection of Jesus (Oxford: Oxford University Press, 1998).

Jack Dominian, *One Like Us: A Psychological Interpretation of Jesus* (London: Darton, Longman and Todd, 1998).

Denis Edwards, *Jesus and the Cosmos* (Homebush: St Paul Publications, 1991).

Walter Kasper, *The God of Jesus Christ* (New York: Crossroad, 1992).

Christiaan Mostert, editor, *Hope: Challenging the Culture of Despair* (Adelaide: ATF Press, 2004).

Malcolm Muggeridge, *Jesus Rediscovered* (Glasgow: Collins, 1976).

Gerald O'Collins, *Incarnation* (London: Continuum, 2002).

Ted Peters, Robert John Russell and Michael Welker, editors, *Resurrection: Theological and Scientific Assessments* (Grand Rapids: William Eerdmans, 2002).

Thomas P Rausch, SJ, *Who is Jesus? An Introduction to Christology* (Collegeville: Liturgical Press, 2003).

Conclusion:
The Fruitful Conversation Between Science and Religion

1. Is science our salvation?

Medieval life was said to be brutal, short, and for most people, impoverished. Towards the end of the medieval period, as some people began poring over thermometers, gas jars, and chemicals, the philosopher Francis Bacon (1561–1626) foresaw enormous possibilities in the application of science for the benefit of society.[1] He thought of many people researching experimentally on projects which would add to many more facts being discovered, and result in benefits for society. He wrote a fictional story, *New Atlantis*, about a utopian society where new discoveries were applied for the welfare of society. He thought the widespread application of knowledge gained by science would so increase the number and variety of products, at very reduced expense, that no one could possibly be in dire need again. Others at various times have echoed similar sentiments.

Bacon saw science as a saviour. Jawaharlal Nehru, the leader of India after independence, looked to science to solve problems regarding poverty, illiteracy and to weakening the hold superstition and customs had over the people. Going further than this, modern scientists like Walter Crick, Peter Atkins and Richard Dawkins have maintained that the answers to all questions were to be found in science.

Question: Media heavyweight, Rupert Murdoch, once lectured on the power of technology to liberate. Does all the technology available to us make us more and more liberated?

....

....

....

....

....

....

....

---

1. Brown, *The Wisdom of Science*, 4–7.

Certainly science has a part to play. But other forces prevent its fruits being applied for the betterment of all. Its fruits can even be applied destructively. Whatever breakthroughs science achieves, the dissemination of its fruits to all humanity depends very much on other factors. Profit taking, power seeking, self-indulgence and heartlessness mitigate against this dissemination. Unselfishness, fairness and compassion are qualities that must be dominant if science is to be employed for the everyday salvation of all humans. These qualities cannot emerge from the scientific method.

2. The many fruits of science

In the sixteenth century neither scientists nor the emerging discipline of science were seen as valuable contributors to society. Yet the findings of these dedicated and single-minded people, and the equations they and their successors have left us, have enabled Bacon's dream of a utopia in some ways to be realised. After discovering electricity and how to generate it, through a simple switch we use it for heating and cooling and many other things: add in magnetism and we have all sorts of entertainment (sound, video, DVD); add in the microchip (which fits a ten storey building of valves into a pinhead) and we have the amazing computing and information revolution. Problems which would either be unsolvable or take decades to solve can now be solved in hours; and we have access to unlimited information and news via the remote control or the internet; even when we are out, absent friends are accessible by pushing a few buttons on the mobile.

When there are problems the experts go to science for solutions, and rightly so. We in the West now have an expanded, generally more comfortable, lifespan. Small pox has been defeated. Polio and measles are no longer grave threats in the West. TB was held in check for decades, though it is making a comeback. Cancer is still a great killer, but many forms, previously deadly, are now often treated with success. By-pass operations give many people extra comfortable years of life. For people with mental trouble, scientists provide medication which controls moods and relieves distress. Actual genes which are responsible for genetic disorders are being located. There is activity to find a cure for AIDS: although the medical profession is not yet near a solution if there is a cure it will come through science. SARS was nipped in the bud by a closely worked international effort. When planes crash, scientists race to the scene, work out the cause and propose remedies for the future. Real food supply difficulties were anticipated thirty years ago, but the 'green revolution' resulted in vastly increased harvests so the world is well supplied with food despite large increases in population. There is enough to go around: though it does not always go around to all for other reasons. When pests occur in agriculture or livestock, the scientist comes in. With pressure on food supplies increasing again the world looks to genetically engineered plants to increase production, yields.

Question: Have scientific achievements increased human happiness?

3. Serious problems remain for a large proportion of the human population

Yet, despite the enormous increase in the number and variety of goods, of the wealth per person, and the information on CD Rom, the world is teeming with undernourished or starving, illiterate, poor and sick people. And there are still significant areas of armed conflict which bring injury, disruption and death to large numbers of people.

Science has not eliminated poverty. There is a huge number of poor, and the gap between rich and poor is not decreasing. The scientific method has enabled the production of enough to save the people of the world from many ills. Food, medicine, shelter and education could be there for everyone, but are not reaching nearly half of the population. Many cannot make enough to improve their lot, nor can they see how to improve their earnings. In the meantime science continues to develop more good things for the fortunate to add to what they already have.

4. Reason in a world of science

Science is a wonderful means of exploring many aspects of ourselves, our world, our origins and our future. It has totally transformed our everyday lives and our relationship to the forces of nature. Science has provided many answers to questions about nature, and to problems troubling the human race. Science is not an arbitrary fabrication of the human mind. Theory is not the result of individual opinion. Science actually tells us about the world; its theories are formed in response to nature's answers, and theories are destroyed by observations running contrary to it. Peer evaluation is essential. Science is objective in the sense that the ultimate source of its knowledge is the physical world. It is a continual response to reality leading us closer to the nature of reality. Its seeming hold over the workings of nature have often been questioned when nature speaks differently: ' . . . the paramountcy of the physical world as itself the ultimate source of knowledge preserves science from being merely a social construction'.[2]

5. A danger emanating from the success of scientific reasoning[3]

The dominance of scientific knowledge and the consequent familiarisation with its method can lead to the downgrading of other forms of coming to the truth.

- If we see that scientific knowledge is provisional then values and morals can be seen as provisional.

    o Science's theories have historically been found to be replaceable, and most have been replaced. If successful scientific theories can be found to be wrong, the conclusion is that there is no real truth in science. If there is no truth in this highly successful mode of knowing, there is no real truth anywhere.

    o Scientific truth, even if provisional, works wonderfully well with all its technological applications, making life better for many. This can be extended to *whatever works for me is right.*

    o If scientific truth is provisional, it means it may well be wrong so that its contradictory may be also be right. So contradictory choices or opinions, in the same circumstances, can both be right. Truth is reduced to mere

---

2. John Polkinghorne, *Beyond Science, the Wider Human Context* (Cambridge: Cambridge University Press, 1998), 18.
3. Bryan Appleyard, *Understanding the Present* (London: Picador, 1992).

opinions. There is no basis for moral right and wrong. We are to become gods, self-defining, free from the mythologies of the past.

- Scientific knowledge is detached, an unemotional search for a grasp on material reality. The search for meaning may also appear detached. There is no passionate conviction. There is no purpose. On the other hand there are and have been many scientists enthusiastically devoted to their search for truth: Albert Einstein, Neils Bohr, Richard Feynman and Fred Hoyle amongst others.

- Science is empirical; its statements come from experience. Thus it can be thought that all true knowledge is empirical. Values and religion are not empirical. It can be seen that there is no possibility of religious truth and then God is condemned to permanent retreat or to *opinion*. In this view we are to become gods defining ourselves our meaning, our purpose.

This can be expressed in the following diagram. The scientific method can be seen to erode other forms of knowledge.

The potential for science to endanger value thinking

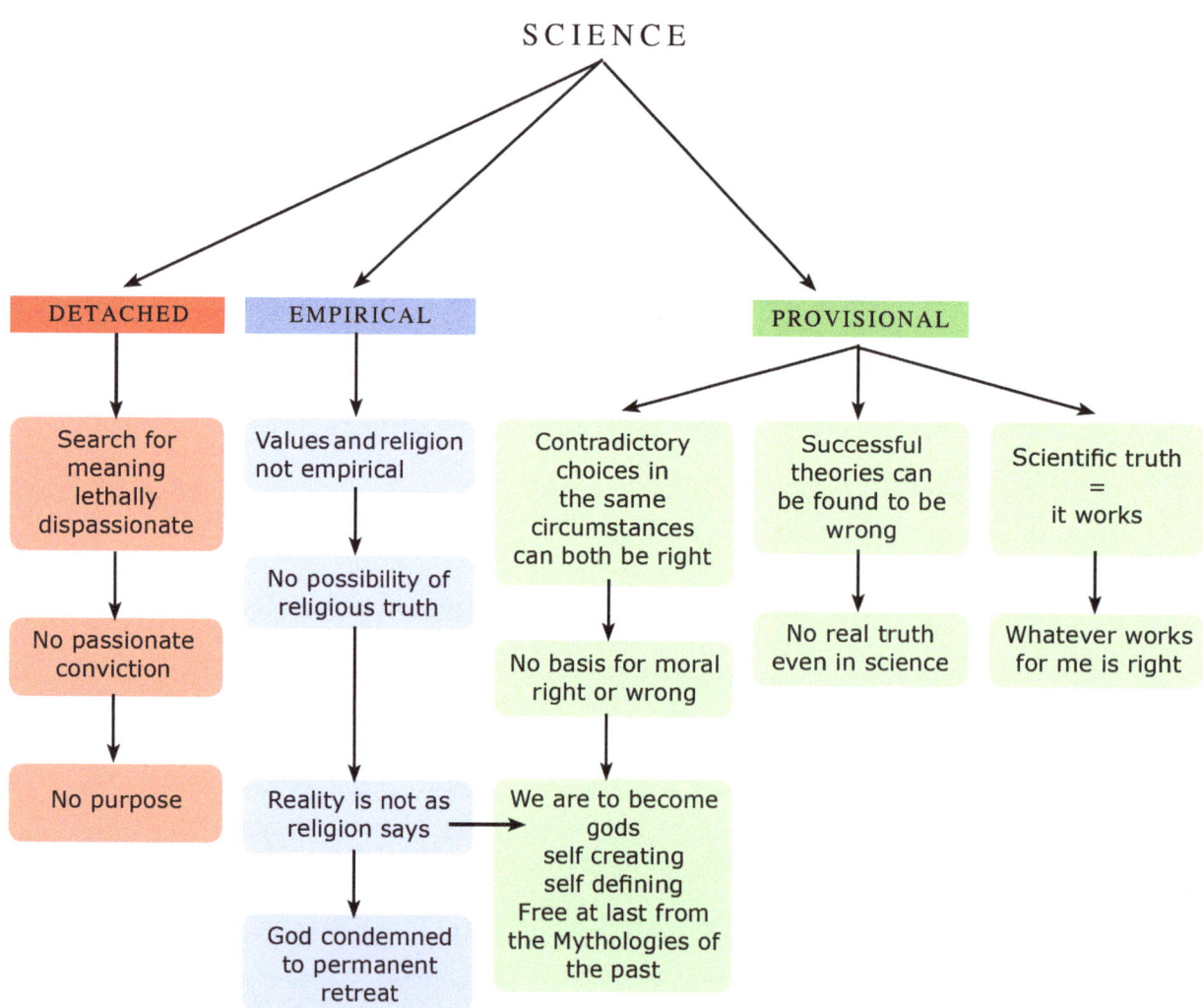

Question: For you, has science downgraded reason? Personal opinions are only as good as the evidence and/or the logic involved in reaching the opinion. Discuss.

....

....

....

....

....

....

....

....

....

....

6. How to view the relationship between science and religion

6.1 The conflict model
Though the relationship between science and religion is often seen in terms of the conflict model[4] this is by no means the only way of looking at the problem.

When science is considered the lone road to truth, the following dilemmas are confronted:

- Firstly, science leads to walls which cannot be scaled by science alone. The beginning of the universe and its contingency (it did not have to exist), the progress of the cosmos from chaos to ever more sophisticated organisation and its overall fine-tuning cannot be answered by science without its venturing into metaphysical territory.

- Secondly, while science delivers us many things for humanity's benefit, it cannot provide the plan and the motivation for the human race to actually use things for the benefit of all. It cannot speak of purpose or of conscience or of the possibility of anything outside the realm of the material.

If religion is regarded as truth's sole benchmark, again there are serious difficulties. When taking scriptures literally, religious fundamentalism flies in the face of reality, dispensing with some well-established findings of science.

6.2 Contact, conversation and confirmation
God speaks through the book of nature as well as through God's biblical word. The contact model acknowledges and respects each, but plays down the speculations of science in

---
4. See Introduction, Section 4.4. John Haught's models: conflict, contact, conversation and confirmation.

dealing with creation. The religious belief of creation in the past has always been associated with the then current scientific cosmic model; the truth of creation was associated with an ancient model in the Bible, and consequent on later advances in knowledge and philosophical speculation, creation was presented in the context of Aristotle's universe. It needs now to be placed within the big bang model of the universe, realising at the same time that this may not be the last scientific word.

Science offers real statements about the cosmos which must be taken account of when discussing reality as God's creation. In this way, science limits religion in its treatment of material reality. Science's findings lead to questions properly dealt with by religion.

Religion can propose to science a world basically hopeful, imbued with purpose, and give nature's processes an overall meaning.

To the believer, scientific revelations serve as a *confirmation*. The contingent beginnings, the wonderful progress to life and mind, all serve to manifest to the believer the purposeful designer, the intelligence of the being said to be the creator. It confirms and broadens the believer's ideas about God as creative power and giver of purpose; God as the one whose message to creation is not yet finished.

6.3 A parallel approach
Ian Barbour, in *When Science Meets Religion*,[5] proposes a similar scheme. He calls the four approaches conflict, independence, dialogue and integration. In 'conflict', there is the option between either 'scientific materialism' or 'biblical literalism'. In 'independence', each field has separate domains, different languages and different functions.

> *Dialogue* may arise from considering the presuppositions of the scientific enterprise, or from exploring similarities between the methods of science and those of religion, or from analysing concepts in one field that are analogous to those in the other.[6]

Barbour's 'integration' follows the path of Haught's 'confirmation'.

7. Concluding comment

Science has confronted religion. Science has achieved so much and has expanded into areas previously within the domain of religion. Religion's past association with myths has told against it. Religion does lack the type of evidence used by science. But religion has an evidence of a kind and it cannot be dismissed merely as the musings of men and women. More importantly, we know that something more than science is needed, for science lacks the power to go beyond the material, beyond things and processes. There is the quest for meaning—conscience, values, the nature of the human person, the very justification of the scientific method itself—which is out of the reach of science. However science can and does provide matters for further speculation; it can lead us to the base of the mountain of meaning.

But science itself has left us with questions. Why is there anything at all? What lies behind the so far impenetrable physics of the big bang? The big bang theory is really a theory of what happened after the big bang. Why has a succession of more ordered states arisen during the history of the universe when the chances are so much against this happening? Why has mind unravelled itself from matter in this unfolding? Can such an extraordinary journey be explained by chance? Does an unending series of universes as another explanation call upon

---

5. Ian Barbour, *When Science Meets Religion* (San Francisco, HarperCollins, 2000). 7–38.
6. Barbour, *When Science Meets Religion*, 23.

too much credulity? Or is matter's fruitful journey a sign of an ultimate designer/power?

The importance of religion in the life of humanity stands: its resilience throughout history; its deep appeal to the human psyche; its capacity to provide a guiding sense of ethics and morals; and its validation of mystical experiences of the 'other' that defy everyday explanations. The resurrection of Christ has as its best explanation that it really happened. Any other explanations for the hope-filled, experiences and attitudes of its witnesses and for the remarkable expansion of Christianity in its early centuries do not do justice to the events, do not proffer a sufficient reason. Jesus' resurrection gives on-going hope that this imperfect, developing, changing cosmos will continue on its optimistic path to a final consummation, when God will be all in all.

Further reading

Jan Barbour, *When Science Meets Religion* (San Francisco: HarperCollins, 2000).

Arthur Gibson, *God and the Universe* (London: Routledge, 2000).

John Leslie, editor, *Modern Cosmology and Philosophy* (New York: Prometheus Books, 1998).

Christopher Southgate and others, *God, Humanity, and the Cosmos: A Textbook in Science and Religion* (Edinburgh: T&T Clark).

Glossary

Absolute	The ultimate being, the ultimate ground of all things, free from imperfection, restrictions or limitations.
Almagest	Book written by Ptolemy*. Its subject was the earth-centred (geocentric) model of the universe.
Andromeda	A large spiral galaxy* containing over 100 billion stars, 2.4 million light years* away. It can be seen in the southern sky. It is the largest member of the 'local group'* of galaxies.
Animism	A belief system that attributes all natural happenings to the work of spirits. There is no hierarchy of spirits.
Anthropic universe	View of the universe whereby the universe's laws are seen as especially suited to guide the universe to the evolution of intelligent life. Anthropos is the Greek word for man.
Apostles	Group of twelve most closely associated with Jesus Christ.
Aristarchus of Samos	Proposed a sun-centred universe in third century BCE.
Aristotle	Greek philosopher and theoretician, 384–322 BCE. Disciple of Plato who eventually parted ways with Plato on key issues. He has left treatises on metaphysics, ethics, biology and physics. Much of his metaphysics was adopted by the church after 1300 CE, and his ethics especially is still widely respected.
Arius	Early Christian theologian of Alexandria, c250–336 CE. Proponent of the belief that Jesus Christ was the incarnation of an angel previously created by God. Condemned as a heretic*.
Ark	A mythical watercraft built by Noah to survive the flood sent by God as a punishment for sin. Its symbolic meaning is that God will save the just.
Astronomia Nova	Publication in which Kepler* reported his finding that the orbits of the planets were ellipses* and not circles.
Australopithecus Afarensis	Earliest bipedal hominid, about five million years ago.
Bedouin	A nomadic Arab, living in arid lands in Asia or Africa.
Bellarmine, Robert	Head of the Inquisition* during the Galileo trials. A Jesuit, cardinal and canonised saint.
Beryllium	Element number 4. Its nucleus has 4 protons.
Big bang	The explosion into existence of the universe 13.7 billion years ago. This term, initially intended as derisive, is the commonly accepted name for the beginning of the universe.
Billion	A thousand million: 1,000,000,000 (10^9).

Black dwarf	A white dwarf* after it has cooled sufficiently to be no longer emitting light.
Black hole	Final state of a very large star after a supernova* explosion. The remnant has imploded. All the matter has shrunk to a point. Light cannot escape (hence 'black').
Brahe, Tycho	Danish astrologer and alchemist, 1546–1601. Made accurate measurements of positions of stars and planets. Developed the theory of the planets circling the sun, which circled the earth, dragging the planets. This accounted for the retrograde motions of planets. Kepler was his assistant.
Brahman	The one transcendent reality behind all local gods in the Hindu* tradition.
Buddha	The ancient Indian spiritual teacher, Siddhartha Gautama, c560–c480 BCE, who left a comfortable life to find by meditation the key to inner peace. 'Buddha' means the enlightened one. Historical founder of Buddhism.
Buddhist	Follower of the teachings of the Buddha*. Pain endemic to human life can be overcome by a victory over desire, and by a following of the 8-fold path.
C^1	The element Carbon. The most common form which has 6 protons* and 6 neutrons* in the nucleus, and hence is called carbon 12.
Cambrian explosion	Geological era approximately 542–488 million years ago. Rocks from this period contain fossilised multicellular organisms. Land and sea organisms witnessed a rapid diversification in this era.
Cassiopeia	Modern constellation also listed by Ptolemy. Spectacular remnant of supernova* 1572.
Cepheid	A star whose brightness varies noticeably with time. The star became brighter and fainter with regularity. The periodic time of the waxing and waning is related to the actual brightness of the star.
Chaos	The unpredictability arising not from quantum theory*, but from insufficient knowledge of deterministic causes.
Cluster	A number of galaxies* grouped gravitationally together.
Commentariolus	A small work published by Copernicus* in 1514 in which he first outlined his ideas about a sun-centred universe.
Copernicus, Nicolaus	Polish mathematician and astronomer, 1473–1543. In *De Revolutionibus Orbium Coelestium* (1543), he developed the model of the sun-centred (heliocentric) universe. This idea was promoted by Galileo* in the seventeenth century.
Cosmic Background Explorer (COBE)	Satellite that measured the intensity of the cosmic background radiation* coming from all directions, and found slight variations of intensity consistent with big bang* theory.
Cosmic microwave background radiation (CMB)	Radiation bathing all space, emanating from the big bang*.

Cosmological constant	Repulsive gravitational force proposed by Einstein to counteract the implosion of the universe.
Cosmologist	Scientist who develops theories about the universe.
Cosmos	The universe. From the ancient Greek for ordered whole.
Creationist	One who interprets the first twelve chapters of the Book of Genesis literally.
Cyclotron	Apparatus in which charged particles are accelerated to high speeds so that they can help in the formation of new particles/nuclei by colliding with other nuclei.
Dark energy	An entity said to be present in all space which is responsible for the acceleration of the universe's expansion rate.
Dark matter	Matter whose existence is necessary to explain why galaxies* do not fly apart as they rotate, why galaxy clusters* stay gravitationally bound, and how visible matter clumped in the early universe to form stars and galaxies. Dark matter has not been directly detected, though its gravitational effect on light has been noted.
Degrees Kelvin	Zero degrees Kelvin is -273° C. This temperature is the situation of no heat. There can be no lower temperature. The differences in degrees are the same as for Celsius. 0° C = 273 K.
Deism	Belief that the God who created all things has, since the initial act of creation, been disinterested in what was created.
Democritus	Greek philosopher, c460 BCE. Proposed an atomic theory, which was generally rejected in favour of Aristotle's infinitely divisible solid.
De Revolutionibus Orbium Coelestium	Book written by Copernicus*. Published as he was dying. In the book, he developed the model of the sun-centred (heliocentric) universe.
Determinism	Doctrine where occurrences and phenomena are seen as being inevitably caused by what has come before. Given initial conditions, certain effects must follow.
Deuterium	A form of hydrogen, with twice the mass of normal hydrogen. Its nucleus contains the normal one proton* and in addition, one neutron*. In sea water (H_2O), one H in every 8000 is deuterium. An absolute essential for starshine.
Dialogue (The)	*The Dialogue Concerning the Two World Systems*. Galileo* was commissioned by Pope Urban VIII* to write an account of the two world systems: the earth centred and the sun centred. His account was not the even-handed one agreed upon, but mocked the geocentric view.
Disjunction	An either/or situation in which one of the two must be right and the other must be wrong.

DNA	Deoxyribosenucleic acid. Chemical on which life depends. A blueprint for a living organism. Contained in the chromosomes which are in the cell's nucleus
Doppler effect	Waves from a source have shorter wavelengths when the source is approaching the observer, and longer wavelengths when the source is receding from the observer. On approach, sound has higher pitch; on receding, sound has lower pitch.
Electromagnetic waves	Waves which go through space: light, heat, microwave, ultra-violet, radio. They are composed of mutually perpendicular oscillating electric and magnetic fields.
Electromagnetism	The property possessed by physical phenomena that involves the mutual influence of electric and magnetic effects. For example, light waves, radio waves.
Electron	A much smaller particle than the proton*. It is said to be in orbit around the nucleus. It has a single negative charge.
Element	A substance whose ultimate particle is one atom only.
Ellipse	An oval shaped geometric figure with a major axis 'a' and a minor axis 'b' such that $x^2/a^2 + y^2/b^2 = 1$
Empedocles	Greek philosopher (c490–430 BCE). All material things were seen as being composed of the four elements of earth, air, fire and water.
'Empty tomb'	The tomb in which Jesus Christ was buried after his death on the cross, found empty by some women disciples on Easter Sunday morning.
Epicurus	Greek philosopher of the fourth century CE who set up a community in which people could find true happiness.
Epicycle	To account for the observed retrograde motion of Mars and other planets, it was thought that each planet journeyed around a short circular path, and that the centre of this circle orbited the earth.
Ether (also aether)	Early postulation of a transparent medium pervading all space. Light was seen as a vibration of this medium. As light was a wave, it could not travel through empty space.
Excommunicate	To expel from the church, depriving the person from the path to salvation.
Feuerbach, Ludwig	German philosopher who proposed that God was the invention of the human mind, the fulfilment of our wishes.
Field	Region of space in which a force will be felt if an appropriate object is introduced into the space. For example, a massive object will experience a force of gravity if introduced into the region around the earth.
Firmament	Feature of ancient cosmology to describe the apparent arch of the sky; transparent dome enclosing the flat earth. Vault*.
Fractal	From the Latin word 'fractus' meaning broken. Describes fancy patterns which can be generated using quadratic equations. For example, the Mandelbrot set.
Fusion	The process of smaller sub-atomic particles joining together to form larger nuclei*, with the loss of mass and the release of energy.

Galaxy	Collection of stars containing typically a hundred billion stars.
Galen	A Greek medical doctor. c130–c200 CE, who studied anatomy and who wrote a treatise on anatomy which was the basis of much medical practice for centuries.
Galileo Galilei	Using a version of the telescope he had constructed, he found significant evidence that the earth was not the centre of the universe. Eventually his robust promotion of this idea precipitated a conflict with church authorities, and he was sentenced to house imprisonment for breaking an agreement. He was never declared a heretic*.
General relativity	Einstein's theory of gravity, space and time, which supersedes Newton's theory.
Gentiles.	Jewish term for those who were not Jews.
Geocentric system	A system where the earth is seen as the centre.
Gravity	Force which makes objects fall to earth. It keeps the moon in orbit around the earth. The sun's gravity keeps the earth in orbit around the sun. Gravity exists between any two masses; but is minute between ordinary objects.
Haught, John	Professor of theology at Georgetown University, USA. A lay person.
Heliocentric system	A system where the sun is seen as the centre.
Heisenberg uncertainty	In the sub-atomic realm the precision with which certain pairs of variables can be measured is restricted. Great precision in the measurement of the momentum of a particle restricts the precision with which you can locate it, and vice-versa.
Helium	Inert gas. Element number 2. Makes up for about 25% of the visible universe. Formed in the first three minutes of the universe.
Heretic	One who has been publicly named as professing a doctrine contrary to a doctrine declared by the church.
Hinduism	Religion common in India. There is ultimately one transcendent reality, Brahman*. Salvation* means awareness of our oneness with Brahman.
Homo sapiens	Species name for the modern human. Literally 'wise man'.
Hoyle, Fred	Twentieth century cosmologist who proposed the theory that almost all the elements were synthesised within large stars, and saw the theory verified. He also proposed the 'steady state' universe: the universe may be expanding, but it is infinite in extent, and new matter is always appearing, so that it always appears the same.
Hubble telescope	Telescope in space, orbiting the earth.
Index (The)	A list of prohibited books, drawn up by the Inquisition*.
Inflation	The universe doubled in size many times over a very small time interval very soon after the big bang, so that its volume increased from less than that of an atom to something like that of a grapefruit.

Inquisition	Roman Catholic tribunal for the defence of church doctrine. Offenders were punished by imprisonment or even by death.
Intelligent Design	The idea that science has revealed there is no possible scientific explanation for some evolutionary developments so that the presence of divine activity is necessary for an explanation.
Irrational number	A number which cannot be expressed as a ratio of another two whole numbers. It is characterised by a never-ending set of numbers after the decimal point in such a way there is no repeatable or predictable pattern in these numbers.
Isotropic	The same intensity from all directions.
Joseph of Arimathea	A Pharisee* who allowed Jesus Christ's body to be buried in his own tomb.
Judeo-Christian	A term applied to Christianity as it sees itself as having emerged from Judaism, and shares many books of the Bible with Judaism.
Kaku, Michio	Prominent advocate of string theory*, a theory proposing the different sub-atomic particles are different vibrations of the one string.
Kelvin	The name of a temperature scale. The zero Kelvin (-273^0 Celsius) is the absolute zero of temperature, corresponding with the condition of no heat. The degree gradations are the same as for the Celsius scale. 0^0 C = 273 K. Named after Lord Kelvin (JJ Thomson).
Kepler, Johannes	A German astronomer, 1571–1630, who was an assistant to Copernicus*. Showed that the planetary orbits were ellipses*, not circles. The sun centred universe, with the planets having circular orbits did not give as accurate an account of their positions as did Ptolemy's* epicycle* model. Kepler's replacing of circles with ellipses corrected this deficiency.
Lambda, ☐	Cosmic repulsive force postulated by Albert Einstein to prevent the implosion of the universe.
Law of nature	Laws are constant ways of behaving of physical systems. A law yields a description of how a physical system is operating. It does not give an explanation.
Leviathan	A mythical Syrian monstrous being dwelling in primeval chaos, and must be slain by a creative god as part of creative activity.
Light year	The distance light travels in one year: $3 \times 10^5 \times 365 \times 24 \times 3600$ km = 9460800000000 km (9.46×10^{12} kilometres).
Lithium	Element number 3. Nucleus* has 3 protons*. Resembles sodium. A very light reactive metal. Dissolves vigorously in water.
'Local group'	About forty-five galaxies of which the Milky Way* is a member. The Milky Way and Andromeda* are the dominant members.
McGrath, Alister	Professor of historical theology at Oxford. He has written in opposition to Richard Dawkins, a populist scientist who writes strongly as an atheist. Books include, *Richard Dawkins' God, The Twilight of Atheism, The Dawkins Delusion*.

Messiah	A figure expected by the Jews who would deliver them from occupation by other powers. Equipped with power from Yahweh* he would establish the nation as a strong kingdom. Christians look on Jesus as having fulfilled this role, but in an unexpected manner.
Milky Way	The name of the galaxy to which our solar system belongs. It is spiral in shape, a hundred light years in diameter, and contains a hundred billion stars.
Microwave	Electromagnetic radiation whose wavelength occurs between radio and infra-red (heat) radiation. It is used in ovens, and for TV transmission.
Monotheism	Belief system admitting of only one god.
Multiverse	A set of universes. An ensemble of separate universes is postulated according to this theory.
Myth	A story which is not literally true but has strong historical and psychological resonances. In modern usage it is often seen as a falsehood. Its literary use refers to a story that while not factually true has a deeper truth within it.
Nebula	Previously galaxies were thought to be clouds of gas within the Milky Way*, and were called nebulae. Today usage is restricted to clouds of gas in space which may house stars being born.
Nestorius	Early church patriarch, (died c451) who was a proponent of the belief that Mary was not the mother of God
Neutrino	Sub-atomic particle with almost zero mass and no charge.
Neutron	Sub-atomic particle also residing in the nucleus*, with the same mass as the proton*, but uncharged.
Nietzsche, Friedrich	German philosopher, 1844–1900, who emphasised 'no pain, no gain' and famously declared 'God is dead'.
Nucleosynthesis	The formation of larger nuclei by the fusion* of smaller ones. Occurs in stars.
Nucleus	The centre of an atom, occupying only a small volume of the atom, positively charged.
Ohm's law	Mathematical law relating voltage and current produced by the voltage.
Paradigm change	The adoption of a completely new set of related theories to explain the same phenomena. For example: the replacement of the earth-centred universe with the sun-centred; the change from Newton's laws to quantum theory*.
Parameter	A physical quantity that can be expressed mathematically. For example: weight, energy, force, speed.

Pharisees	A lay group in Judaism who adhered closely to the Law, respected the Law, the first five books of the Jewish scriptures (the Pentateuch), and the oral traditions of the elders. An influential group, who alone survived the destruction of Jerusalem in 70 CE.
Philosophy	The arrival at conclusions through logic and reasoning alone. The premises may come from experience.
Phlogiston	Before the discovery of oxygen, combustion was thought to be the driving off of an entity called 'phlogiston'. Each substance was thought to be a combination of 'calx' (ash) and phlogiston which held the ash together to form a solid substance. Because the substance then gained weight during combustion, phlogiston was said to have negative weight.
Polygenism	The multiple origin of the human race. Intelligence evolved within a group.
Polytheism	Belief system that admits of many gods.
Pressure	Force per unit area.
Primum mobile	The first mover. The one from whom all movement in the heavens (sun, planets, stars, moon) received their movement.
Proton	The sub-atomic particle which determines an element's nature. Hydrogen has one proton, helium two, iron 56, uranium 92. It resides in the nucleus and each proton has a single positive charge.
Ptolemy, Claudius	Influential Alexandrian astronomer, c90–c168 CE. His description of the universe had the earth as centre, the sun and moon circling the earth, and the planets orbiting the earth tracing out an epicycle* whose centre circled the earth. Author of the 'Almagest'*.
Pulsar	Very dense 'star'. What remains after a large star ends its life in a supernova* explosion. It is a mass of neutrons*. A teaspoon weighs a billion tonnes. Spins rapidly, emitting radio waves.
Quantum theory	Theory describing the behaviour of atoms, molecules and sub-atomic particles. Mathematically flawless, but difficult to interpret physically.
Quantum uncertainty	Given initial equal conditions in the sub-atomic realm, there can be many outcomes. Each possibility may be accorded a probability. Given large numbers of reactions in an event under examination, the different probabilities given to different outcomes are mirrored exactly in the proportions of reactions resulting in those outcomes.
Quark	Protons* and neutrons* have been shown to be made up each of three smaller particles called quarks. They cannot exist except when bound together in the sub-atomic particle.
Quintessence	Substance out of which anything else in the universe besides the earth was made. Heavenly, perfect substance.
Rahab	A monster of chaos slain by the creative deity in ancient Semitic myths.
Ramapithecus	Ancestor of apes and humans.
Red dwarf	A slow burning small star, much smaller than the sun. None are visible to the naked eye, although 70% of stars are red dwarfs.

Red shift	Light waves have longer wavelengths if the source of light is receding from the observer. All wavelengths are shifted towards the red (which is the longest visible wavelength).
Resurrection	The arising of Jesus after his death. He was then seen by his disciples. He was the same person, but transformed. (This is not the resuscitation of a corpse.)
Saducees	A group within Judaism comprising the priestly aristocracy, their supporters and dependents.
Salvation	Materially: the state of being delivered from poverty, oppression and ignorance. Spiritually: the state of being freed from inner forces which aim the person towards evil, and, ultimately, the conquest of death.
Scalar field	The physical quantity described by the field*. This does not involve a direction.
Scientism	The belief that the only truths available are those obtained through the scientific method.
Scribes	Scholars of the Law in Judaism. A respected position of leadership.
Semi-conductors	Elements such as silicon which partially conduct electricity. They are vital in computers.
Simplicio	A sixth century commentator on Aristotle. A leading character in Galileo's* *Dialogue*.
Steady state	Theory of the universe advanced by Fred Hoyle: the galaxy density of the universe never changes, as matter is always being created to fill the gaps caused by the expansion of space. The universe is infinite in extent. There was no beginning.
String theory	A recent theory where the basic physical entity is postulated to be a string (not a particle), 10^{20} times smaller than a nucleus*. Each particle is said to be a unique vibration of the string.
Strong force	The strong nuclear force which holds protons* and neutrons* together in the nucleus*. It is much stronger than the repulsive electrostatic force so that it can hold protons together in the nucleus, provided that there are neutrons there as well.
Supercluster	A number of galaxy clusters* grouped together.
Supernova	The explosive end of life for a large star. Emits the light of a billion suns for a few months.
Supersymmetry	The existence of certain undetected particles is demanded by a certain sub-atomic theory. They have not actually been found. The conditions for finding them have not yet been realised, but new accelerators could provide the conditions.
Tao	The ultimate principle of the universe in Taoism, which originated in China in the sixth century BCE. Means 'the way'. Non-personal ultimate, a self-existent one, a supreme force, itself formless, unable to be spoken.
Theory	A scientific model. Theories are mental constructs intended to account for the way physical systems behave.
Thermodynamics	The physics of heat.

Transcendent	Above and beyond the material universe.
Trinity	The one God of Christianity who is three distinct persons sharing the one divine nature: Father, Son and Holy Spirit.
Urban VIII	Pope during the Galileo* controversy. He firstly encouraged Galileo, but finally referred him to the Inquisition after Galileo broke an agreement to present an even handed account of the two possible world systems in *The Dialogue*.*
Uncertainty	See 'Heisenberg'* uncertainty, or 'quantum uncertainty'*.
Uranium	Element number 92 whose nucleus* contains 92 protons*. Very heavy. One isotope, U238, makes up over 99% of a sample and is radioactive. Another isotope, U235, can undergo nuclear fission. It is the fuel for nuclear reactors and bombs.
Vault	Feature of ancient cosmology; transparent dome enclosing the flat earth. Firmament*.
Virgo cluster	Group of 2000 galaxies 100 light years from the Milky Way*.
Vital principle	That which imparted life to inert matter. It could be vegetable, animal or human. All living things were once thought to contain an appropriate vital principle, or 'soul'.
Weak nuclear force	A second nuclear force. It acts on electrons*, positrons (positive electrons), neutrinos*. Its most well-known effect is to regulate the rate of radioactive decay.
White dwarf	Remnant of a sun-sized star remaining after it ends its life as a red-giant*. About the size of the earth, but 100,000 times as dense. Emits light, hence 'white'.
Wilson cloud chamber	Apparatus designed to show trajectories of sub-atomic particles.
WMAP	Wilson microwave anisotropy probe. This satellite measured the intensity of the cosmic background radiation* with great precision, improving greatly on the measurements made by the COBE* satellite. It showed slight variations in intensity which allowed conclusions to be made about the very early universe.
Yahweh	Name for God in the Hebrew culture.

Lightning Source UK Ltd.
Milton Keynes UK
UKHW052008070122
396782UK00004B/59